THE CRISIS OF MEANING
IN CULTURE AND EDUCATION

PEDAGOGY AND CULTURAL PRACTICE

Edited by Henry Giroux and Roger Simon

Recognizing that pedagogy begins with the affirmation of differences as a precondition for extending the possibilities of democratic life, the series analyzes the diverse democratic and ideological struggles of people across a wide range of economic, social, and political spheres.

THE CRISIS OF MEANING
IN CULTURE AND EDUCATION

DAVID TREND

PEDAGOGY AND CULTURAL PRACTICE
V O L U M E 3

University of Minnesota Press
Minneapolis
London

Chapter 2 first appeared as "Nationalities, Pedagogies, and Media," *Cultural Studies* 7, no. 1 (1993), published by Routledge; chapter 4 first appeared in *Afterimage* 19, no. 3 (1991); chapter 5 first appeared in *Afterimage* 19, no. 7 (1992); chapter 7 first appeared as "The Politics of Philanthropy: Cultural Policy and the Public Interest," *Afterimage* 20, no. 8 (1993); chapter 8 first appeared in *Socialist Review* 92, no. 3 (1993).

Published by the University of Minnesota Press
111 Third Avenue South, Suite 290, Minneapolis, MN 55401–2520
Printed in the United States of America on acid-free paper

Library of Congress Cataloging-in-Publication Data
Trend, David.
　　The crisis of meaning in culture and education / David Trend.
　　　p.　cm. — (Pedagogy and cultural practice ; v. 3)
　　Includes bibliographical references and index.
　　ISBN 0-8166-2522-0 (alk. paper). — ISBN 0-8166-2523-9 (pbk. : alk. paper)
　　1. Critical pedagogy—United States.　2. Educational sociology—United States.
　3. Politics and education—United States.　4. Discrimination in education —United States.　5. Minorities—Education—United States.　I. Title　II. Series.
　LC196.5.U6T74　1995
　370.11'5—dc20　　　　　　　　　　　　　　　　　　　　　　　　94-19504

Contents

In developing this book, I received a great deal of help from the people around me. First, I must thank my friend and colleague Henry A. Giroux for his encouragement and critical guidance. Significant credit is also due to Dennis Carlson, Peter McLaren, Richard Quantz, and Susan Reilly for their engagement with the theoretical aspects of this book. Important advice on selected chapters came from Grant Kester, Nadine McGann, and members of the *Socialist Review* collective. Finally, and most importantly, I want to express my gratitude to Patricia Lester for her ongoing intellectual and moral support and to my mother, Jean Trend, for being a teacher to me in the finest sense of the term.

ONE

THE CRISIS OF MEANING IN CULTURE
AND EDUCATION

> Cultural identity . . . is a matter of "becoming" as well as "being."
> It belongs to the future as much as to the past. It is not some-
> thing which already exists, transcending place, time, history and
> culture. Cultural identities come from somewhere, have histo-
> ries. But, like everything which is historical, they undergo con-
> stant transformation. Far from being eternally fixed in some es-
> sentialized past, they are subject to the continuous "play" of
> history, culture, and power.
>
> —Stuart Hall[1]

Pick up any newspaper and it is clear that the United States is facing a democratic crisis. Conventional definitions of citizenship and national identity have been thrown into question by ruptures in the global political landscape, changing postindustrial economic relations, shifting racial demographics, and new attitudes toward sexuality and religion. In a post–cold war era lacking in superpower conflicts, old fears of foreign insurgency have been supplanted by anxieties about trade deficits, declining educational standards, and a loss of common purpose. As social inequities continue to increase, citizens are losing faith in the government and in the master narratives supporting it.

Few could have predicted the speed with which Europe would be reconfigured by the collapse of the Eastern Bloc. Yet rather than easing international tensions, these events have triggered new forms of national chauvinism and regional antagonism. Complicating matters further is the so-called post-Fordist restructuring of global capitalism. Because the world is evolving into a transnational marketplace and the production of goods and services is becoming more fluid and decentralized, the distance between rich and poor nations has continued to widen. Meanwhile, in the United States, the white majority's historical dominance is quickly diminishing as communities of color claim a greater role. Factor in the growing influence of feminism, challenges to the traditional nuclear family, and more recent activism supporting the rights of lesbians and gay men, and it becomes clear that a massive movement—indeed, *a majority movement*—is rising to confront the reigning order.

Not surprisingly, these shifts have produced considerable public tension, along with a disturbing tendency to reach for quick and easy ways to settle disputes. Witness recent social unrest in cities from Los Angeles to Atlanta, the broad-based hostility toward legislative and judicial figures, and the remarkable popularity of such fringe personae as Rush Limbaugh and Ross Perot. Claiming to appeal to populist sentiments, this new breed of would-be demagogues has emerged to push for stricter laws, more difficult tests, and an ever more puritanical set of cultural standards.

More disturbingly, this reactionary climate creates a desire to find people to blame for the nation's problems. In foreign policy, this translates into the construction of an endless chain of foreign conflicts into which the United States must intervene in its new role as global peacekeeper. In each instance the U.S. military portrays itself as the force of reason in a world overrun by savage tribes and insane dictators. Even as the efficacy of old legal conventions and bureaucratic structures is thrown further into doubt, new justifications are advanced for consolidated power and political control on a global scale. For a growing number of conservative ideologues, these new international dynamics call for a simple and familiar strategy: the return of colonialism.[2]

At home the process of national identity formation is less obvious, particularly as the country continues through the Clinton era. Lacking the threat of the Red Menace, neoliberals and conservatives find common ground in assaulting the very underclass that the dominant culture exploits most. In a post–civil rights era, bigotry is executed in new and sometimes subtle ways. Rather than being viewed as victims of discrimination and inequality, the poor and disadvantaged are cast as the source of a decaying national infrastructure. Too sophisticated to name specific groups directly, this new rhetoric frames its objects by allusion and exclusion. Within this discourse, policy makers even appropriate the vocabulary of "empowerment" and "free choice" once thought to be the province of radical activists.

These rhetorical strategies fall into two interrelated categories, involving presumptions about national *strength* and *unity*. In the first category, the nation's declining prowess is attributed to a weakening of will and standards as evidenced in such expressions as "welfare dependence," "school truancy," "drug addiction," and "gang warfare." This thinly veiled vocabulary of racism has become a defining element in the negative identification of the modern citizen.[3] Its coded terminology defers blame for structural inequalities while simultaneously discrediting both foreign nationals and recent immigrants (or their descendants) in a single gesture. The second category—the threat of disunity—derives from the presumed divisiveness of such practices as "affirmative action," "multiculturalism," and "gay rights."[4] Here accusations are cast on the polluting influence of external others who fail to assimilate appropriately. Ironically, a nation founded by immigrants has come to view immigration as a threat to its "unique" character, as the nation's newest residents are blamed for crime, disease, and social decay. This is apparent in recent legislative calls to tighten border patrols and to expel political refugees.

Of course, liberals and conservatives have always fought over issues of nationalism and national identity. But in the current era there is a further distinction. Unlike ideological conflicts of the past, which focused on tangible issues, the new political warfare is conducted over the more subjective terrain of identity and representation. Battles once restricted to laws and money are being waged over ideas and symbols. It is this enlarged sphere of political conflict that this book addresses. More than ever these struggles entail the discourses through which subjectivity is formed—as evidenced in the current debates over political correctness, literary canons, and arts censorship. The stakes of this battle are well characterized by Pat Buchanan, who urged his fellow conservatives to launch "a cultural revolution in the 90s as sweeping as the political revolution of the 80s."[5]

In the broadest sense, these contests can be construed as issues of pedagogy. They signal efforts to control the ways people come to know who they are and what they can become. This broadened notion of pedagogy was an important element of the political philosophy of Antonio Gramsci, who wrote that "every relationship of 'hegemony' is necessarily an educational relationship."[6] In this context Gramsci was referring not simply to the forms of teaching that one commonly associates with the classroom, but to the profoundly political process through which citizens are socialized to recognize and validate state power. This process infuses all components of the social apparatus: the office, the church, the museum, and, particularly, the school. If these institutions are recognized as sites of potential ideological persuasion, then Gramsci's theory of education assumes great political significance.

This expanded view of education entails more than merely acknowledging the pedagogical implications of everyday actions.[7] It means admitting that many areas that claim neutrality in our lives are in fact sites of profound ideological struggle. Television newscasts, educational syllabi, art museums, scientific breakthroughs, "great" works of literature—these are not "objective" phenomena that somehow exist outside the realm of politics. They are forms of representation invested with specific interests in every manifestation. Through these texts dominance strives to replicate itself, often disguising its actions in the process. As Russell Ferguson put it, "The place from which power is exercised is often a hidden place. When we try to pin it down, the center is always somewhere else."[8] This invisibility of the center is often accompanied by a quiet exclusion of otherness. People may be concerned about the violent suppression of certain dissenting voices, yet at the same time they may be unaware of those consigned to the "structured absences" of discourse. In this sense every act of writing, of film production, of curriculum design, of institutional organization is an act of inclusion and exclusion. As Edward Said has suggested, the process of "representing (and hence reducing) others, almost always involves violence of some sort to the subject of the representation."[9]

Exacerbating this problem are the ways representations are internalized as somehow "natural" by both oppressors and oppressed. This is how even the victims of racism, sexism, and homophobia can become complicit in their own victimization. Here again, Gramsci's broadened notion of education can be important in helping people see the unnaturalness of categories of domination and inequity. Pedagogy becomes a driving mechanism of political agency, as citizens come to recognize the potential of a new social order and are thus compelled to challenge what exists.

Central to this formulation is the theory of power developed by Michel Foucault. For Foucault, power is not simply a substance that one person exerts on another, but a circuit flowing between oppressor and oppressed:

> If it is true that at the heart of power relations and as a permanent condition of their existence there is an insubordination and a certain essential obstinacy on the part of the principles of freedom, then there is no relationship of power without the means of escape or possible flight. Every power relationship implies, at least in potential, a strategy of struggle, in which the two forces are not superimposed, do not lose their specific nature, do not finally become confused. Each constitutes for the other a kind of permanent limit, a point of possible reversal.[10]

Hence power is a continually negotiated relationship that can be enhanced or negated by either side.[11] The issue becomes more complex both in the range of factors that come into play and in the varying degrees to which pedagogical actors (both students and teachers) become complicit in the maintenance of hegemonic relations. This is not to deny the material oppressions that stand in the way. It is simply to suggest that fissures and breaks exist for resistance, and that a shift in consciousness is the first move toward change. Within these breaks and openings lie the source of revolutionary possibility and hope. Taking this notion a step further, Ernesto Laclau has suggested that all entities involved in a struggle are enabled and disabled to some extent by each other: "Every identity is dislocated insofar as it depends on an outside which both denies that identity and provides the conditions of possibility at the same time."[12] The exploitation practiced by the factory owner both disables workers and enables their revolutionary sensibility. Viewed from this perspective, any antagonism always contains within it the seeds of its resolution.

This attitude toward social possibility derives from a recognition of the partial and fragmented character of subjectivity. It constitutes an argument against the pessimism that would reduce the world to black-or-white, all-or-nothing dichotomies. Needed instead is an understanding that people and institutions—including such categories as "liberal" and "conservative"—are not monolithic capsules of homogeneity, but complex and often contradictory assemblages of many ideas and attitudes. Thus a "bad" person can possess "good" qualities, a regressive movie can yield emancipatory meanings, and an oppressive organization can offer revolutionary opportunities. An important goal of critical education is to help reveal these possibilities.

In what follows I discuss this pedagogy of possibility in terms of three central concepts.[13] The first is the interaction between difference and democracy. Almost every contest in contemporary culture pits an argument for normative conformity against efforts to legitimate diversity. This translates into confrontations between forces that foreclose or encourage democratic exchange among diverse interests. The second concept is a theory of culture as a reciprocal substance that citizens both receive and produce.[14] As in Foucault's theory of power, within this formulation ideas and images do not flow unproblematically from dominant to subordinate groups, but are created in the relations among them. As citizens come to recognize their capacities in the power/knowledge equation, the generative character of this enterprise evolves.[15] The third issue addresses pedagogy as the motor force for developing productive culture. By necessity this calls for an examination of the complex role of the cultural worker in the process, not as a vanguardist, but as an agent for expanding the space of discursive possibility. By encouraging the critical agency of a citizenry, cultural workers can help develop a people's abilities to maximize their positions in negotiating relationships of power. Asserting authority in the use of representations and commodities means asserting authority in political life.

DEMOCRACY AND DIFFERENCE

In large part debates over the character of U.S. democracy derive from the philosophical split between idealism and realism. Conservative groups, though varying considerably in style and motivation, tend to support a faith in timeless, unchanging truths to be learned and obeyed. They see a fundamental correctness in existing arrangements, but fear that its enabling values are eroding. Within this logic assertions are made that job discrimination, sexual harassment, and unfair housing practices really are not that much of a problem, and the government programs to rectify them provide inegalitarian preferences on which "minority" groups become dependent. Liberalism, a similarly diverse and contradictory category, frequently embraces a concept of truth that is revised in each new application. As a consequence, liberals are often critical of a society they believe emphasizes greed and competition rather than social justice. Hence, they promote government programs to correct the inequities produced by market forces.

These positions yield radically different views of moral authority, resulting in conflicting attitudes toward the way people should act. Increasingly, such differences manifest themselves in intense struggles to organize and control national culture—struggles that have become all the more intense in the current transitional era. As relationships toward work and leisure shift, and as national and international relations change, unprecedented openings have appeared for new definitions of social forms. Prior accords between competing groups have become unsettled, and new kinds of antagonism have begun to develop. For example, the once stable accord that developed between business and labor in the post–World War II years has deteriorated. Implemented by collective bargaining, the implicit agreement had been that management could call the shots if labor received an ever increasing paycheck. Now that economic recession has made such largesse impossible, business and labor are in conflict.[16] These factors have shaken long-shared understandings of how citizens should live together.

Exacerbating these circumstances even further in recent decades have been changes in the nation's moral infrastructure. As the role of organized religion in public life has decreased, a void has opened around ethical issues involving charity, human compassion, and social justice. The former national consensus on these matters—loosely organized within Protestant, Catholic, and Jewish ethics—has come undone. And with it has vanished a range of agreements over social accountability and mutual concern. While this Judeo-Christian consensus has come apart, the organizing principles of American pluralism have changed. The weakening of the religious center has increased the anxiety of its remaining proponents, resulting in a new breed of constituency-based organizations competing for public accommodations. Indeed, the number of entities like Operation Rescue and the American Family Association has doubled in the post–World War II years.[17]

Answering these fundamentalist groups has been an expanded range of newly strengthened entities such as the American Civil Liberties Union, ACT UP, and the National Organization for Women. In part the growth of such progressive groups can be seen as a response to the narrowness of both the "old" and "new" Left. The development of these single-issue entities has produced an environment in which conflicts are organized, funded, and promoted as never before. Yet rather than as a negative phenomenon, these new social movements should be viewed as a potentially useful development. The acknowledgment of diverse needs and concerns presents the possibility of shaking loose archaic forms of social control based on cultural conformity.[18]

Effecting such changes will not be a simple process, for the positions from which people engage these struggles for power are fraught with inequity. Worse, recognition of this inequity is often unacknowledged or suppressed. Meanwhile, the Right argues that in a land of purportedly "equal opportunity," hardship should be attributed to individual weakness or lack of will. Differences are often viewed by the conservative camp as obstacles to be suppressed in favor of the common culture, rather than as potentially liberating attributes.

Special interests are measured against the standard of the social "mainstream." Entitlement claims of different constituencies are neutralized in appeals to "traditional values" and "general interests." But what are the grounds on which such notions are based? Although this imaginary mainstream purportedly includes a majority of people, in fact, it excludes everyone. Instead of functioning as a marker of the civil middle ground, it works as a mechanism to naturalize social hierarchies. When stripped of its mystifying pretensions, the mainstream can be seen as an abstract representation that at best describes a rather small minority of people. Nevertheless, its primary referent of male European heterosexuality marks the coordinate around which Western law and culture are organized. This structural hegemony converts efforts to contest, infiltrate, or subvert it into acknowledgments of its dominance. In this manner the relation of margin to center has been maintained.

As recent political campaigns have pointed out, liberal arguments present equally problematic attitudes toward difference. Liberalism constructs a comparably normative model of an American middle class to which citizens should be economically reconciled. Differences are obstacles to be overcome or "tolerated," as citizenship is collapsed into a single category based on individual rights. Often evoking the evils of "the market," this rhetoric fails to acknowledge systematic oppressions related to gender, race, and sexual orientation that install people within relations of wealth or poverty.

To achieve these monolithic visions of national identity, both liberals and conservatives have assaulted as divisive the proponents of multiculturalism, or identity politics.[19] Ignoring historically entrenched power asymmetries among social groups, they have argued that such "separatist" and "ethnocentric" views subvert the potential of a national accord.[20] Promoted instead is a monolithic definition of citizenship that dismisses the specificity of human variety as either irrelevant or selfish. Ironically, much of this is carried out in the name of a "freedom," which would claim to protect each citizen from interference by others, while leaving intact the mechanisms through which that freedom is selectively denied to certain groups.

The danger of such high-minded universalizing was demonstrated three decades ago, when even the concept of democracy was challenged in the name of coherence and order. In the midst of the 1960s, when elements of cultural diversity and social change were gaining momentum, the unsettling of conventional authority was labeled "an excess of democracy" by a group of business leaders and government bureaucrats known as the Trilateral Commission. Largely forgotten today, the Trilateral Commission was assembled by David Rockefeller in the wake of an era, like today's, of activism by students, women, and people of color. Its infamous report by Samuel P. Huntington, entitled *The Crisis of Democracy*, argued that unbridled freedom breeds anarchy, loss of common purpose, and, more to the political point, economic decline.[21]

In the last decade these dusty arguments have been brought forward again. As Allan Bloom pointed out in his classic attack on liberal education, *The Closing of the American Mind*, "Democracy liberates from tradition, which in other kinds of regimes determines the judgment."[22] To Bloom this democratic liberation from regulation throws the rules of civic reason in jeopardy: "Since very few people school themselves in the use of reason beyond the calculation of self-interest encouraged by the regime, they need help on a vast number of issues—in fact, all issues."[23] Rather than acknowledging the democratic potential in multiple, conflicting viewpoints, the conservative program's pessimistic view of human agency brands such diversity a danger.

The democratic stakes in the debate become particularly clear when the discussion involves education. The Right seems incapable of reconciling its political appeal to a mainstream identity and its cultural appeal to idealized notions of "the best" of Western culture. Implicit in recent school reform plans—with their programs of universal testing, their implication of a national curriculum, their invitation to business interests to cash in on public education, and their failure to commit an extra dime to child poverty and health care—is the belief that the nation has spent too much time pursuing educational equity and too little time advancing rarefied standards of "world class" excellence.[24] These attitudes have helped produce an atmosphere in which today's young people—the so-called Generation X—feel powerless and alienated from society.

In the cultural world these debates have taken a similarly vicious turn, as the Right has seized the offensive. No longer content to play the role of defender of conservative values, the Right has moved to eliminate dissenting opinion with a more direct assault on democracy and cultural diversity. The parameters of the argument are framed well by Samuel Lipman: "Culture and democracy cannot co-exist, for democracy by its very nature represents the many, and culture, by its nature, is created for the few."[25] Lipman's conservative proclamations notwithstanding, one should recognize that the problematic stratification of high and low culture is not only promoted by the Right. Whether oriented toward politics or tradition, much of that reified substance called art is produced and consumed by a rather small minority. To the vast majority of citizens, the objects that hang on museum walls are artifacts of someone else's culture. Indeed, at the height of the recent controversies over the National Endowment for the Arts, polling data indicated that although most people opposed the idea of arts censorship, few felt compelled to do anything to stop it.[26]

Radical activists would do well to rethink their practice along more egalitarian and politically savvy lines. What is required is a new radical democratic imaginary capable of reclaiming concepts of "citizenship" and "community" within a reconfigured—and flexible—framework of social inclusiveness. Recent events have demonstrated the failure of the institutions of the old Left (primarily trade unions), a failure due to their inability to accommodate the needs of groups defined by noneconomic issues. Part of the answer lies in fashioning the type of movement Jesse Jackson inspired based on people's common estrangement from power. The simple idea that groups could share a political ideal without surrendering their differences—an idea so fundamental to the concept of a "United States"—has been lost in the appeal to cultural verisimilitude from both conservative and liberal camps. Such a movement has a tremendous moral appeal among both the oppressed and the privileged. Its ethos of *justice* is a trigger to forms of collective agency for which people yearn.

The result will not be the type of naive democracy based on unexamined notions of "free expression" or "equal rights." Nor will it ever claim to be a perfect democracy in the idealized sense. A working democracy is a dynamic and clamorous process that does not ask groups either to compromise their needs or to level their differences. What it does, however, is ask groups to assume a degree of collective agency of exactly the sort the Right's program of privatized individualism seeks to undermine. In the writings of Ernesto Laclau and Chantal Mouffe, among others, this concept of a radical democracy entails a renewed commitment to community on a number of levels, an understanding that despite their varied interests, needs, and demands, all individuals and groups share a common interdependence.[27] This interdependence is the very glue that reconciles individual freedom with collective responsibility. Each supports the other in a strong *affective* relationship that has the power to lend new meaning to terms such as *heroism, patriotism*, and *human compassion*.

PRODUCTIVE CULTURE

As political struggle has shifted to the cultural terrain, its rules of engagement have changed. Whether the topic is television or textbooks, contests of meaning are governed by the normative conventions of different "interpretive communities" and inscribed in relations of power.[28] For this reason it is important to emphasize to students or audiences that although political power is often presented as monolithic and absolute, it is quite frequently fragmented and vulnerable. As one activist video collective puts it, the media are but a "paper tiger"—easily dismantled with the proper interpretive tools. The task for radical cultural workers is to reveal the constructed character of received meanings, the ways such meanings are secured, and how they can be revised or rewritten. Why, for example, has the Left permitted conservatives to determine the dominant meanings of symbols such as the flag? The American flag is an extremely powerful metaphor in the collective unconscious that the Right has used to mobilize vast areas of support. But just as the flag has stood for militarism and global conquest, it can also stand for justice and equity.

The task ahead involves taking back symbols and reclaiming their emancipatory meanings. In this sense the mutability of cultural signs should be seen as a point of political strategy and, ultimately, of democratic possibility. In the continual process of reinventing itself, a free society admits many viewpoints. By studying the ways representations are actually deployed within communities, cultural workers can encourage productive means to interpret and use them. What is the relationship of textual encoding and decoding on both individual and collective levels? How do patterns of consumer buying and product use influence the behavior of industries and governments? Not only do these questions bear heavily on issues of identity and agency, but they are also important in the articulation of emancipatory public spaces.

Linked to the job of recoding cultural signs is the mission of opening such "free spaces" where unencumbered discourse can begin to emerge.[29] Historically, these free spaces have been key staging grounds for interventionist politics—from the small group meetings of the early women's movement, to the "free pulpits" of black churches in the Deep South during the civil rights era, to the "liberated zones" of independence movements in the third world. In the art community, this notion motivated the formation in the 1970s of the "alternative space" movement.[30] These organizations evolved in response to the exclusionary practices of large museums, symphonies, and public television stations. Indeed, as public institutions supported by tax revenues, civic cultural organizations wield considerable symbolic and actual authority.[31] To the founders of the alternative space movement, such government-financed entities were thought to exemplify the principles of democratic discourse and cultural diversity. Not surprisingly, it is exactly such alternative organizations that conservatives have found so troubling in recent years, as evidenced in efforts to muzzle the recipients of grants from the National Endowment for the Arts.

Producing new and emancipatory forms of culture means leaving behind binary oppositions of text and materiality. A major charge leveled against academic cultural criticism has been its tendency to define social change in linguistic terms. These divisive sentiments are typified in arguments splitting concerns over language from the very circumstances that language describes. Consider the recent comments of Steven Watts: "For small farmers holding a notice of loan foreclosure, for the urban underclass, for unemployed steelworkers, the glib liberationist claim of poststructuralism—that a decentered discourse will set you free—must seem puzzling indeed. Here is a feeble politics of words."[32] Besides dangerously essentializing categories of theory and practice, such attitudes have produced a split between so-called culturalist camps that privilege representation and more materially based economist groups. Although a degree of reconciliation has been achieved between these positions in interdisciplinary fields such as cultural studies, within more reified domains such as education, polemic attitudes remain entrenched.[33] This rift has seriously frustrated understandings of the way culture works as a dialectical process.

As Watts suggests, one need only look to the hardships of farmers facing foreclosure, of urban youth subjected to structural unemployment, or to communities of color brutalized by daily racism and discrimination to appreciate the physical realities that exceed any text. But it would be a grave mistake to invalidate the importance of signification when oppressed peoples' stories are being heard for the first time.[34] This privileging of material instrumentality over the "politics of representation" further precludes access by women, people of color, lesbians, and gay men to suppressed histories and narratives of emancipation. Not so coincidentally, this antinarrative posture is being promoted largely by Anglo-American and European male intellectuals at exactly the time when their primacy is being challenged. Just when new forms of nationalism are emerging and new domestic entitlement claims are being advanced, the academy has begun to legitimate a formulation of the subject as devoid of moral agency or political grounding.[35]

Because of the persistence of this economist/culturalist divide, it is worth reviewing the history of the split in some detail, as it relates both to cultural studies and educational theory. The difficulties originated in orthodox Marxist claims of a direct correspondence between the relations of the economic base and superstructure. Within this scheme, culture was perceived as little more than an advertisement for capitalism, and thus directly reflected the manipulative interests of the market. Frankfurt School scholars Max Horkheimer and Theodor Adorno, among others, described a system in which the masses were systematically duped into lives of servitude and consumption. Within such apocalyptic logic, cultural objects functioned as propaganda, and the citizenry was incapable of resisting the seduction of the dominant "culture industry." Although useful in the broad mapping of ideological reproduction, this totalizing position refused to grant makers or audiences any autonomy whatsoever. Unabashedly elitist in its views of "the masses," the resulting "reflection theory" readings of art and entertainment invariably produced predictable evidence of existing class inequities.

Alternatives to reflection theory date to the 1940s, although until recently many were unknown to wide audiences. Some of these works emphasized the independent character of cultural practices, apart from the presumed overdetermination of the economic base. Others focused on audiences. Louis Althusser's work in particular sought to undo myths of unproblematized transmission and reception. In his paradigmatic essay "Ideology and Ideological State Apparatuses (Notes Toward an Investigation)," he argued that subjectivity is socially inscribed in the relationships *between* individuals and organizations.[36] Institutions such as the school and museum construct systems of meaning that install people in imaginary relations to the real situations in which they live. Identity is recognized as a fictional text on which various forces exert influence.

More significantly, Althusser proposed a revision of reflection theory that assigned a quasi autonomy to cultural works. No longer a mere superstructural manifestation of the economic base, culture was seen to operate in a complex dialectic with the market. In other words, a space was acknowledged between the oppressive institutions of the state and the consciousness of individuals. Within this space, resistances could form that were capable of destabilizing ruling power structures. These sentiments were echoed in the writings of Herbert Marcuse, who likewise argued against the classical Marxist doctrine that material relations alone were responsible for producing consciousness. Emphasizing the role of human agency, Marcuse said: "Radical change in consciousness is the beginning, the first step in changing social existence: emergence of the new Subject."[37]

A further refinement of Marxist cultural theory came in 1970 when Hans Magnus Enzenberger proposed in his "Constituents of a Theory of the Media" that the Left had been misguided in its understandings of how culture actually works.[38] He suggested that instead of tricking the masses into a web of false desires, media actually find ways of satisfying real (but often unconscious) desires. This position was later elaborated on by poststructuralist Marxists such as Fredric Jameson and Roland Barthes, who further considered the negotiable possibilities of signification. If cultural signs could be interpreted variously, their meanings assumed a "floating" character as individuals assigned them different readings. From an understanding of the contingency of meaning has evolved a complex discourse on the many forces that struggle to influence it. The very way one sees the world becomes a matter of strategy.

A comparable evolution occurred within education, although somewhat later. In the 1960s and 1970s political economists like Samuel Bowles and Herbert Gintis were pointing out the ways that schooling replicated the economic base by teaching students to assume worker/manager roles.[39] This so-called reproduction theory of education was later refined to critique not only the contents of books and curricula, but the "hidden curriculum" that taught students how to behave.[40] Missing from this analysis was a way to account for student aberrations and failures, an absence corrected in the subsequent development of "resistance" theories.[41] This formulation afforded students a hitherto unacknowledged agency in resisting or rejecting school authority, even if this behavior did little to change their class positions.

A turning point came in the early 1980s, as educators in the emergent "cultural studies" movement in Great Britain and the United States began to recognize the potential for channeling resistant impulses in positive ways. Rather than simply accepting lessons as given, students would be encouraged to bring their own insights to the pedagogical encounter. No longer did texts need to be interpreted as intended by their authors or manufacturers; they could be revised, combined, or contested according to the reader's interpretive capabilities. This led to broadened considerations of the many issues that contextualize culture and education. Factors hitherto subsumed within base/superstructure objectivism like history, social formation, and class struggle began to be examined in relation to language, identity, technology, and power. Moreover, this discursive expansion challenged strictly aesthetic definitions of culture by reading into the very fabric of all political and social relations. Because cultural works are subject to multiple readings, meaning became a matter of contest on the broad terrain of politics.

Crucial to these theoretical developments was the evolution of what has been termed "critical pedagogy," an amalgam of radical philosophies that first gained wide recognition in the 1970s through the writings of Brazilian expatriate Paulo Freire.[42] As practiced by Freire in countries throughout the third world, the doctrines of critical pedagogy were used by colonized citizens to analyze their roles in relations of oppression and to devise programs for revolutionary change. During the 1970s and 1980s the philosophies of critical pedagogy were adapted throughout the industrialized world as a means of addressing power imbalances there. Significant in this regard are the writings of such scholars as Michael Apple, Henry Giroux, Peter McLaren, and Ira Schor.[43]

Much of the movement's vocabulary of "empowerment," "dialogue," and "voice" has entered the lexicon of Western social reform movements. At the same time, the principles of critical pedagogy have undergone significant modifications that adapt them to the needs of contemporary technocratic societies. In a world that is rapidly redefining relations between its centers and margins and questioning the legitimacy of master narratives, critical pedagogy's analytical strategies have been modified with theories of postmodernism, feminism, and postcolonial theory.[44] In different ways each of these discourses has advanced the concepts of critical pedagogy by challenging it to be more self-reflexive and attentive to its own internal biases, hierarchies, and solipsisms.

The issue of power should be stressed here, because it is not enough simply to encourage students and audiences to celebrate what they study and watch. One of the important lessons of Paul Willis's ethnography *Learning to Labour*, a lesson repeatedly confirmed in subsequent studies of sexual and racial identity, is that there is nothing inherently progressive in the attitudes of "the people."[45] More often than not, political appeals to populism amount to little more than ploys encouraging citizens to relinquish entitlements and government protections. Asserting that human agents are not the robotic servants of cultural reproduction is *not* to say that they are free from histories of dominance or submission. This is the very baggage that constructs internalized oppression.

For this reason, proponents of critical pedagogy attach great political significance to cultural matters. By affording audiences a role in the communicative transaction, one does not deny the overwhelming influences culture commands. Instead, this view suggests, consumers of culture have a stake in the process that can be enhanced through education. Culture is as much *descriptive* as it is *prescriptive*, existing in a dialectical relationship with lived experience. Culture and experience inform and are informed by each other. Needed are pedagogies that encourage the production of diverse identities and knowledge forms, rather than restricting such possibilities. The concerns of such pedagogies are well summarized by Henry Giroux and Roger Simon:

> Do such practices open up new notions of identities and possibilities? What identities and possibilities are disorganized and excluded? How are such practices articulated with forms of knowledge and pleasure legitimated by dominant groups? What interests and investments are served by a particular set of popular cultural practices and critiqued and challenged by the existence of such? What are the moral and political commitments of such practices, and how are these related to one's own commitments as a teacher (and if there is a divergence, what does this imply)?[46]

Answering these questions involves finding the means to interrogate and revise textual and material codes. It means revealing the ways received meanings are bound in specific histories and modes of address (or use) that act as limits to human possibility. Thus, the pedagogical task is to demystify these codes in the interest of new methods of production and consumption.

In this sense *production* refers both to the fabrication of ideas and things. It evolves from the understanding of the mediated character of all representation and consequent ability of human agents to create new or alternate interpretations. This more active posture of reception implies that viewers, users, or purchasers of texts and objects need not accept the subject positions they have been assigned by an author or manufacturer. Consumers possess the capacity to subvert given interpellations or create new ones. Ultimately citizens can invent their own stories, write their own texts—make their own gardens, sculptures, or stamp collections.

These matters hinge on relations of *consumption*. Human agents need to recognize both the extent and limits of choice in the selection of narratives and consumer goods. Obviously, one is always constrained by the range of texts, ingredients, and commodities that are available and affordable. To paraphrase Marx, indeed one does invent one's life from a limited range of possibilities. Yet at the same time, within these parameters options exist with tactical applications. As Mica Nava argues, it is time to move beyond the reproductionist "consumer-as-victim" mentalities that characterized much early writing on advertising.[47] Such negative discourses range from overdetermined suggestions of "false consciousness" to psychological claims of "subliminal seduction." What ought to be stressed instead

THE CRISIS OF MEANING IN CULTURE AND EDUCATION

is the degree to which audiences are not always fooled by the media. People *do* exercise agency in the acquisition and use of products; consumer advocacy groups and product boycotts *have* had an impact on what gets shown on television and what ends up on store shelves.[48] The corporate production of texts and objects does not exert a total authority over buyers, but functions in a relationship of exchange.

Since reception and use are active gestures, activists need to recognize that the potential for productive culture inheres in the very fabric of life. Like talking, it lives in the ways people communicate with each other, in the objects they make, and in the stories they tell. It permeates the rituals of meeting, listening, dancing, telling jokes, playing sports, and making pictures. It lives in the sophisticated meanings people generate from their work, parenting, cooking, letters, record collections, parties, cars, yards, gardens, hairstyles, photo albums, wall posters, sketchbooks, home videos, and so on. Most importantly, it inheres in the ways people make choices, invent their lives, and adapt to difficult circumstances. In this last sense culture is, as Paul Willis has stated, the very stuff of survival.[49]

PEDAGOGY, NATIONALITY, AND COMMUNITY

Cultural workers in many segments of the Left can stand united in the principles of democracy and pedagogy if they can reclaim these values on their own terms. At the same time, steps need to be taken to reconstitute alliances among radical and progressive groups inside the academy and outside. Accomplishing these tasks requires a democratic imaginary that speaks in the tradition of history's great emancipatory struggles, even in the face of enormous pressures to forget them. Many postcolonial critics argue that it is endemic within modern imperial states to enforce a denial of people's past histories in the name of an illusory national unity of the present. Homi Bhabha speaks of the "daily plebiscite" that renews the consent of the governed while erasing dangerous memories of former oppressions and struggles.[50] This process tends to privilege the imagined community of the "homeland" over other forms of affiliation.[51] Clearly this will to nationality is not to be taken lightly. More significantly, this ethos is not restricted to mainstream or traditionalist movements. It is partly an appeal to nationhood that is evidenced in movements for Black Nationalism and in the names of such groups as Queer Nation.[52] (The mutability of national identity and its mobilization across multiple fronts are addressed in detail in the next chapter.)

The important point here is that a radical democracy premised on a respect for difference needs both to encourage dangerous memory *and* to recognize the populist will to nationalism. This political philosophy requires a pedagogy that supports the production of diverse knowledge as a prerequisite for an egalitarian civic order. While honoring diversity, a radical democracy resists the temptation to romanticize difference into equivalence. It recognizes that identities often are shaped in asymmetrical power relationships and that the resultant conflicts give democracy its dynamic character. In the context of cultural struggle, this involves a critical reexamination of the way textual signification is constructed, as well as an acknowledgment of the frequent indeterminacy of narrative representations.

What is the appropriate role of educators and other cultural workers in this process? How does one use authority without subsuming the interests of others into one's own? What is the role of identity and history in this process? In part the answers lie in questioning Enlightenment definitions of terms such as "civilization" and "progress." In the sciences and the humanities such impulses resulted in the reification of disciplinary knowledge into hierarchies of certification and control. Such chauvinistic attitudes fostered a faith in a single vision of utilitarian purpose embodied in the common enterprise of the state. Both views were premised on utopian speculation based on generalized assumptions of social planning. This modernist program of human unity and singularity of purpose assumed its greatest appeal after the turn of the century as World War I physically splintered and brutalized Europe. But times change. In recent decades the world has witnessed the consequences of this modernist program exhausting itself, as industrial superpowers decay from the inside and the world remains poised at the brink of environmental disaster and nuclear war. From Europe to the United States it has become evident that the historical grand *récits* of reason are not enough. The near-universal failure of master narratives—whether in art or politics—has created a suspicion of totalizing paradigms. This has produced two distinct actions: a movement to unseat the unified modernist establishment, and an effort to efface modernism's protective boundaries, particularly those that separate it from mass culture.[53]

This has resulted in a crisis in conventional conceptions of "leadership" based on Enlightenment notions of vision, genius, and individuality. It has brought about a revision of leadership that is facilitative rather than prescriptive. For first world educators and cultural workers this means engaging the project described by Gayatri Spivak of "unlearning our privilege as our loss" by realizing that positions of dominance often are insulated from unpleasant realities.[54] From this perspective the "transformative" intellectual is one who provides the catalyst for change.[55] Yet as Jennifer Gore has recently pointed out, no matter how versed one may be in the precepts of critical pedagogy, care must be exercised in seeking answers *with* rather than *for* the groups one wishes to support.[56] This might involve encouraging a community to look into its own past to resuscitate lost narratives of emancipation. Certainly this is the case with current efforts to combat the systematic erasure of the labor movement from textbooks. In other instances activists in school districts are engaging in local campaigns to rewrite the struggles and gains of African American, Asian, and Latino peoples into school curricula. Similar motivations have brought together dozens of groups to explore the literacies of folk culture or mass media.

Not that such cultural affirmation is without its complications, for activists inherently run the risk of advancing their own concerns in the name of the disempowered. Indeed, the very construction of such generalized categories as "the oppressed" establishes a simplified dominant/subordinate relationship that elides the subtle ways in which different forms of power circulate. The same can be said of "resistance." Such terms can reduce the lived world of multiple, overlapping, and fragmented subjectivities to little more than binary oppositions on paper.[57] Thus one can no longer speak of a singular "hegemony" to which all groups respond in the same way. Nor can there exist singular definitions of liberation or progress. What can be discussed are the conditions for developing human capacities and sites of possibility.

As cultural activists are continually examining the limitations and blind spots of their own subject positions, they should be wary of anyone who asserts a privileged relationship to cultural knowledge based on social location. This is the one regrettable consequence of the now familiar call to "voice" that romanticizes personal perspective as automatically sacred and true.[58] Indeed, as Lawrence Grossberg suggests, the "politics of any social position is not guaranteed in advance."[59] This essentialization of knowledge based on racial, sexual, or economic identity generally produces two detrimental effects. First, it silences and invalidates external perspectives by refusing the applicability of partial or mediated experience. This can cause a failure of communication, as well as the type of moral solipsism characteristic of a single viewpoint. Second, the privileging of one form of identity tends to discount others. Therefore, a focus on race can easily elide any consideration of gender, sexual orientation, or class—and as a consequence overlook the imbricated character of these issues. While affording a form of provisional (perhaps strategic) closure, such an emphasis can produce a distorted view of the ways ideologies and oppressions operate.

With this in mind critical educators and cultural workers need to be attentive to the subtle ways in which oppressions creep into the discourse and practice of reform. They also need to support each other to establish coalitions for breaking down the debilitating separation that occurs in the workplace and between workplaces. Ultimately the university and the community are not segregated realms for theory and practice, but integrated components of a single system. Theory has to be redefined as the everyday instrument that it is, namely, a tool that is only as good as its uses make it. The new pedagogy of difference is dedicated to such an enterprise—to an explication of the ways theories of materialism, modernity, difference, culture, democracy, and education intersect the lived world of students, teachers, gallery goers, TV watchers, and so forth. This is not to imply anything like a unified set of answers to the questions that have plagued society for generations; it is only to suggest that strength and empowerment derive from seeking them out.

TWO

WHAT'S IN A NAME?

NATIONAL IDENTITY AND MEDIA LITERACY

> To encounter the nation as it is written displays a temporality of
> culture and social consciousness more in tune with the partial,
> overdetermined process by which textual meaning is produced
> through the articulation of difference in language. . . . Such an
> approach contests the traditional authority of those national ob-
> jects of knowledge—Tradition, the People, the Reason of the
> State, High Culture, for instance—whose pedagogical value
> often relies on their representation as holistic concepts located
> within an evolutionary narrative of historical continuity.
>
> —Homi K. Bhabha[1]

Nationality is a fiction. It is a story people tell themselves about who they are, where they live, and how they got there. As such it is a complicated and highly contested text. In the contemporary United States, issues of national identity resonate in debates over educational reform, literary canons, multiculturalism, political correctness, and artistic freedom. All of these result, at least in part, from the paradoxical manner in which "nations, like narratives, lose their origins in the myths of time and only fully realize their horizons in the mind's eye."[2] One's location in this narrative, one's ability to write oneself into the text of nationality, constitutes a form of literacy. It is an acquired language of belonging in space and time to an imaginary community. Increasingly, both the Left and Right have recognized the educational importance of this process of national identification, as young people are socialized to understand their roles as citizens. Opinions differ radically over both the form and content of this language. Some argue that in an increasingly complex and multicultural society there is a need for a common literacy; others propose that we are moving toward a culture of many literacies. Yet as suggested in the preceding chapter, one fact is relatively certain: the attachment to national identity is an incredibly powerful means of political organization. Unfortunately, it is all too often used to suppress other, equally powerful identities.

Media figure prominently in all of these debates. Without doubt, substantial ingredients in the process of national identification are delivered through newspapers, magazines, television, and movies—not to mention the plethora of instructional materials, catalogues, billboards, and junk mail that bombards citizens daily. There is a growing sense that these media constitute the primary source of identity formation, supplanting roles formerly held by school, church, and the family. Rather than seeing this as a negative phenomenon, educators and parents should acknowledge the importance of media in cultural life, and work to harness this power in productive ways. Like it or not, young people are as much educated, albeit informally, through daily encounters with media as they are in the formal environment of school.[3]

It is argued that even the concept of a national identity is a product of media. Some historians link the development of the modern nation-state to the evolution of European "print capitalism."[4] Prior to the mass dissemination of newspapers, books, and pamphlets, people rarely imagined a collectivity on a scale broader than local. It does not take much insight to recognize the current role of network television and movies in constructing the illusion of connectedness among citizens thousands of miles apart. As Benedict Anderson puts it: "An American will never meet, or even know the names of more than a handful of his fellow Americans. He has no idea of what they are up to at any one time. But he has complete confidence in their steady, anonymous, simultaneous activity."[5]

Moreover, the reach of contemporary electronic media is hardly bound by a country's geographical borders. The ability to broadcast across national boundaries, even in the face of government resistance, motivated the electronic warfare waged by the U.S. Information Agency in nations around the world. Not that media imperialism is typically so belligerent. On the contrary, the mass marketing of U.S. productions throughout the world is customarily viewed as a positive function of the "free market." Due to the scale and technical sophistication of the American media industry, Hollywood films and television programs constitute the nation's second largest source of foreign income, just behind aerospace technology.[6] Moreover, the mass dissemination of U.S. movies and TV abroad helped provide an important context for the foreign consumption of American products—from McDonald's burgers in Russia to Marlboro cigarettes in Thailand to Euro-Disney entertainment in France. Although this ability to profit in the media trade helps the nation's sagging economy, the massive influx of American media into other nations is not always viewed as positive. The now-familiar image of *Dallas* glowing on television screens throughout Europe, Africa, and Asia has triggered mass resentment about the transmission of Yankee culture throughout the globe. As a consequence, government-sponsored media education programs in nations that import significant amounts of film and television are far more advanced than in the United States. Foreign nations perceive the need to protect themselves from the boundless expansion of American capitalism.

People at home are not entirely thrilled by media either. Almost since the inception of television, a diverse assortment of educators, parents, and religious groups have warned of the corrupting influence of commercial media. Like critics of media dissemination overseas, domestic opponents believe it has an irresistible control over its consumers. Those on the Right see media as the conveyors of moral depravity. On the Left media are believed to transmit oppressive ideologies. Both views are unified by their belief that media must be resisted at all costs.[7] All of these arguments against the media—both international and domestic—share a common flaw: they assign a range of social problems to the media that originate elsewhere by assuming both that media representations invariably correspond to outcomes and that viewers exert no license in the viewing process. In part the problem stems from a lack of understanding about how media are received and interpreted. Intellectuals, parents, and clergy make assumptions about the media practices of the less powerful. This results in a condescending series of judgments about the capabilities of viewers to evaluate what they see.

The solution to the perceived tyranny of the media lies in turning off the tube or girding oneself to resist its mendacity. This has been the premise of media education, the rationale for the development of public broadcasting, and even the motivation for several United Nations resolutions. Obviously such beliefs do not give viewers very much credit, nor do they recognize that meaning develops in the relationship between text and reader, with readers actively comparing narratives to their own experiences. This position also neglects to acknowledge viewers' ability to accept portions of a text while discarding the rest. In short, this negative view of media insists that audiences are incapable of telling the difference between images and life itself.

In what follows I review media attitudes both at home and abroad, by raising questions specifically focused on issues of national identity. How do contemporary media define public perceptions of nationality? What role do media play in developing citizenship and collective agency? How do media influence relationships among global powers? Addressing these questions entails both institutional and textual analysis of the way the nation has been constructed in an international context. Such analyses are particularly needed at a time when the United States is asserting its right as the only legitimate superpower in the New World Order. My central premise is that, although the material and textual power of the communications industry is indisputable, the authority of media is not absolute. Although audiences possess the ability to creatively mediate the texts they receive, they do not necessarily exercise that option with skill or consistency. Through a concerted media education program, the practice can be cultivated. Models for such pedagogies already exist, but they are few and far between. In describing the ways some of these new media curricula operate I will also explain why they have been so poorly received, particularly in U.S. schools. In an era in which schooling is increasingly driven by a corporatist agenda of basic skills, interdisciplinary studies such as media are seen as both frivolous and subversive. Nevertheless, arguments for media education can be made that are both powerful and progressive.

THE BIG PICTURE: INTERNATIONAL PERSPECTIVES ON MEDIA IMPERIALISM

The problems started after World War II. What began with the seemingly innocent export of commercial media products evolved over time into a global ideological offensive. Of course, U.S. business interests had long promoted American capitalism with a religious zeal. But it was not until the cold war era that politicians and entrepreneurs like publishing magnate Henry Luce began urging Americans to spread the gospel of capitalism across the globe by accepting "wholeheartedly our duty and our opportunity as the most powerful and vital nation in the world and in consequence to exert upon the world the full impact of our influence, for such purposes as we see fit and by such means as we see fit."[8]

Complementing such attitudes was a U.S. diplomatic policy promoting a "free flow of information" throughout the world. This transparently self-interested stance was asserted as a protection against the resurgence of fascism and the outbreak of future wars. Yet it also represented a direct assault on the protectionism practiced by the Eastern Bloc. Such expansionist sentiments were well characterized by another influential publisher, Palmer Hoyt, who described the world in 1946 as headed for "destruction unless steps are taken to insure the beginning at least of freedom of news—American style—between the peoples of the earth. A civilization that is not informed cannot be free and a world that is not free cannot endure."[9]

This fusion of profit and politics fed a news and entertainment complex that was already the largest in the world—and that was one of the first domestic industries to restructure itself along transnational lines. In the 1940s and 1950s, U.S. wire services, magazine publishers, television studios, and movie companies quickly achieved global control. By the 1960s, concerns about American media hegemony had reached such a magnitude worldwide that the United Nations convened a special series of conferences to investigate the media market. Charges were made that the United States had stepped well beyond the realm of simple profiteering. At one of those early meetings Finnish president Urho Kekkonen expressed the thoughts of many gathered when he asked, "Could it be that the prophets who preach unhindered communication are not concerned with equality among nations, but are on the side of the stronger and wealthier?"[10]

As a consequence of the ubiquity of American products, the United Nations Educational, Scientific, and Cultural Organization (UNESCO) issued a series of policy statements intended to protect discrete cultural identities. Despite the nonbinding character of such directives—and despite attempts by the United States to discredit

UNESCO as "partisan"—the documents demonstrated the seriousness with which many nations viewed cultural imperialism. These concerns related to two fundamental tenets of national self-definition: limits (the ability to maintain clear boundaries) and sovereignty (the authority to govern within those boundaries).[11] Hence, a 1972 Free Flow of Information declaration pertaining to broadcast technology stated that nations must reach "prior agreements concerning direct satellite broadcasting to the population of countries other than the country of origin of the transmission."[12] In 1973, UNESCO issued the first of several statements of the New World Information and Communications Order, again calling for equity. These documents culminated in the 1980 report by the International Commission for the Study of Communication Problems known as the MacBride Report.[13] Some nations ignored such declarations in part because of lack of enforcement, and both the United States and Britain eventually withdrew from UNESCO.

In the years since the MacBride Report matters have worsened. As borders continue to soften within the Americas, the European community, and throughout the world, cultural imperialism—led by a few dominant nations—continues to increase. A global economy may indeed open the door to an electronic global village. The question is, what can be done about this? Part of the answer lies in education, in the recognition that the cross-cultural exchange of media is not an inherently negative phenomenon. Old notions about the unilateral imposition of ideology from the strong to the weak need to be rethought. Understandings need to be developed of the complex and often contradictory ways that weak and strong powers enable each other. Assertions of cultural sovereignty are difficult to maintain in nations whose populations are clamoring for Madonna tickets. This is because typical cultural imperialism discourse fails to adequately theorize viewing/consuming subjects—their needs, desires, and pleasures. Instead of mediating the oppressive logics of capitalism and modernization, conventional cultural imperialism discourse offers a reactionary mix of humanism, chauvinism, and nostalgia. It fails to recognize how cultural imperialism works and what can be done pedagogically to help citizens resist it. For all of its good intentions, the UNESCO program was structurally incapable of exceeding a humanist appeal to universal merit. Implicit was the assertion of an essential sameness of all people in the "brotherhood" of nations.[14] This position was easily collapsed into the U.S. argument for universal trade rights in the presumed interest of international cooperation.

In the years after the UNESCO declarations, the United States redoubled its cultural assaults, which culminated in the passage of the 1989 Free Trade Agreement with Canada and its subsequent expansion to include Mexico.[15] In that accord Bush and Clinton administration officials established what they considered a precedent-setting legislative rationale for limitless export. By legally affording "corporate speech" the same status as "personal rights," the government gave transnational corporations authority to override any efforts to block the flow of not only media, but also computer data, electronic communication, or commodities of any kind.

This has only increased long-standing worries about U.S. cultural imperialism among its other allies. Since the end of World War II, for example, values of "Americanization" have been regarded widely as a threat to the purity of British national culture and tradition. Speaking of soap operas, George Orwell and Richard Hoggart both wrote of the erosion of working-class strength that might result from such a "feminine" medium.[16] To F. R. Leavis, the danger was less specified, but more sinister. Leavis pointed to "the rootlessness, the vacuity, the inhuman scale, the failure to organize cultural life, and the anti-human reductionism (of) the American neo-imperialism of the computer."[17]

Such criticisms of the media were justified, but misdirected. In Leavis's comments, one finds a nostalgic yearning for authenticity that often characterizes cultural nationalism. This is a longing for common origins in a world seemingly run amok with difference.[18] Racist innuendos aside, such romanticism is patently antimodernist, more pitted against notions of change than against media.[19] Like many cultural nationalists, Leavis was lamenting the threat to traditions posed by an American media of rock and roll, fast cars, and plastic plates. Ironically, this disposable modern culture was a great deal more appealing to the British working class than was the pastoral nostalgia associated with British aristocracy. It was not Leavis's traditions that Britons found exciting, but the newness offered by icons such as Elvis Presley and Marilyn Monroe.

Similarly it has been argued that much of what is customarily identified as cultural imperialism is really a function of change itself. John Tomlinson asserts that national identities defined purely in spatial terms fail to realize the temporal character of culture.[20] Simply put, no single national culture remains the same year after year. Nations are constantly assimilating, combining, and revising their national "characters." Moreover, even spatial boundaries rarely correspond to the demarcations among racial and ethnic groups, speakers of various languages, and even families. Thus the heterogeneous and changing nature of nations raises the question of who is authorized to speak on behalf of a national identity and when.

All of this suggests that solutions to cultural imperialism are far more complex than the establishment of trade barriers and import quotas. The answers involve helping people to understand how and why media imperialism works, both in general and on them.

HOME VIEWING: DOMESTIC MEDIA AND NATIONAL IDENTITY

No one needs reminding that similar debates over media texts continue to be waged within the United States, as antagonists on both the Left and Right have recognized the capacity of images to assume a symbolic meaning in the national consciousness. This is a function of the way signs become unhinged from their references in the age of the simulacrum. The resulting slipperiness of meaning has been exploited by various groups, as in debates during the last decade over schoolbooks, motion picture ratings, and arts funding. By focusing on particular films or photographs as ideological emblems, public figures have used these discourses for political gain. But whether or not these critics have had an impact on the content of TV and movies is still an open question.

Domestic complaints about media fall into three categories.[21] The first might be called the moral crisis argument. Its proponents assert that the violent and sexual content of television, movies, and recordings causes deviant behavior in viewers. They insistently overlook the absence of any empirical validation of their beliefs, despite countless studies on the subject. They also refuse to recognize both the complexity of young people's viewing practices and the kinds of pleasure derived from such viewing. Most significantly, by blaming social problems on the media, moral panickers divert attention from root causes of crime and violence such as racism and structural poverty.

The second category of criticism frames the activity of television viewing as a form of narcotic that dulls the senses, encourages laziness, and confuses the viewer's sense of reality. This includes the well-known labeling of TV as "mind candy," the "idiot box," or the "plug-in drug." The medium is blamed for ills ranging from poor academic performance to obesity to voter apathy. Not only do the media become scapegoats for other problems, but they are condemned for their basic function of providing relaxation and entertainment that bring people pleasure.

The third category of criticism poses media as extensions of a consciousness industry that exerts a virtual authority over consumers. Viewers are seen as passive recipients of instructions that they are powerless to challenge. Like those taking the moral panic stance, people who assume this position choose to overlook the growing body of research suggesting that audiences use media in extremely diverse and complex ways. They fail to see that there is no such thing as a homogeneous "public" for media, but instead a variety of audience configurations with different needs and desires.

It is worth remembering that recent debates over media censorship were not initiated by an outraged public or concerned scholars but by religious extremists and headline-hungry politicians. Even though the potential has always existed for partisan misreadings of cultural signs, until the late 1980s the political incentive (and strategic wherewithal) was insufficient to elevate the practice above name calling. It took the catalyzing influence of forces outside the cultural mainstream to capitalize on domestic fears and to cast cultural workers as the terror of the heartland.[22] Religious fundamentalists and political conservatives linked their accusations of immorality to a populist resentment of artists, intellectuals, and the "minority" interests the cultural community represented. Rather than proffering an inherently "false" message, the Right successfully linked its program to existing attitudes via a series of displacements that associated Martin Scorcese, Karen Finley, and 2 Live Crew with such perceived threats to traditional values as atheism, socialism, homosexuality, racial difference, and gender nonconformity.

Ironically, while the conservative program makes surface appeals to a nationalistic populism, it simultaneously promotes a cultural elitism that excludes the identities and histories of most citizens. This is a function of the often contradictory deployment of power in contemporary society. As Homi K. Bhabha has suggested, the continuing renewal of national identity—the will to nationhood that is reaffirmed each day—requires an erasure of past origins, ethnicities, and places. The obligation to forget in the name of unity is a form of "violence involved in establishing the national writ."[23] It is a matter to which national subjects consent and with which they struggle. Culture can no longer be seen as simply rooted in the kinds of "functionalist" views of social reproduction to which the Right has clung for much of the past century. It can no longer be attached to elite ideals to which the unwashed masses should aspire. In such thinking learning is regarded as a process of adaptation to a stable array of social mandates, and personal agency inevitably succumbs to the will of existing institutions and behavioral norms. Instead, culture should be seen as a set of social transactions that are negotiated and exchanged over time.

At the same time, as important as it is to see culture as a network of negotiated texts, it would be foolish to discount the role of the political economy in which they reside. The sustenance of academic and political conservatism lies in the consolidated corporate strength supporting it. No amount of theorizing by itself will place an alternative record album on a store shelf or an independent video on television. Those institutions are firmly under the thumb of an economic power structure that functions strictly in its own interest. Utopian speculations of the 1960s promised to replace alienating written texts with a humanizing electronic network. But such aspirations of technological determinism could not forecast that the mere exchange of medium would not disentangle the message from the capitalist order.[24]

This effect of economic reproduction across a range of productive fields was documented by Ben J. Bagdikian in his often quoted study of the early 1980s, *The Media Monopoly*.[25] Bagdikian described the near-complete control of U.S. publishing, movie making, and broadcast media by a handful of multinational conglomerates. Fewer than twenty companies (Westinghouse, Paramount, Time, ABC, CBS, McGraw-Hill, New York Times, and General Cinema, among others) control all leading television networks, 70 percent of the major book publishers, 45 percent of the dominant magazine companies, 75 percent of the leading movie companies, and 70 percent of the major radio networks. In orthodox leftist analysis this monopolistic control of media was believed to promote an ever-increasing textual homogenization that promoted the consumption of mass-produced goods and the delegitimization of alternative thinking. At the other extreme, the Right argued that the expansion and differentiation of capitalist production ensured an ever-widening choice of goods and texts. Both positions failed to account adequately for differences among consuming groups in their willingness and ability to engage or not engage in consumption. However, what can be asserted is that the bulk of Hollywood products contained more variety than critics of homogenization were willing to recognize and more sameness than conservatives were able to see.

Further analysis has revealed that media tend to address what has been termed an "ideal spectator," someone who possesses a particular set of interpretive capacities and preferences. The appeal to an ideal spectator is made in the form of a "preferred reading" that asks the viewer to identify with particular values and beliefs. These preferred readings rely on "dominant codes" of semiotic meaning. As a subset of this process, television has its own special forms of address, related to its ability to communicate to national and international audiences. This address assumes four basic functions in national identity formation.[26] First, it replicates and thereby reinforces hierarchies of capital within a given society. Major media networks are owned and controlled by a small elite who dispense information to multitudes. Second, television is structured to accommodate what Raymond Williams termed a "flow," that is, the tendency of viewers to watch a chain of programs, commercials, and news without switching from discrete program to program. Over time this flow creates the impression of a unified theme. Third, television's direct address to viewers (who are often isolated) positions them as "the public" looking over a commentator's shoulder. This positioning implies a controlling gaze through which viewers survey and control a world of difference. Fourth, television often depicts "ordinary" people in a fashion that implies populist consent to this controlling gaze.

Because communications industries are predicated on maximizing audience shares, they tend to address a normative spectator profile. Yet, particularly in recent years, this approach has been complicated by a growing recognition of different audiences identified by such factors as age, race, gender, and region. Further exacerbating this fragmentation has been the consumer flexibility afforded by cable television and home cassette viewing. These factors have encouraged large-scale producers to search for issues that transcend audience divisions. And indeed, many of the biggest-grossing films address themes with a national or nationalist appeal.

One form this chauvinism takes is the nostalgic appeal to origins mentioned earlier. From the misty romanticism of *Driving Miss Daisy* (1989) to the soft-core social critique of *Dances With Wolves* (1990), filmmakers seek to conjure up a shared national past. Literally or symbolically the specter of an ominous *other* often lurks in the background, encouraging viewers to draw their nationalistic wagons in a circle of defense. Not surprisingly, Hollywood villains and real-life political scapegoats often are indistinguishable: the implied ethnic criminality of *Boyz N the Hood* (1991) and *Bugsy* (1991) mirrors contemporary prejudices, and the foreign menace of *The Hunt for Red October* (1990) and *Shining Through* (1992) is hardly pure fiction. On one level, it is argued, such films help to coalesce an audience around the fear of a common demon that throws national parochialism into relief. But this analysis fails to account adequately for the complex economies of attraction and desire that also characterize constructions of difference. As discussed in chapter 1, any entity is both defined and limited by objects of alterity.[27] Because the externalized other is simultaneously a figure of antagonism and radical possibility, it constitutes a part of the self that the self both wants and fears.

This ambivalence toward otherness finds its most instrumental expression in colonial narratives. Here, difference is both material substance and textual sign. The short distance from nationalistic pride to imperialistic aggression, from patriotism to racism, is demonstrated in a comparable range of films celebrating colonialism past and present, including *The Gods Must Be Crazy* (1981), *A Passage to India* (1984), *Indiana Jones* (1984), *Out of Africa* (1985), *Club Paradise* (1986), and *Heat and Dust* (1988). In each instance the world becomes a stage for an alternating program of benevolence and conquest.[28]

In an age increasingly defined by limits, the commercial discourse of the West anxiously calls for continued expansion in the name of social betterment. This compulsive drive for the proliferation of Western capital is manifest in a plethora of recent ads baying at the threat of international competition. The U.S. trade deficit mounts ever higher as Buick touts its "commitment to world-class quality" and AT&T's business service offers "To Help Herman & Son Take On the World." While the pressure from foreign trade competition continues to grow, the rhetoric of global domination heightens. Nowhere is there evidence of the spirit of interconnectedness that a true international community requires. Is it any wonder that the programmatic dissemination of hegemonic capitalism has become the very emblem of the United States abroad?

From the War of 1812 to the present, the United States has maintained an image of military invulnerability and global sovereignty. Although recent examples abound, one of my favorite illustrations of such propagandizing involved a domestic program of the 1980s, the comical publicity campaign waged for Star Wars—not the film fantasy of director George Lucas, but the political fantasy of Ronald Reagan. Inasmuch as both film and defense program were popularized via the media, their differences became exceedingly difficult to discern. Interchangeable subject matter, terminology, and hardware blurred the line between science fiction and fact—and the Reagan administration took full advantage of it. Narrowing the gap between futuristic fantasies and world events permitted the reduction of complex international issues into a realm of simplistic figuration: Manichaean battles of light against dark, tales of wilderness conquest, and Manifest Destiny. Comparable narrative displacements were called into service to popularize the invasions of Panama, Grenada, and Kuwait.

The Star Wars mythology was powerful medicine indeed, which both Reagan and Bush were able to translate into budgetary success. One might logically ask why the voting public was so willing to swallow so "unreal" an explanation for the expenditure of billions of dollars that might otherwise have served more humanitarian purposes. In part the answer is the circumspect pathways that propaganda travels in Western society. As the sophistication of the film industry's illusionistic capabilities pushes the public's fantasy quotient to all-time highs, the press increasingly encourages a language of euphemism and analogy, a distancing from the real. In this vocabulary, war is not fought, but "prosecuted," and citizen massacres are rendered invisible by terms such as "collateral damage."

Within this mediated view, world peace is enforced through the benevolence of a single superpower. Despite its utopian intentions, the United States has carried out this role with an irrational ruthlessness with three primary characteristics: (1) a desire for absolute freedom from any outside control, (2) a privileging of unilateral action over extended diplomacy, and (3) a tendency to use military force to resolve political or economic problems.[29] Although this attitude has been manifest in recent U.S. interventions in Central America and the Middle East, it culminated in its most explicit form in the 1992 Pentagon plan for a "New World Order" calling for all nations except the United States to demilitarize.

Implicit in this stance of benevolent world domination is a vision of global agreement and sameness similar to that purportedly existing within the United States itself. This is a world of total conformity to a single standard of beliefs and principles—as represented in a presumably perfect U.S. system. As Reagan put it, the ethos "for which America and all democratic nations stand represents the culmination of Western Civilization."[30] Whether the subject is education or foreign policy, in such an environment dissent becomes no longer appropriate or acceptable. Agreement to standardized norms, held in place by elaborate social technologies, becomes the only permissible option. Unilateral action on the international front is therefore always permissible because the United States is always correct. The spread of U.S. culture throughout the world is viewed as healthy and just.

BACK TO SCHOOL: THE EVOLUTION OF MEDIA IN THE CLASSROOM

Television entered the pedagogical picture in the decade following World War II, but critical viewing was the last thing on its proponents' minds. As the first wave of the baby boom hit the classroom in the 1950s, video was instantly seized upon as a means of increasing teacher productivity. Simply by eliminating the need for duplicate presentations, video was credited with reductions in labor of up to 70 percent.[31] It was also recognized as a powerful tool for observation and evaluation.[32] Concurrent advances in computer and telecommunications industries prompted more elaborate speculation. While in residence at Fordham University in New York during the late 1960s, Marshall McLuhan attracted a quasi-religious following for his vision of a global telecommunications network designed on biological (and therefore "natural") principles that would undermine all hierarchical structures. At the core of McLuhan's program lay a concept of media as "information without content" that defined international turmoil as the result of failed communication rather than ideological confrontation.[33]

This pop-philosophy approach to new technology fit perfectly into 1960s educational reformism, while also complementing U.S. cultural policy. In a domestic atmosphere of desegregation, urban renewal, and other liberal initiatives, efforts were made to eliminate the biases inherent in standard pedagogies. As a means of deemphasizing differences of race, gender, and class, theories of educational formalism were introduced in many schools to stress the structure of learning over culturally specific content. As John Culkin put it in 1970, "One doesn't have to know all about a subject, but one should know what a subject is all about."[34] Educators saw photographic media as tools for directly engaging student experience. They developed concepts of "visual literacy" to compete with what some viewed as oppressive print-oriented paradigms.[35] In the introduction to their 1971 book *Need Johnny Read?*, Linda Burnett and Frederick Goldman explained that many students "demonstrate a lack of proficiency and lack of interest in reading and writing. Can we really expect proficiency when interest is absent? To what purpose do we force students through traditional subjects in traditional curricula?"[36] Within this movement, many teachers adapted photography and video equipment to their purposes.

With the economic downturns of the 1980s and the ascendancy of the Reagan/Bush government came sweeping indictments of liberal programs. Supply-side analysts blamed schools for the nation's inability to compete in world markets while, ironically, arguing for reductions in federal education and cultural budgets. Because they often required expensive equipment, media programs were terminated in the name of cost reduction, as emphasis was placed on a "back to basics" curriculum. This did not mean that television disappeared from the classroom, only that its more complicated, hands-on applications were replaced by simple viewing.

The reemergence of the television as teacher in the 1980s paralleled distinct shifts in its production and distribution. These were outgrowths of large-scale changes in the film and television industries brought about by the emergence of affordable consumer videocassette equipment. For the viewer, home recording and tape rental allowed hitherto unknown control over what was watched. The same was true in the classroom. For the instructional media industry, the costly process of copying 16mm films was now supplanted by inexpensive high-speed video duplication. The entire concept of educational media products began to change, as films could be mass-produced on a national scale (in effect "published") like books. Market expansion in this type of video was exponential. So profound was the technological change that 16mm-film processing labs from coast to coast went out of business overnight.

In many respects, the real beneficiaries of this video proliferation have been consumers, along with the profiteering business interests who serve them. Beyond making available a wide variety of materials—from Hollywood movies to aerobics lessons—the VCR revolution has afforded viewers an unprecedented degree of autonomy. With the options of time-shifting, editing, and even producing videotapes, the average television user has become significantly more involved in TV culture. The creative potential of orchestrating video within family life, building tape collections, and documenting important programs or personal activities is enormous—all are active gestures of cultural production and practices that media educators can encourage as means of promoting citizen agency and voice.

There is also a negative side to the VCR boom, particularly in the classroom. Beyond obvious arguments that pit time efficiency against human interaction lie the more subtle issues of subjective address. Unlike home viewing that affords a degree of flexibility and choice, the use of educational media does indeed position students as passive receivers of information, while at the same time validating an intellectual process based on stereotyping.[37] This replicates the most conservative forms of transmission learning and teacher-centered pedagogy. Such an approach is typified in the flood of slickly produced and moralistic videos for the school market from such entities as the Children's Defense Fund, the Center for Humanities, and Guidance Associates. These organizations offer an enormous range (the current Guidance Associates catalogue lists over five hundred filmstrips, slide series, and tapes) on topics from drug abuse to "values clarification," all stressing a prescriptive and normative ideology.

Such appeals to moral norms characterize a discourse of nationalism obsessed with a "national family" and the sanctity of its procreative capacities.[38] Indeed, the correspondence between home and country as "domestic" regimes becomes literalized in the figure of the motherland, the fertile ground of the nation where "to govern is to populate."[39] This metaphor of woman-as-nation hinges on a representation of a specific female personality: chaste, dutiful, and maternal. Like other tropes of nationalism, it establishes itself relationally within a system of differences. Its identity is determined as much by exclusion as inclusion. This nation is not the motherland of aggressive sexuality, homosexuality, or sex outside the legislated precincts of marriage.[40]

Lorraine Kenny has detailed the efforts of educational media producers to construct a normative national subjectivity for young women based on fear and coercion.[41] In one of the most insidious examples, the Children's Defense Fund evokes the dual specters of teen pregnancy and HIV contagion as consequences of sexual transgression. In such materials both adolescent sexuality and homosexuality are equated (metaphorically or literally) with illness, humiliation, crime, poverty, or death, as in this excerpt from a Children's Defense Fund report: "Teen pregnancy affects everybody's family, community, neighborhood, and region. Like the prospect of nuclear war, illegal drugs, and Acquired Immune Deficiency Syndrome (AIDS) and other sexually transmitted diseases, teen pregnancy is becoming an equal opportunity threat."[42] Kenny asserts: "Given that AIDS and teen pregnancy are seen to result from amoral sexual practices, i.e. homosexuality and sex between 'children,' in both cases legally unmarried partners, it is perhaps not surprising that public response to each issue falls within a similar domain."[43] Both are referenced in terms of "epidemics" or "crises" that threaten personal well-being and the social totality. Clearly, such media materials do more than merely teach students about the consequences of unprotected sex. They constitute elements of a broader mechanism of social control in which young people are socialized into specific belief systems and institutionalized behaviors.

The renewed use of such instructional aids has increased in recent years, as corporate educational reformers reach for technological solutions to school problems. Witness the phenomenon of Channel One. Since going on-line in 1990, the Whittle Communication Corporation's Channel One has been piping its MTV-style blend of news programming and commercials for corn chips and acne medicine into twelve thousand secondary schools. In exchange for up to fifty thousand dollars in free video equipment, schools agree to present the twelve-minute programs to their students. As explained by company president Chris Whittle, normally "you can't make people who don't watch television watch television."[44] In school you can.

As programs such as Channel One have grown, a number of grassroots groups have worked to produce alternative teaching aids. Countering the influx of conservative industrial material have been the classroom programming services of the Media Network (New York) and the Video Data Bank (Chicago); the role model project organized by Women Make Movies (New York); the media for the handicapped project of the now defunct Film in the Cities (St. Paul); and the juvenile court school program of the Masada Community Day Center (Los Angeles), to name but a few. The Media Network's *Images of Color* directory and the Video Data Bank's *What Does She Want?* series take different approaches to placing noncommercial work in an educational marketplace overwhelmed by corporate production. *Images of Color* is a reference guide of productions and distributors from and for communities of color. Films and tapes by makers such as Ayoka Chenzira, Lourdes Portillo, and Luis Valdez are listed according to categories such as civil rights, health, housing, immigration, and work. *What Does She Want?* is a series of feminist video works assembled into packages addressing themes of history, the family, and media representation.[45]

A recent pilot program organized by Women Make Movies brought filmmakers Christine Choy, Jacqueline Shearer, Sharon Sopher, and Peggy Stern into contact with students at Manhattan's Muse School. Muse is part of the Pompeii Youth Program, an off-site education service of the New York City Board of Education that works with long-term truants and dropouts. The project sought to foster a nonsexist media curriculum by introducing participants to the filmmakers and their films. By doing so, it furnished positive role models for women, including those engaged in nontraditional occupations and from different racial and ethnic backgrounds. As the screening series progressed, Women Make Movies instructors overcame the resistance with which students often greet liberal pedagogy. Project coordinator Margaret Cooper explained, for example, that in the prescreening discussion of Sopher's *Witness to Apartheid* the class doubted the ability of a white filmmaker to adequately analyze South African race relations.[46] Yet after seeing the film and discussing the issues with Sopher, the group was sufficiently moved to draft a series of letters to the president. Obviously these programs brush against the grain of both conservative ideology and bureaucratic organization, and as such they are anomalies. At the same time such programs provide models through which the promise of progressive views of national identity is kept alive.

Clearly, the importance of audiovisual materials will continue to grow in school, in the workplace, and at home with the proliferation of videocassette equipment, cable channels, home shopping networks, computer information services, telecommunications linkups, interactive texts, and games. We should not delude ourselves that these new technologies by themselves are capable of changing social relationships or economic structures. As quickly as a new gimmick is developed, Madison Avenue finds a way to turn a profit from it. Yet these new tools offer potential for innovative subversive use, and for the establishment of new forms of alliance, and for the creation of new strains of cultural production.

THE NEW MEDIA LITERACY MOVEMENT

As with regressive written texts, the key to emancipatory use of media in the classroom is helping students locate progressive readings to the materials offered. Particularly in settings with students from diverse backgrounds it is important to stress that culture is not limited to what is legitimated in books and other instructional materials. It includes what is "ordinary."[47] Culture is a sociological substance produced every day by each of us. This is especially true with everyday texts, and it is what makes a static view of national identity problematic. People's narrative relationships are constantly in flux—both those we find in books and the diverse narratives we encounter in items such as movies, television, clothing, appliances, food, and housing. Understandings of these texts are always partial and incomplete, always in need of some revision to adapt them to change and circumstance. As people continue to adjust their interpretations, they are making the meaning that is culture.

In radical circles of education a growing body of literature has developed in recent decades to contest hierarchical models of schooling.[48] Partly informed by critical pedagogy and cultural studies, the new "media literacy" movement (as opposed to its older "market research" counterpart) is an amalgam of reader response theories and institutional analyses. While acknowledging the persuasive properties of images, practitioners of media literacy emphasize individualized ways viewers use media. Moreover, because moviegoers and television watchers can recognize the artifice of representation, they need not always be fooled by it. The concept of literacy is central in this pedagogy, as explained by Cary Bazalgette:

> Most people agree that fully literate readers bring many understandings to a text: they can recognize what kind of text it is, predict how it will work, relate it to other texts in appropriate ways. They can thus understand it critically, enjoying its pleasures, engaging with its argument, reading "between and beyond the lines" . . . Every medium can be thought of as a language. Every medium has its own way of organizing meaning, and we all learn to "read" it, bringing our own understandings to it, and extending our own experience through it.[49]

The media literacy movement has political significance in the ways it connects theory and practice—often by attempting to explain or demonstrate complex theories to young people. By doing this it diplomatically reconciles opposing concepts of the viewing subject. In textual terms, the media literacy movement argues that our abilities to mediate dominant readings and spectator positionings can be improved with study and that these skills can be taught to children regardless of age or grade level. One can teach young people to use media for their own ends by actively interpreting how media function and choosing how to read them. Put another way, the movement proposes to begin identifying strategies for contextual reading, thereby suggesting changes to the "institutional structures" that condition spoken and interpretive norms.[50] One method is encouraging viewers to look beyond specific texts by asking critical questions such as "Who is communicating and why?" "How is it produced?" "Who receives it and what sense do they make of it?" A characteristic exercise for younger children asks what TV programs they like and dislike. In the course of the discussion the class quickly divides into groups of Voltrons, Noozles, and Smurfs. What becomes apparent is the relatively simple yet important notion that media texts are not uniformly received. By examining their own preferences, children come to recognize that mass media do not define a unified national audience but rather a heterogeneous universe of spectator groups.

From this a discussion can evolve on the ways advertisers and media producers tailor their programming based on media consumption.

In a class conducted by the San Francisco–based group Strategies for Media Literacy, students[51] compare pictures of their own families with ones they find on TV. By making visual comparisons between the Huxtables, the Keatons, and themselves, kids are asked to ponder "Which is real?" Of course the answer is "None," because depictions—private and public—are fictional. Through this exercise youngsters begin to learn not only how they are interpellated by the forces of media myth making, but also the ways they have internalized received narratives of family. Again, the lesson is that children are part not of a unified "national family," but of many different communities and affinity groups. By drawing attention to students' own attitudinal biases and stereotypes, the lesson underscores the relationship of self to image.

Beyond such textual issues, media education can also interrogate the concrete ways that television, radio, and movies structure audiences and their material surroundings. For example, the address of TV has evolved in part to cater to a domestic audience and to encourage certain patterns of television use within the home. It serves as breakfast entertainment, evening family ritual, or weekend sports gathering. These functions have influenced the layout and use of spaces within the home as well as appointments within individual rooms. Consequently, TV has both a direct and indirect impact on a broad range of commodities, a point hardly lost on the merchandisers of goods ranging from popcorn poppers to easy chairs. John Fiske has written of the way people employ television to modulate the "texture" of living environments, which people create and alter as a means of laying claim to social space: "Television is used to increase, enrich and further densify the texture. It is typically left on all the time, adding color, sound and action to apartment life; it is used to frame and cause conversations, to fill gaps and silences. It can provide both a means of entering and intensifying this dense everyday culture and a way of escaping it."[52] Again, use becomes a matter of strategy and intent.

Such consumer activism hardly characterizes most media literacy curricula. All too often in conventional pedagogies such emancipatory forms of media literacy are discounted as inconsequential, banal, or unhealthy. Offered instead is a program of viewer "empowerment" with a free-market attitude of audience "choice," in which viewers become reconciled to the options available to them. This has been the rationale of numerous recent prescriptions from the mainstream, as typified in the National Endowment for the Arts's landmark overview of arts education in the United States, *Toward Civilization: A Report on Arts Education*. In it NEA pedagogues suggest that the value of media studies lies in creating smarter shoppers:

> Every child growing up in the United States is bombarded from birth with popular art and artful communication over the airways and on the streets.

The purpose of arts education is not to wean young people from these arts (an impossible task even if it were desirable) but to enable them to make reasoned choices about them and what is good and bad. Art education can help make discriminating consumers.[53]

The attitude concerning media in *Toward Civilization* is consistent with the view of culture in general in the report, which promotes a single, "good" standard of visual literacy to which all Americans should subscribe. The overall goal is the production of a national identity of verisimilitude, wherein all citizens share the same competencies, values, and rights.

This conservative view of media education on the national level results from the unwillingness or inability of many localities to integrate media into their curricula. In part this is due to the relative intransigence of North American education markets and to the economic difficulties many school districts face. Also, as an interdisciplinary field largely devoted to popular culture, media studies is often dismissed by school administrators as an educational frill. "Back to basics" advocates vehemently oppose media courses, claiming that they undermine traditional culture and values. (The difficulty, of course, is that the popular appeal of mass-cultural texts derives largely from their anti-educational character.) Finally, it hardly goes unnoticed that media courses are by definition student-centered and subversive in their critiques of capitalism and patriarchy. The resulting rejection of them is a form of institutional control that limits the extent to which criticism can be raised or even discussed.

When media literacy does find its way into the school curriculum it generally takes one of two forms: vocational education or an enhancement of an existing course in another discipline. Media education in a vocational context is generally driven by a job-preparation mandate lacking in any critical consciousness. At Cincinnati's Hughes High School for the Communications, a Scripps-Howard Foundation–sponsored national model in vocational media education, students engage in a rigorous four-year curriculum of media writing and production. In addition to cable-television programs, photography projects, and public-relations materials, students work on a special school newspaper covering controversial issues such as student race relations, homosexuality, and drug use.

Yet, while providing technical training and a forum for airing social issues, the overall curriculum promotes an unexamined image of commercial media and journalism. As in the U.S. "free flow of information" doctrine and *Toward Civilization* cultural prescriptions, the media landscape in the Hughes program is presented as an inherently even terrain where choice is open and access unstymied. Little acknowledgment is given to the extremely unequal positions from which people enter this terrain, the continuing discriminations they suffer, and the power structures that benefit from these arrangements. An unproblematic image is promoted of a nation where all citizens have equal opportunities—regardless of race, gender, or sexual orientation—if only they have the gumption to follow their dreams. Failure is thus personalized as an individual shortcoming rather than recognized as an institutionally programmed necessity.

As enhancements to existing courses, studies of television, movies, or print media are most likely to be found in English, art, or social studies classes where textual reading and production already have a footing. Unfortunately the atmosphere often locked in by canonical regimens can stultify critical thinking. Regarding media education in English classes, Len Masterman has suggested that "an emphasis upon links and parallels with literature and a reliance upon student response via the limited form of the literary review suggest that the realities of curricular life . . . may act as a brake upon achieving the fullest potentials for media education."[54] When constituted as an add-on to existing courses, media education has been extremely limited in its ability to challenge forms of identity, national or otherwise, perpetuated in schools.

TEACHING TEACHERS

Change requires effort. One place to begin is within schools of education, where the curricula of teacher preparation continue to reproduce very traditional attitudes toward media. The introduction of media literacy into existing courses need not rely on special texts or instructional materials. Like other critical pedagogies, it hinges more on the way a teacher handles all materials. On a primary level, media education within a given curriculum entails a greater attention to photographs, films, or videos as producers of meaning. This requires abandoning assumptions that particular readings are self-evident or that a medium itself is a neutral carrier of information. Such views are rooted in the same subject/object dualisms that foster transmission theories of teaching. In contrast to these views, it should be pointed out that truth does not pass perfectly through a video to a student, nor knowledge through a teacher. Both require the engagement of students in receiving messages and making sense of them. Therefore, beyond course content and the forms of its delivery, schools should focus on developing competencies of reception that permit students to make choices and exercise agency in learning.

This form of media education capitalizes on what students already know about the vocabulary and syntax of media, while encouraging them to become more critically conscious of "how they know what they know."[55] In history classes, this might involve a content analysis of the images in a textbook. What kinds of people are pictured and in what numbers? Who seems to be in control? Similar questions can be asked in geography. In social studies, current events often are used as a springboard for discussion. But do newspapers and television report the facts with complete objectivity? What parts of the story have been highlighted or ignored? In an

English class using required texts, a teacher might spend time talking about the limits of specific genres, the economics of publishing, and the separation of "high" culture from the everyday.[56]

In each of these instances media literacy instruction begins to ask students to question the way their identities have been shaped as subjects in the school, the neighborhood, the nation, and the world. The point is that whether or not viewers realize it (in fact because they often do *not* realize it) they are always being interpellated by the media into quite specific roles. Every movie, every textbook, and every magazine addresses an ideal audience that is most often defined in terms of a national collectivity. This interpellation is so ubiquitous that it seems nonexistent. It is simply assumed.

More than in the brazen chauvinism of Rambo and Ralph Lauren, the country-as-consumer-collective exists in an advertising industry that pictures the world as its playground; in a commercial ethos of economic dominance rather than cooperation; and now, in a military attitude of complete global control rather than negotiation. Images aside, the question these attitudes leave begging concerns the future role of the United States in the world community. Indeed, what is the relevance of any national identity in a world of transnational capital? The combined effects of the free flow of information and the breakdown of national boundaries have caused changes in the centers as well as the margins of international culture. Media products from the United States now reach larger audiences abroad than at home. For this reason production companies (many of which are foreign-owned) now tailor programs for international audiences. Increasingly, the choices offered to U.S. viewers are determined by audiences located elsewhere. As the United States loses strength as an economic power, the influence of external cultures will continue to grow.

These realities come into direct conflict with a foreign policy based on the eternal correctness of the United States and its "right" to unilateral action throughout the globe. Sooner or later the United States will need to recognize the inherent partiality of any single perspective and the imperative for cooperation in global affairs. One place where this awareness can begin to be introduced is the classroom. By learning the limitations of any particular viewpoint or reading, students can develop literacies that value difference, and can use the awareness of difference in creating a moral vision that a single perspective can never offer.

THREE

Ordinary People

Material Culture and the Everyday

> What kind of life can it be, I wonder, to produce this extraordinary fussiness, this extraordinary decision to call certain things culture and then separate them, as with a park wall, from ordinary people and ordinary work?
>
> —Raymond Williams[1]

In the preceding quotation from his often cited 1958 essay "Culture Is Ordinary," Raymond Williams posed a defining question for cultural studies. Why indeed has culture been conventionally defined in such narrow terms, and why are those terms endlessly reconstituted in successive discourse? What is behind the compulsion among traditionalist historians, curators, and journalists to separate the "extraordinary" in their writing from the common stuff of daily existence? How does the competitive structure of a market economy extend even to its most progressive quarters?

Every day another salvo is fired in the ongoing battle between defenders of "the best and brightest" and proponents of the liberating possibilities of the "ordinary." Implicit in the valorization of high culture is its presumption of a moral standard, an exclusive set of truths to which all people should aspire. Coupled with this idealism is a claim to represent the values of mainstream America. In public debates over political correctness and arts censorship, reactionary ideologues have exploited this position to mobilize mass resentment toward experts, academics, and government bureaucrats. Ironically, while the Right valorizes the uncontrived pleasures of the "average" citizen, it simultaneously promotes a cultural policy that excludes the histories and identities of most people. The Left has proffered its own contradictory version of such populism, with well-meaning artists and intellectuals romanticizing rituals of the ordinary. But thus far most of these efforts have backfired, as the progressive call to "the people" increasingly is read either as opportunistic vanguardism or as intellectual tourism.[2]

Steeped in politics, this problematic relationship with the ordinary is a function of cultural difference. It results when one group possesses the means and resources to reduce the life of another to a text. In public policy, this is the process by which human capacities and needs become translated into budgets, regulations, and laws. The bureaucratic analysis of ordinary lifestyles reveals a compulsive preoccupation with difference, which, despite its well-meaning intentions, results in a form of discursive management. It maintains a normative "everyday" against which other cultures are measured. Within this scheme, the very markers of group identity and solidarity become curiosities to the examiner. This objectification of the ordinary has an aestheticizing character that strips these markers of any emancipatory possibility, in effect replacing them with new meaning.[3]

In the professional realm of the academy, social domination is part of the scholarly obsession with those Enlightenment inducements to capitalist differentiation: progress, innovation, and originality. In a competitive atmosphere that requires constant achievement, the modernist demand of the new becomes the highest of intellectual values. In art history, anthropology, sociology, and now, to a certain extent, cultural studies, this translates into a relentless search for the exotic. In a revisionist era in which tracking foreign "primitives" is out of political fashion, the hunt for unspoiled territory is carried out on domestic soil. Like the birds an ornithologist must kill so that they can be studied, everyday behaviors that seem different are organized into narratives of control. This has changed a focus on the banal habits of lower and middle classes into a search for their more anomalous subcultures. Witness the recent spate of research projects on Trekkies, hackers, cyberpunks, and New Agers. Such is the character of disciplinary reification in the "post-disciplinary" era.[4]

Actually, this practice of consuming and reconstituting the everyday as a text has a long history, with origins in eighteenth-century "pastoral" writing that celebrates the simple pleasures of the "common peasant."[5] In the pastoral tradition, everyday themes and subject matter are reproduced, but in language and syntax of such sophistication that only an educated reader can appreciate them. This gesture of condescending empathy serves to identify and acknowledge the visceral pleasures of the body and the earth, while simultaneously marking a distance from them. In this sense it constitutes a ritual performance of detachment. Rather than drawing the washed and unwashed together, it employs a narrative that reinforces the boundaries between them. More importantly, instead of giving voice to the peasant's crudeness and complaints, this gesture of appropriation envelopes potentially disruptive speech, cleansing it of any truly subversive potential. Such is the colonial moment.[6] A dominant culture, or any culture for that matter, requires a recognizable Other so that it can see itself. As Stuart Hall has put it, through difference the self is thrown into relief: "The English are racist not because they hate the Blacks but because they don't know who they are without the Blacks. They have to know who they are not in order to know who they are."[7]

In contemporary life the process of pastoral rendering takes many forms—from cinematic representations of working-class life, to tourist excursions to tropical lands, to the postmodern fascination with kitsch. Each signifies the translation of cultural otherness into a usable stereotype. Difference is comfortably transmuted into a wrapping for a commodity or a commodity itself. The most prevalent instances of the pastoral in bourgeois life occur in people's homes, as the text of the ordinary is assigned a decorative function. Perhaps there is a souvenir salt-and-pepper set on the kitchen table, or a whimsically collected postcard on the refrigerator. More likely one finds an antique chair or cupboard, an "Oriental" rug, or a hand-thrown ceramic bowl. All of these things reference an attraction for an aesthetics of the commonplace, of the authentic, and even, at times, of the natural.

This appropriation of the pastoral is thought to be a function of the broader process through which material objects are elaborated as signs and identity becomes a matter of representation.[8] Although such a view is helpful in unpacking certain functions of signification, it can also lead to adopting uncritically the superficial "culture as signifier" approach to materiality.[9] As Dick Hebdige's early work on style illustrates, often missing in these linkages among signs are the activities and outlooks from which styles emanate.[10] Detached from its referent, the interpretive text takes on a life of its own, as academic treatises generate other academic treatises with little regard for the origins of their subject matter.

The next question is whether such a descriptive practice can have a prescriptive effect. Certainly, the overarching influence of texts has underscored recent debates over their role in establishing identity. Debates over multiculturalism and canon formation reflect the widely held view that what people think and do is largely influenced by the stories they see, hear, and tell. Within this self-justifying logic, language is credited with the ability to determine not only what one does, but who one is. Any visceral experience of the world is supplanted by its symbolic representation.[11] More than a few poststructuralists go as far as suggesting that within this environment the human subject ceases to exist, as identity becomes synonymous with narratives written elsewhere.

Needless to say, this view of textual authority is not held universally. A sign's link to its referent can never be absolute, and its influence on the subject must always be a mediated one. Although human identities are shaped by culture and history, undoubtedly there exists an accumulated narrative of self that can be named, albeit provisionally. But as noted earlier, compromises between positions that privilege either text or the material world have been surprisingly difficult to reach. Instead, there has been a tendency in cultural criticism to split discussions into polar oppositions. Either the world is rendered as a subset of language, or it is explained entirely in economic terms. New approaches should reach beyond this binary construction by discussing relationships among discourse and commodity, desire and consumption, subject and object, and all the kinds of difference that inform these terms. This might produce mechanisms to establish links to materiality by acknowledging and further developing the social spaces surrounding production, exchange, and consumption. What are the needs and texts that mediate these relationships? How does power operate in these processes?

Such an inquiry suggests a recognition of the necessarily reciprocal character of the speaking subject and the spoken-about object. Indeed, the choices people make cannot be explained as functions of text alone. As Susan Strasser has noted in discussing product development and marketing, new commodities do not emerge from a corporate black hole. They are more than simple media concoctions to be foisted upon unwitting consumers.[12] Such innovations succeed and fail according to their ability to complement genuine human desires.[13] Appreciating this process requires a critical sensibility about the ways meanings are attached to objects.

In this chapter I present a range of theoretical approaches to materiality as they relate to a contemporary culture. Instead of offering the material as a fetish set apart from language, I discuss the necessarily imbricated character of the two within social relations. Without denying the influence of texts on human agents, it is important to acknowledge the dialectical character of this exchange. Culture is a process that simply cannot be reduced to its objective or subjective forms. The tendency to separate text from materiality is most profoundly manifest in recent accounts of the ordinary. Hence, in exploring the heterogeneous category of everyday life within this model, I place particular emphasis on domestic artifacts such as furniture, cookware, and household appliances as they have been utilized as display objects. In particular the discussion examines the role of nostalgic icons that conjure up for their owners a pastoral past. This includes the entire range of "natural" wood furnishings, antiques, and folk crafts that so typify thirtysomething yuppie aesthetics. As an ensemble they prop up a mythic cult of authenticity that functions as a mask for deeper ideologies.

As these rocking chairs and spinning wheels have been appropriated into institutional academic culture they are frequently textualized and reified in the ways just described. In contemporary life very few objects maintain a stable meaning for very long. With this in mind I conclude this chapter with an analysis of one commodity form—the quilt—and trace its changing signification through a range of domestic, institutional, and aesthetic discourses. The seemingly innocent ethos of "Americana" quilt production occupies a position of profound contradiction in the hierarchies separating fine art and crafts. Within this contradiction exists the potential for using such domestic objects for emancipatory ends. They can be employed to inform taken-for-granted relationships of subjects and objects. This process of appropriation and emancipation is far from a simple one, for it is characterized by an ambivalence: a simultaneous affection and conceit belies its cultural construction and calls for a rethinking of the ways crafts are commonly understood.

Object Lessons

It is difficult to approach material culture without acknowledging the theoretical contributions of Karl Marx. More than any other thinker, Marx insisted on grounding social thought in the lived relations people have with actual things. Marx's famous formulations of the commodity form evolved from Hegel's phenomenology, which mapped out a basic theory of subject/object relations. Hegel postulated an abstract dyad of the self and other, constructed in the consciousness of individuals. Within this idealized rendering the subject envisions an external object that it comes to recognize as different from itself. This difference produces a dissatisfaction that prompts the subject to absorb the attributes of the external other. Hegel termed this process "sublation," and theorized that sublation is the motor force of human learning, as the subject is changed through the appropriation of new ideas and objects.[14] What is important to remember is that this dialectic was, for Hegel, a pure function of metaphysics.

Marx extended this metaphor by insisting that philosophical ideas must have applications in physical reality. For this reason Marx literalized the idea of the externalized other to represent actual commodities.[15] Thus he attributed the processes of acquisition, growth, and change through sublation to the relations between people and actual goods. In a utopian communist environment, workers would have unstymied access to the products they produce, and the process of social development would advance unproblematically. Under capitalism, this process is distorted as workers become estranged from their creative products by the operations of the market. To generate profits the market must interfere with sublation. This causes a frustrated mode of consumption, in which the commodity is fetishized and the consumer willingly pays more than a product is worth.

In the context of this chapter, Marx's ideas hold a special significance in their insistence on the simultaneous existence of commodities in both material and cognitive realms. Yet as Marx's ideas were reinterpreted and adapted to changing historical circumstances of the twentieth century, the dual character of commodities often was forgotten. The phenomenological side of the equation that privileged the direct experience of the subject was split from the side of cognitive objectivism. Unexamined experience of the subject was critiqued by the emergent discipline of structuralism as being unscientific, ahistorical, essentializing, and "subjective." Structuralists perceived a need for systems that "objectively" organized and rationally explained experience. As important as these developments were in correcting the solipsistic tendencies of phenomenology, they often were taken to extremes that afforded the subject no role whatsoever.

Jürgen Habermas described this split somewhat differently, as a division between positivism and hermeneutics. In this view the orthodox notion of the subject defined through productive relations was deemed too deterministic, for it subsumed all aspects of communication and culture within an overriding economism. Human evolution was reduced to a physical science. Without fully discounting the importance of Marx's latent positivism, Habermas proposed a hermeneutic practice to analyze more carefully the nonscientific and discursive aspects of daily life. To Habermas, hermeneutics addressed a different form of "knowledge-constitutive interest" than positivism.[16] Both were seen as partial (and interdependent) approaches to social analysis, applying different logical forms to the disclosure of reality.[17] Important in Habermas's formulations, and what brought him into conflict with poststructuralists, was his desire to retain partial autonomy for the subject as an entity that is constantly reconstituting itself in relation to external objects. Subsequent thinkers have made similar efforts to resolve seemingly mutually exclusive attitudes toward culture.[18]

The early writing of Jean Baudrillard continued this struggle to maintain a tension between subjective and objective theories. For Baudrillard these dual logics fused in the figure of the "commodity sign." Like Marx, Baudrillard blamed the textualization of commodities for generating an "abstract" exchange value from a "concrete" use value.[19] In this manner Baudrillard identified signification as the central logic of late capitalism. As seen in Americana folk art, the *rendering of the commodity as text* becomes the driving force of objectification, surplus valuation, and, ultimately, alienation. The much maligned pessimism of Baudrillard's work emanates from the next step in this logic, in which he asserted that signs take on a life of their own. These textual abstractions begin to generate an artificial intelligence that detaches itself from its material moorings. Soon signs are referring to other signs, as access to concrete materiality is endlessly deferred. Physical production becomes a redundant support of the system that eventually permeates every social institution and human relationship. To Baudrillard there is no escaping this process that assigns values, not only to objects and institutions, but to people and groups as well: "The system no longer requires universal productivity; it only requires everyone to play the game."[20] The only way to revolt is to quit the game.

Regrettably, Baudrillard's critique of the political economy of the sign failed to go much further in offering a way out. Instead his later work elaborated on both the mediation of the signifier and the death of the subject. This is unfortunate considering the important observations Baudrillard provided about the textual mediation of materiality. His understandings of the role of the sign in the assignment of value to commodities offer valuable pedagogical insights. They can help provide the means by which people oppressed by such texts can learn to work collectively to name, analyze, and change the conditions of their lives.[21]

As a point of tentative closure, I will proceed with this model of reciprocal subject/object relations. Discussion will focus on the uneasy relationship between "ordinary" folk cultures of past eras and the range of divergent narratives into which they have been appropriated. My fundamental premise is that popular knowledge of the material is not always identical to the texts used to describe these artifacts. Over time, human subjects accumulate identities that can be recognized and acted upon. Far from being static or unified constructions, these identities are constructed in language and are continually evolving in response to social changes. From this evolving narrative, diverse subjects can articulate themselves in relation to other texts. These identities achieve an individual character because human agents are always inscribed in multiple asymmetries of power. They exist in a multitude of social fields that unseat simple subject/object dualisms, replacing them with constellations of constituting differences.

Taking this model of multiple subject/object relations a step further is the porous nature of any self or other. As Renato Rosaldo has explained, the objectivist separation of the observer from the observed is a fiction, deployed in the colonial interest of distinguishing "us" from "them." It serves only as a clinical boundary to protect the anthropological researcher. But as Rosaldo suggests, "The objects of analysis are also analyzing subjects, who critically interrogate ethnographers, their writings, their ethics, their politics."[22] That subjects and objects are always partial provides the potential for forming new identities and for supporting the struggles of others in new ways.

At the risk of promoting a form of intellectual vanguardism, I want to emphasize that in each of these struggles one is ethically bound to acknowledge one's position and to act. In many instances, to remain passive in response to an asymmetry is to encourage its continued existence. For cultural workers this ethical task is at least partly a pedagogical one, because citizens need to become aware of the problems surrounding them. In modern hegemonic societies organized by purportedly democratic principles, consent to oppression and inequality cannot be overtly enforced. Instead consent is manufactured through idealized representations of harmony, justice, and national pride—representations that are often inscribed on material goods.

But since people are capable of recognizing a world of lived circumstances in relative distinction from the idealized world of signs, the contradictions between the two can be underscored. For every conservative proclamation of cultural populism, there is a conservative institutional reality of aristocratic elitism. For every idealized White House pronouncement of unbounded opportunity and freedom, there is an unidealized scene of lived oppression, discrimination, and economic violence.[23] With each passing year the distance between the dream and the reality widens. The reckoning that is coming holds both responsibilities and possibilities for pedagogical cultural workers.

These responsibilities extend beyond the mere identification of inequity or "false consciousness." Although each individual or class of individuals is located in a relation of both complicity with and opposition to oppression, these differing and overlapping subject positions do not ensure a necessarily productive response. As

Meaghan Morris has suggested, there are no advance assurances that citizens will find the means of subverting the antagonisms that surround them.[24] In fact, the idealistic faith in the inherently progressive character of social location itself has been used to obscure an awareness of "real" racism, sexism, homophobia, or economic injustice. For this reason cultural workers have an important role in opening conversations and discursive forms for the interrogation of oppressive antagonisms. Within this dialogue new articulations can emerge of the motivations and means of restructuring public life.[25] This constitutes the first step in the development of a critique and, ultimately, in the construction of a positive plan for a new order.

JUST PLAIN FOLK

The institutionalization of folk craft offers an important lesson about textualization within the political economy of the sign. In revealing the unstable meaning of the very term *folk*, one can see the ways such constructions are evoked in the service of hegemonic interests. Consider the collective connotations of the frequently used terms *primitive, natural, ethnic, outsider, rural, amateur, popular, vernacular, grassroots, homemade, naive, innocent, childlike, anonymous, unschooled, unsophisticated,* and *nonacademic*.[26]

The amalgamation of these terms under the general rubric of folk emerged while utilitarian objects from different regions and historical periods were being recoded as display items. The complexity of this recoding reveals the often contradictory character of U.S. national identity, in part suggesting a nostalgic return to frontier origins, a yearning for a cultural anchor. But as in pastoral renderings, this desire also signifies a disdain for the crudeness of those origins. As discussed by John Frow, these nostalgic sentiments structure a peculiar paradigm of absence,

> a sense of historical decline, giving rise to various social theologies of lost grace; a sense of the absence or loss of personal wholeness and moral certainty (the fracturing of the canopy of religious and moral value by the growth of capitalist relations and of urbanization); a sense of the loss of individual freedom and autonomy (the disappearance of genuine social relationships; and the bureaucratization of everyday life); and a sense of the loss of simplicity, personal authenticity, and emotional spontaneity.[27]

What results from this sense of loss is a "sadness without an object," a longing for a past that never existed except in narrative form (and that, for that reason, remains eternally absent).[28]

This longing is always ideologically charged, for it beckons representations of a specific utopia with a particular design. Hence, the nostalgic impulse often is charged with class and ethnicity, manifest in varying positions of acceptance or denial. The regressive side of such romanticism frequently expresses itself as an appeal to notions of the "authentic" and the "natural." This thinking has its roots in the biological determinism of Jean-Jacques Rousseau and the precapitalistic agrarianism of Martin Heidegger. Both men suggested a return to an unproblematic past of endlessly reproduced patriarchy—a sentiment extended in the implicit racism, classism, and homophobia of contemporary conservatives. As critiqued by Theodor Adorno in *The Jargon of Authenticity*, within this logic the laws of God and nature are continually evoked to justify the exploitation of cultural Others.[29] Existential truths are posited to mask social antagonisms and inequities.

Although folk art has been a recognized part of U.S. culture for nearly a century, the category is currently enjoying a renaissance in the public imagination. In the post–Kuwait era this resurgent interest in Americana parallels the cosmetic ascendance of the United States in the "New World Order." Despite (or because of) a failing economy and a crumbling social infrastructure, positive images are all the more sought. As anti-Japanese bigotry increases in Detroit and would-be demagogues call for walls along the Mexican border, the yearning for a reassuring American history is fed by Ralph Lauren and Martha Stewart.

Not that such political innuendos are especially new to folk craft. The impulse for collecting weather vanes and rocking chairs took root in earnest in the decades following World War I, when the United States emerged as the dominant hemispheric power. This was also the culmination of a period of great economic and social transition, as workers from abroad and from the Deep South began massing in the new industrial centers of the Northeast and Midwest. Anxieties in the emergent middle class of bourgeois Protestants were fed by this shift from a farm economy, by the depersonalization of urban life, and by the increased presence of ethnic minorities.

The link between class and commodity use was discussed by Basil Bernstein in his model of restricted and elaborated codes: "The simpler the social division of labor, and the more specific and local the relation between an agent and its material base, the more direct the relation between meanings and a specific material base, and the greater the possibility of a restricted coding orientation."[30] Conversely, elaborated codes evolve in people with more complex and distanced relations from the material, as those with more money are not as immediately concerned with obtaining the necessities of life. As a consequence, their needs are deferred in aestheticized rituals such as collecting objects that once served a utilitarian function. The institutionalization of such rituals in the museum, the home, and the school constitute what Bernstein termed an "invisible pedagogy."[31]

The emergence of the managerial class lent a new impetus to broad-scale collecting, which offered a particular brand of bourgeois conceit. Eugene W. Metcalf explains:

> As with fine art, the possession of folk art is an honorific sign of conspicuous consumption, and spending one's time collecting it serves as a symbol of

conspicuous leisure. . . . Those who have been able to redefine—and thus revalue—these objects enjoy increased social power; for they have turned these low status objects into high status art and have rescued them from their primitive makers, who were reputedly too childlike and too naive to realize the aesthetic value of their productions.[32]

The fetishization of handmade objects from the past offered a comfort to some and an investment to others. The move to collecting encapsulated the decline of use value into commodified exchange value—the narrativization of everyday objects as texts.[33] It also fed a residual xenophobia and a mythic belief in what current-day conservatives term the "common culture," an idea that emerged as diverse styles and forms of objects were merged into a unifying Americana that stripped the notion of folk of any differentiating characteristics. This phenomenon was exacerbated by the tendency for common objects to be exchanged informally, one by one, and without provenance. The very ubiquity of folk materials made their decontextualization and dehistorization almost an inevitability.

The absence of a studied history of folk may well have contributed to its affective populist appeal. In the early part of the century, folk objects were completely ignored by the university, as historians were obsessed with texts, and art connoisseurs cared only about "genius." Intellectual elitism toward folk exemplifies the class-bound character of aesthetic consumption; preferences for cultural styles and genres reflect the education and social standing of those holding them.[34] Therefore, everyday objects would never be considered appropriate material for "refined" sensibilities unless they were institutionally imbued with an additional legitimacy.

This process of certification began in the 1930s, as New Deal sponsorship by the federal government gave rise to projects documenting and preserving U.S. culture. This was also when the art world began to take notice: in 1932 the Museum of Modern Art (MOMA) inaugurated *American Folk Art: The Art of the Common Man in America, 1750–1900*, curated by then-museum director Holger Cahill. The show instantly established a place for folk in the art world by assigning high cultural value to common objects. Cahill described the exhibition contents as "the simple, unaffected and childlike expression of men and women who had no school training in art," and explained that in selecting the works on display he had "stressed aesthetic qualities rather than technical proficiency. We have tried to find objects which illustrate not only excellence in craftsmanship, but particularly those which have value as sculpture."[35]

Thus began the art world's appropriation of folk, a practice predicated on the suppression of utilitarian purpose in the name of aesthetic form. Later MOMA deployed this strategy to subsume all manner of artifacts—from documentary photographs to furniture to cars—into a universalizing narrative of modernism. It was paradigmatic of the modernist ethos to engulf disparate elements into an ever-expanding humanism. This emphasis on aesthetics downplayed social function and historical context, thus neutralizing any political meaning. After all, in the modern era genuine art was defined by its distance from daily instrumentality. Thus pitch forks and spittoons were imbued with the icy transcendentalism of museum objects.[36]

Certainly the MOMA exhibition did not emerge from a vacuum. In Europe the postwar avant-garde had for some time emulated "primitivist" styles. This fashion can be attributed to many of the anti-industrial impulses mentioned earlier, as well as to the growing science of anthropology and the growth of tourism. By the 1930s audiences on both sides of the Atlantic had been made aware of aboriginal peoples by popular documentary films and the paintings of artists including Georges Braques, Paul Gauguin, and Pablo Picasso. Within this discourse, cultural otherness existed only to be consumed by the colonial subject. Perhaps anticipating the speculations of a nascent structuralism, scholars pointed to the formal similarities between native renderings and the reductionist abstractions of cubist painters. As primitivism was giving new life to folk craft in the art world, appreciation was also gaining momentum in more popular quarters. Given folk craft's obvious ideological attractions, it should come as no surprise that civic-minded businessmen would come to view it as an appropriately patriotic and not-too-esoteric object of philanthropy.

From the 1940s through the cold war years, dozens of national- and regional-history institutions appeared, such as John D. Rockefeller's Williamsburg and Henry Francis DuPont's Winterthur. These well-meaning endeavors often took considerable license in their presentations of material culture. The two primary interpretive strategies were inherited from art history and social science, respectively: objects as masterpieces or objects as normative exemplars. The former tended to valorize historical anomalies or objects produced for the wealthy; the latter would overgeneralize about the use of everyday commodities. Aside from the fetishization of objects outside their original settings, these procedures led to a number of often misleading display conventions. In the interest of contextualizing objects, curators would go too far by massing representative samples in single "period rooms." In other instances, complicated technical routines such as blacksmithing or daguerreotyping would be simplified into processes of a few minutes.[37]

Such practices have been defended in the name of educational expediency. And certainly that argument has merit, inasmuch as any historical interpretation is a fictional text. But this line of reasoning gets considerably more complicated in circumstances where the political economy of the sign begins to influence the actual production of folk craft. Early on it became apparent that the public demand for vintage artifacts would far outstrip supply, and thus the manufacture of historical objects began on both an individual and industrial scale. At its more innocuous levels, this phenomenon inspired the handmade trinkets of sidewalk vendors and craft show entrepreneurs, but merchandising became more serious in the increasingly cash-driven context of the museum store. In an era of limits, in which philanthropy is dwindling and acquisition costs are escalating, museums feel increasingly under pressure to generate income. In the context of pastoral collecting, this means encouraging museum visitors to take a little piece of the institution home—to own a bit of history.

This impulse reaches its quintessential expression in the manufactured nostalgia of Ralph Lauren. What began for Lauren as a clothing line of "traditional" style has evolved into a brand of home furnishings and total environments—from country stores to hotels and resorts. As described by *New York Times* architecture critic Paul Goldberger, Lauren's vision "is fundamentally conservative. His work does not so much break new ground as reinvent the past, turning it into a siren call—soft, alluring, and absolutely free of blemishes."[38] In this scheme the real world does begin to recede in the presence of the copy, which is so much more appealing. The uncomfortable question that arises is whether such artifice is the only authenticity our culture is capable of producing. Consider the following description of the Polo/Ralph Lauren Country Store in East Hampton, New York:

> There is no better stage-set version of an old country store anywhere— sweaters are piled up on old country tables, shirts stacked in old cupboards, old postcards, photographs, and a handful of household antiques are carefully positioned to look as if they had always been there. You are walking through a miniature theme park of Americana, filled with attractive pieces of clothing, any one of which you can have if you present a credit card.[39]

As with most merchandising, the Lauren ethos capitalizes on the human impulse to self-identify through the acquisition of material goods, a process that encourages people to display their social location through choices of clothing, furniture, automobiles, or home decorations. Rarely are such decisions innocent manifestations of essential aesthetics or "taste"; usually they function as specific markers of economic status and education level. They are the very articulations of cultural difference.[40]

Viewed from this perspective, the consumption of Americana—either in its "authentic" or in its simulated form—constitutes a type of cultural "writing" in which the subject represents itself as an array of objects. Unfortunately, in its nostalgic modes this tends to result in a narrative that celebrates reigning interests at the expense of oppressed groups. In many cases, this ideology is written directly on the surface of the objects employed, as in "Banana Republic" clothing, which evokes the name given to nations exploited in the 1920s by the United Fruit Company, or in the Lauren perfume "Safari," which celebrates a comparable legacy of colonial trophy hunting. A recent ad for the fragrance featured travel postcard images of foreign deserts and tropical beaches, and was captioned: "Safari by Ralph Lauren. A world without boundaries. A personal adventure and a way of life."

Given the pervasiveness and strength of such narratives, it is no surprise that social critics on the Left once posited the intractability of capitalist media and culture. In recent decades, however, overdetermined models of false consciousness and ideological reproduction have given way to more contingent theories of culture. It is now broadly recognized that consumers are capable of making choices about appliances, clothing, cars, and movies—the way they are used, altered, combined, rejected, or spoken about. Such an attitude augurs against the apocalyptic inevitabilities that Marx identified.

One of the earliest proponents of an alternative view was Georg Simmel, who proposed a value-neutral theory of money itself. Simmel argued that an egalitarian capitalism is conceivable within a web of protective restraints.[41] To Simmel money is just another medium of abstraction into which goods and services are translated for exchange. By itself such abstraction implies no automatic exploitation for either producers or consumers. In fact, Simmel went so far as to suggest that money is an inherently democratic medium in that it offers a universal currency with no extrinsic meaning. Obviously a danger exists in romanticizing the capabilities of consumers in a society in which systematic exploitation *does* exist. The flaw in Simmel's reasoning was not acknowledging adequately the unequal access of people to production and consumption. He failed to recognize the inequalities of power and access at either end of the monetary system. Yet Simmel's critique of essentialized views of capitalism makes an important point about material culture. His ideas suggest the theoretical possibility of enhanced sublation through consumption and exchange, if the means can be found to forestall inequity.

Again this implies a role for cultural workers. Given that commodity relations and the discourses surrounding them do not simply reflect the mandates of a Madison Avenue monolith, spaces exist for creative and emancipatory possibilities. Artists, teachers, writers, and others can help by encouraging critical approaches to cultural consumption. This means suggesting that people can assume more autonomy in the construction of their cultural lives. Engaging this responsibility requires the recognition that culture is not only something that hangs in galleries, but is a substance that inheres in the very fabric of life.

Although this broadened approach to culture has always been the subject of anthropology and sociology, it typically has been directed toward disadvantaged or "foreign" peoples. Before the growth of hybrid disciplines such as communications and cultural studies, only others were deemed to have a "culture" interesting enough to examine. In focusing their gaze, social scientists usually studied normative gestures and ritualized customs in the interest of establishing empirical validity; that is, they chose behaviors that occurred in clearly predictable patterns.[42]

What often went undocumented were the anomalies of daily life in which people spontaneously responded to circumstances requiring them to adapt, improvise, or negate a standard action. This resulted in a failure to see that culture inheres in the ways that people invent their lives or adjust to changing situations.[43] For the cultural worker these pedagogical forms present new challenges that might enlarge definitions of what counts as knowledge and where it can be found. Rather than perpetuating types of expression that tell people that everyday forms of culture lack value, one should try to find ways to develop these forms.

Pedagogies and Quilts

To illustrate more specifically the transmutations of "ordinary" material culture in the service of consumer capitalism, one can trace particular commodity forms, such as quilts, through different contexts of production, consumption, and exchange. This is especially pertinent in the transformation of folk craft objects from the banal instrumentality of the domestic sphere to the rarefied aestheticization of the museum. But beyond this the quilt is also instructive as a pedagogical form employed by artists and teachers to reverse many reifying and dehumanizing commodifications.

In her essay for the catalogue *The Artist and the Quilt*, Lucy Lippard asserts that a revisionist history of the quilt might inform "relationships among producer, receiver, and object that the art world rarely acknowledges," since these relationships are the "product of both class and gender separation, and of the degree of economic support for the art in question."[44] From the earliest days of the republic, quilt making was a heavily gendered task, practiced in all but the most aristocratic households. Because factory-made blankets and comforters were scarce, and new fabrics were often unavailable in rural regions, women developed methods of reusing scraps and pieces of old clothing in quilt production.[45] They made decorative appliqué quilts for show and more informal patchwork quilts for everyday use; the patchwork quilt came to embody the pioneer virtues of thrift and industry so important to U.S. national identity.[46]

The tradition of public exhibition of these domestic products is coextensive with the evolution of the craft. Not produced strictly for private use within the home, colonial quilts often were signed and dated by their makers for exhibition at church bazaars and county fairs.[47] Contrary to some historical accounts, quilting was influenced by a reifying aestheticism from the beginning. Moreover, as a skill passed from mother to daughter, quilting became a distinctively female pedagogy. In an androcentric culture, needlework was "one art in which women controlled the education of their daughters, the production of the art, and were also the audience and critics."[48]

Public attitudes about quilting began to shift in the late nineteenth century, with the nationalistic self-consciousness of the 1876 centennial provoking a heightened interest in collectible Americana. Like other folk art forms, quilts inevitably were discovered by the art establishment, albeit somewhat later. In 1971, the Whitney Museum of American Art celebrated domestic needle craft in its exhibition *Abstract Design in American Quilts*, curated by Jonathan Holstein. Not unlike the MOMA folk art exhibition several decades earlier, the Whitney show equated the formal motifs of quilts with the geometric abstractions of minimalist pattern painters such as Frank Stella, Kenneth Noland, and Barnett Newman. The profound irony of attributing quiltlike intentions to an exclusive clique of male painters was not lost on women artists of the period. Indeed it was during this era that feminist critics and cultural workers, organized in groups such as the National Organization for Women (NOW) and Women Artists in Revolution (WAR), began to mount protests against the exclusive practices of art institutions in general and the New York gallery scene in particular.

Feminist artists of the 1960s and 1970s recognized handicrafts as both literal and symbolic ground to reclaim. The very forms of domestic work were being quickly appropriated and commodified by a modernist art establishment premised on the distancing of art from everyday experience. This vision of aesthetic contemplation apart from any social or political contingency was not-so-coincidentally promoted by an institutional complex devoid of women, people of color, and homosexuals. A group of artists comprising Cynthia Carlson, Joyce Kozloff, Kim McConnell, Robert Kushner, and Miriam Shapiro, among others, coalesced in the mid-1970s to establish the pattern and decoration movement. By reclaiming "debased" expressive forms such as traditional handicrafts, the group sought to reestablish the connections between form and tradition, process and product, and technique and social meaning that the modernist art establishment seemed bent on obfuscating.

The quilt became the quintessential object of the pattern and decoration movement. In the words of Shapiro and Faith Wilding, "Transcending boundaries of class, race, country of origin, and history, the quilt is a humanized, democratized art form. Even its subject matter—weddings, commemorations, friendship, freedom, political loyalties, family records—reflects rituals of community life. Once coveted as prized household possessions, quilts are now exhibited as art works in museums and galleries."[49] This message of liberal humanism was delivered through the similarly liberal strategy of consciousness-raising via a conventional institutional form: young upstart artists produced radical artworks for display within the existing structures of the New York art world, but did little to challenge its parameters. Initially shown and publicized in nonprofit art spaces, many of these pattern and decoration works were quickly co-opted as exchange objects of the first order. Nevertheless, they served an important function in breaking down the rigid separation of "fine art" and "crafts" in museum and gallery contexts. By recoding quilts as emblems of liberation and solidarity, these artists demonstrated that the mutability of the sign need not always serve reigning hegemonies. Even objects as commonplace as domestic commodities could be inscribed with revolutionary meaning.

Perhaps the most influential fabric artist to emerge from this period is Faith Ringgold, who began her first quilt in 1970 in collaboration with her mother, Willi Posey. The youngest of three children, Ringgold has stated that she never had the chance to tell stories when growing up.[50] Issues of narrative and voice figure prominently in Ringgold's quilts, in which heroine-narrators recount stories ranging from the historical to the personal. Often this involves extensive written texts juxtaposed to illustrative panels. *Slave Rape Story* (1985) tells the story of Beata, a young slave girl on a South Carolina plantation whose pregnant mother was raped by a drunken sailor on board a slave ship. After giving birth to Beata while still on the ship, the mother later pulls the sailor overboard, and they both drown. Years afterward the adolescent Beata is herself raped, yet she is sustained by the memory of her mother's resistance. The story ends with Beata concluding, "We don't belong nowhere Mama. But we staying Mama. Rebecca an me ain gonna have to die like you Mama. We gonna live an be free."[51]

Slave Rape Story depicts an intergenerational struggle for spiritual autonomy in a world of white male domination. In its narrative of suffering and strength, the quilt brings to light the little discussed but extremely prevalent crime of slave rape. The bringing forward of underexamined narratives typifies works by Ringgold, notably *Flag Quilt* (1985) about a Vietnam War veteran, and *Change: Faith Ringgold's Over 100 Lbs. Weight Loss Story Quilt* (1986), an autobiographical piece. As described by Thalia Gouma-Peterson, in the *Change* quilt Ringgold "most forcefully asserts the subversive 'I' as a Black-woman who refuses to be categorized and through her art and life opens possibilities for female representation and definition."[52] Ringgold employs the traditional medium of the quilt to displace conventional views of gender and the everyday. More importantly, Ringgold's work exposes the issue of race, underscoring the existence of differences within feminism.

As important as infiltrations by iconoclasts were within the commercial gallery world, some quilt artists began seeking ways to circumvent institutionally bound contexts where the legacy of avant-garde elitism still lingered. In 1975 Charlotte Robinson embarked on what would become a seven-year project to further undermine the separation of the gallery from the everyday. Robinson's efforts culminated in a project entitled *The Artist and the Quilt,* for which twenty quilts were commissioned and produced by teams of women artists and vernacular quilters. Although the traveling exhibition and widely circulated book gave new credence to domestic cultural production, the project did more than support an emergent feminist populism. On a broader level the effort began to unpack the differentiating narratives of the public and private spheres. It offered possibilities for collective reinterpretation of tasks previously performed by isolated agents. Regrettably, like many early feminist projects, it also reinforced essentialized views of "women's work."

Several projects organized by Miriam Shapiro also involved joint enterprise. After incorporating quilting techniques into her own paintings, Shapiro recognized the organizational potential of the traditional quilting bee. Historically these events had functioned as one of the few opportunities for women to gather outside the home, and as such were seen by Shapiro as forerunners of contemporary consciousness-raising sessions. In addition to producing collaboratively made quilts, Shapiro extended the metaphor of collective paneling and patchwork in orchestrating thematic exhibitions such as the 1983 *At Home* show at the Long Beach Museum of Art. In quilting-bee spirit, Shapiro invited women artist friends to complete an installation of room environments she had begun with fabric paintings.

Although the group-installation concept informed the activities of many feminist artists in the 1970s, some of its most public applications were developed by Suzanne Lacy. In the late 1960s, Lacy began organizing large-scale public artworks in which groups of women confronted domestic violence, incest, immigration, aging, and other issues. Staged in office buildings, in parks, and on city streets, Lacy's choreographed "actions" combined the energy of the political demonstration with the aesthetics of performance art. In one of her largest projects, *The Crystal Quilt* (1987), 430 black-clad older women formed a living quilt in the Philip Johnson-designed IDS tower in Minneapolis. After a ceremonious entry, the women unfolded black tablecloths on scores of card tables, revealing the cloths' brilliantly colored other sides. They then sat at the tables in groups of four, talked among themselves, and arranged and rearranged the tables in unison as thousands of spectators watched from balconies above. The proceedings were accompanied by a taped audiocollage of Native American and Hmong songs, thunderclaps, and birdcalls combined with prerecorded comments by some of the performers.

The Crystal Quilt developed symbols of handicraft and group work into what historian Moira Roth has termed a "pageant-like gathering of women celebrating their differences, their commonalties, their survival, and their wisdom—performances with enormous poetic impact. . . . These performances inspire their participants and audiences with feminist visions that help sustain feminist energies and hopes."[53] In addition to being a direct gesture of activism, *The Crystal Quilt* project was able to jump-start a sequence of subsequent events by virtue of its organization and size. What began as a single performance snowballed into a two-year series of exhibitions and discussions throughout Minnesota addressing women and aging. Thus, an event that was, in fact, *not* a quilt drew upon the unifying feminist ethos of quilting to generate a community response. The figurative evocation of a material form carried sufficient symbolic capital to generate a mass reaction. This is the inverse of the Ralph Lauren strategy of grafting regressive nostalgic signs onto copies of antique objects. Rather than evoking a false authenticity to call forth an unproblematic mythic past, in this context the quilt was used as a fulcrum for opening a critical discussion. Instead of smoothing over difference, the issue of aging was foregrounded as a point of ritualistic celebration and an issue of serious concern.

Transmutation of the quilt-as-sign reached its highest expression in the development of the NAMES Project. In 1985, San Francisco AIDS activist Cleve Jones established a community workshop for the production of fabric panels to memorialize those who had died of causes related to the disease. Within two years the project generated thousands of three-by-six-foot quilt panels adorned with ribbons, poems, photographs, and pieces of clothing. In gymnasiums, convention centers, and football fields across the nation, showings of the AIDS Memorial Quilt were accompanied by commemorative readings of the names of the dead. Following is one of the inscriptions on the panels:

> This the way I felt about Paul in the beginning: (April 1981): "What is it I like about Paul? His devastating smile for one thing. Also, his smooth tight body. Beyond all that, he is intelligent (which somehow surprises me) and supremely confident (which excites and perhaps intimidates me). At 35, he is a marvel. I think I am in love." And this is the way I felt at the end (March 1987): "This is a man I once loved above all others, remember. This is a man I once would gladly have spent the rest of my life with. Now he is dead and I never counted on this. I just can't cope—and for the time being, I refuse to try."[54]

In this further transformation of the quilt format, the NAMES Project accentuates the historical implications of an everyday object. Adorned with trinkets and mementos, the panels become shrines to banality itself. Indeed, it is the nonspectacular character of these simple (and complex) memorials that lends the AIDS quilt its powerful emotionalism. This displacement of the domestic as a memorial device again roots the meaning of the quilt in commonplace experience, an image made all the more potent by its multiplication in thousands of panels.[55]

The NAMES Project is diametrically opposed to conventional memorials that formalize and contain responses of grief in reified forms. Unlike monuments created to celebrate victories (typically in wars), memorials commemorate lives lost. Thus, memorials evoke a different tenor of historical memory. They are, according to Charles Griswold, "a species of pedagogy that seeks to instruct posterity about the past and, in so doing, necessarily reaches a decision about what is worth recovering."[56] Central to the NAMES Project's effectiveness as a mass display and an assemblage of individualized tributes is the authorial character of the panels. Unlike the monolithic and totalizing narratives of conventional monuments, the AIDS quilt offers multiple texts, each one linking its absent subject to a community of family and friends.[57] The very particularity and nonconformity of the panels bespeaks a personal connection with domestic handicraft made all the more meaningful by public display.

The AIDS quilt and other quilt projects discussed here function to reconnect subjective ties with the production of commodities. This has a powerful effect in an age in which so few commodities are actually produced in the home. But I do not mean to suggest a naive escape from the market via a romantic return to the homemade. Rather than pure products fashioned with the pretense of authenticity, these new cultural objects are made by appropriating bits of existing meaning. Like early patchwork ones, these quilts are bricolages, made not from "raw" materials, but from scavenged goods brought together. In this way the panels highlight the everyday processes of collection, assembly, and display that typify seemingly mundane activities such as decorating a room, preparing a meal, or planning a garden. What I am suggesting is that these daily routines hold enormous potential as sites of personal and collective agency. Needed are pedagogies to enable the process.

In the controlled atmosphere of the classroom, Marianne Sawicki uses the quilt in a direct educational context. Sawicki obliges students in her feminist-pedagogy classes to engage in quilt production as a means of getting closer to subject matter. Although the course follows a reading-and-discussion format, Sawicki insists that students refrain from note taking while in class. In fact, she confiscates pencils and pens as students arrive at the room, replacing them with knitting needles. While in class students are required to produce panels of collective quilts to be delivered to expectant mothers. As Sawicki explained:

> Knitting was meant to remind us, in the midst of our intellectual work, that we were responsible for concrete needs felt by people beyond the classroom walls. It was also meant to position us to grasp the kind of knowledge that is unavailable to those who do not labor. And it was a gesture of solidarity with women of other eras who never talked to one another without taking their handiwork along.[58]

Though somewhat extreme in its methods, Sawicki's exercise is instructive in bringing this discussion of material culture, folk art, and quilts back to the production of domestic goods as ends in themselves. Surely the home is one of the first sites where subjective authority in material relations needs to be reclaimed. As I have made apparent throughout this chapter, material culture cannot be viewed as an isolated array of old spoons and bicycle parts, but must be seen as a substance that is defined by people in what they do with these things and what they say about them. In the specificity of everyday life, material culture is the very marker of difference itself.

Textuality and materiality are mutually constitutive concepts, reflecting the identities and ideologies of those who use them. To be sure, these elements operate in a system that is stacked in favor of industrial producers and predicated on denying difference, exaggerating inequality, and mystifying its means of operation. Yet at the same time, diverse communities continue to grow in both strength and numbers, calling for new entitlements and inventing new relations to material goods. The point to remember is that, like resistance, these new claims and relations are not automatically progressive or even helpful to the groups making them. They need to be backed by the understandings and competencies required to forge revisions that work. In this sense the cultivation of enlarged fields of social possibility must be informed by a series of ethical commitments that enable change. For educators this means not a condescending populism that romanticizes or exploits the ordinary, but a pedagogical practice that dissolves the concept altogether.

FOUR

A Change of Address

Homelessness and the Politics of Voice

> There are some folks for whom openness is not about the luxury of "will I choose to share this or tell that," but rather, "will I survive—will I make it through—will I stay alive?" And openness is about how to be well and telling the truth is about how to put the broken bits and pieces of the heart back together again. It is about being whole, being wholehearted.
>
> —bell hooks[1]

"**R**emember when we thought we could make a difference?" asks a recent advertisement from the Plan International foster parents program. "When I was in college we fought every kind of social and economic injustice. We sang songs like 'He Ain't Heavy. He's My Brother,' and we thought we could change the world. Then I started having other responsibilities."[2] The ad tells the story of Adrienne, a woman in her mid-thirties. "She's bright, concerned, hardworking. She has a loving husband and a good job. Yet she has never lost her awareness of problems like poverty in the world. Nor that deep need to make a difference."

Naturally, Plan International has an answer, a solution tailored for an upwardly mobile generation of young professionals. For seventy-two cents a day it offers Adrienne and her husband a child in Guatemala, a helpless baby of color that they need never actually meet. In effect, the organization relieves the couple of any procreative or charitable concerns in a single gesture, while subtly alluding to their political powerlessness. As Plan International puts it, "You can reach out to a child who really needs you . . . because you believe in each child's value in the Family of Man."

The Plan International campaign is noteworthy for a number of reasons, not the least of which is its size. Though not exactly a household word, the organization boasts six thousand employees and an annual budget of over $100 million, making it one of the largest nonprofits in the nation. More significantly, Plan International's success derives from its ability to complement the methods and ideologies of U.S. business interests. Its emphases on personalized charity (rather than collective action) and child/family aid (rather than population control or reproductive choice) are hardly accidental, for they neatly elide the thornier conditions of exclusion and exploitation produced by global capitalism. Thus the campaign distorts both causes and remedies for human suffering. As do current discourses on homelessness, drug abuse, crime, illiteracy, and AIDS, it frames social problems as historically de-contextualized and depoliticized phenomena that inexplicably strike "some people" who are inept, in trouble, or simply out of luck.

But this view of human tragedy is more than a conservative conceit. In different forms it permeates perceptions of poverty that infuse much of the language of the political Left. It results from the way ideology installs people in imaginary relations to the conditions in which they live. Within this scheme, a program placing selected groups at the bottom of society is naturalized into a benign, even virtuous, entity. It forms a fictional narrative in which a universal "we" is counterposed to an imaginary "them." This ubiquitous binarism has a major influence on public policy and popular opinion. It is reinforced in the roles of expertise assigned to social workers, teachers, cultural producers—in fact, to everyone except the disadvantaged them-selves. These practices sanction a view of economic catastrophe as a "personal" consequence of human existence, often equating it metaphorically with illness or mental impairment. As in the Plan International ad, the remedies typically offered are personal as well. In a world where "making a difference" in political terms has become a utopian anachronism, social responsibility is consigned to the individual sympathies of "a thousand points of light." By focusing on an isolated problem, peo-ple can ignore the structural necessity and deliberate creation of poverty in an eco-nomic order that requires losers so it can produce winners.

In this chapter I discuss the links between work, welfare, and public discourse, particularly as manifest in recent journalism, advertising, and documentary prac-tice. The discussion will entail an analysis of the ways exploitive political instru-mentalities are rationalized by business interests, supported by government policy, sanctioned by popular opinion, and reified in media texts. Special attention will be paid to the ways well-meaning liberal/leftist organizations inadvertently support re-gressive and damaging views of the poor. This is partly a function of representa-tional conventions that distort through stereotyping and objectify in their form of address. But it also results from attitudes about charity and social reform that priv-ilege singular views about change and progress. This promotes an atmosphere in which white middle-class academics both speak for disenfranchised groups and prescribe particular regimens of behavior for them. This Enlightenment program of social amelioration and betterment continues to pose problems in social docu-mentary practice, welfare reform literature, and educational theory. More-demo-cratic models are needed that can describe complex relationships while admitting a diversity of voices to the conversation.

THE PRODUCTION OF POVERTY

The United States is currently facing an economic crisis of unprecedented propor-tions, characterized by a catastrophic trade deficit, spiraling social problems, and a radically unequal distribution of resources. Yet, while timidly taxing the rich, the Clinton administration has failed to address adequately the politically difficult issue of genuine income distribution. In the face of foreign competition and declining productivity, business has reacted by squeezing more work from employees. One way they have accomplished this has been drastic *disincentives* to joblessness. The most powerful of these have been policies that set public-assistance levels far below even the most unfair wages.

Within this context the relationship of labor to welfare becomes apparent. An equitable system of public assistance would strengthen employees' bargaining position with employers, affording workers choices. Business opposes this for obvious reasons, arguing that welfare encourages people to go on the dole. But it rarely acknowledges the increasing pauperization of the wage earner. For example, in California the current average salary in the retail trade is $9,036 per year. Although this is $3,000 below the poverty line for a family of three, it is significantly higher than the *maximum* welfare benefit of $7,956.[3] What is startling is the number of people who live at this income level. In recent years, subpoverty employment has accounted for a fifth of all full-time jobs and nearly a third of new jobs.[4] Nevertheless the working poor and near poor usually are overlooked in the agendas of social activism.

In recent years, the preponderance of indigent people in major metropolitan centers has underscored the issue of homelessness. As evidence of poverty became more public, it also provided fodder for countless news reports, documentary films, television specials, and photography projects. Examples of this work include books such as Philip Farnsworth and Vernon Baker's *Under the Bridge*, Howard Schatz's *Homeless: Portraits of Americans in Hard Times*, and exhibitions such as *Homeless in America* organized by Families for the Homeless and the National Mental Health Association and *Shooting Back: Photography by and about the Homeless* from the Washington Project for the Arts.[5]

The rising visibility (and simultaneous distortion) of poverty has contributed to the commodification of reformist literature, both in popular and academic publishing. Although hardly a new phenomenon, the reification of the image of the poor has increased in the current electronic age, in which distance between economic classes continues to widen. One need only consider the popularity of the books I have discussed to realize that talk about misfortune functions as both entertainment and social critique. In the process careers get built, bank accounts grow, but very little changes for those written about.

Estimates of the number of homeless vary considerably due to the intrinsic difficulty of measuring a population without phones and addresses and to the fact that many people are on the street for only a short time. Federal Housing and Urban Development (HUD) figures place the number of people homeless each night at 250,000; other estimates run as high as 3 million.[6] As tragic as this problem has become, its scale is dwarfed by the numbers of people who are chronically mal-nourished, in ill health, or living in substandard conditions. Although 35.5 million people are classified as poor, an additional 31 million officially would be considered poor without government help.[7] Despite the logical need for an adequate program of government assistance, such initiatives are regularly blocked by legislators and voters. More than a consequence of corporate hegemony, it is a matter of public consent.

The most significant factor in the rationalization of poverty is the historic con-signment of the poor to categories of social exclusion and otherness. The second el-ement in the ideological assault on the poor is moral censure. With the transition to industrial capitalism in the early nineteenth century, scientific theories by Thomas Robert Malthus, Herbert Spencer, Charles Darwin, and Francis Galton provided a logic for blaming the economically oppressed for their own hardship. These atti-tudes were but slightly (and briefly) displaced in the depression era.

In the neo–social Darwinist ethos of the 1990s, poverty is discussed in the media as almost an individual failing. A recent issue of the *New York Times Magazine* car-ried a disturbingly typical example of this entitled "The Story of a Street Person: Remembering My Brother."[8] The first-person narrative recounts avant-garde play-wright Elizabeth Swados's observations of the decline of Lincoln Swados, a suicidal double amputee diagnosed since childhood as a severe schizophrenic. Although he had financial resources and a family to assist him, Lincoln availed himself of nei-ther, preferring to struggle to become a writer in New York. Over time his psycho-logical and physical condition declined, and he died at age forty-six as he was about to be evicted from his apartment. His demise is conveyed as a consequence of ill-ness and choice. Ironically, Lincoln Swados was never homeless.

As with much journalism of this type, emphasis in the *Times* article fell on the au-thor of the story, with the magazine's cover depicting a preoccupied-looking Eliza-beth Swados standing by a graffiti-covered building. In fact, we never see the "street person" Lincoln until the end of the article. The title, "The Story of a Street Person," implies that the narrative is somehow typical. But clearly it is not. Yet rather than acknowledging the unusual character of Lincoln's story, Swados em-phasizes the fundamental uniqueness of all such tragedies:

> Some people romanticize the plight of homeless as if each life were the con-tent of a folk song. Others point to Reagan and maintain that he broke the back of the poor in our country. Still others understand enough to see that some people are on the streets because of cutbacks during the Koch admin-istration and the resulting lack of hospitalization, care and housing for the mentally ill. But generalizations are worthless. Every person has a different story. Each of them was brought low by a specific personal demon.[9]

Such remarks miss the point. In wiping away generalizations one also disregards the common external forces that cause personal misfortune. The real issue here is that truly typical stories of ordinary people who lose their job and home are too boring to print in the *Times*. The magazine would rather highlight the extraordinary story of a profoundly handicapped "artistic" individual who dies as the consequence of his demons

To counter this sort of personalized essentialism, liberals began to develop alternative formulations in the 1960s. A functionalist approach to poverty was offered in books such as Michael Harrington's *The Other America*.[10] The title of Harrington's book is significant, for its rediscovery of urban ghettos objectified the unemployed and homeless as never before. In this newer, more anthropological, formulation, the poor were cast as out of step with mainstream America and bound within an inescapable "culture of poverty." Rather than the consequence of external economic and political factors, poverty was seen as a propensity for failure passed from parent to child. In its liberal incarnations, culture-of-poverty theories attempted to shift the emphasis from eugenic beliefs in inherent inferiority to environmental causes. Unfortunately, this assessment still attributed the source of poverty to the victim. Though caused by past experiences, the living defect was within the poor person.

More significantly, all notions of agency were absent. The urban poor were seen as incapable of resisting the powerful forces of cultural impoverishment. The goal of the liberal change agent was to rescue the failing individual, with salvation possible only through intervention.[11] Although developed by liberal/leftist activists Harrington, Oscar Lewis, Frank Reissman, and others, these ideas were easily co-opted by the conservative establishment to further essentialize notions of economic misfortune. To Edward Banfield the poor were unable to recognize future needs and defer gratification.[12] To George Gilder the threat was promiscuous sexuality and a deteriorating family.[13] To Lawrence Mead the issue was one of generalized permissiveness.[14] These attitudes became manifest in the fragmented, highly regulated, and parsimonious assistance programs of the Reagan and Bush administrations, programs that have remained virtually unchanged in the Clinton presidency. Currently, federal welfare programs (such as Aid to Families with Dependent Children) account for approximately 2 percent of the gross national product and less than one-sixth all government assistance expenditures (including Social Security and Medicare).[15]

REPRESENTATION AND RATIONALIZATION

Distorted representations that naturalize poverty abound in the mass media, from movies such as *Trading Places* (1986), *Ironweed* (1989), *Down and Out in Beverly Hills* (1989), *Life Stinks* (1991), and *Falling Down* (1993) to nearly every law-and-order TV show. One-dimensional news broadcasts and documentaries, ad campaigns by corporately driven philanthropies, books and exhibitions by politically uninformed cultural producers—all of these contribute to the public's misunderstanding of poverty. Although photographic depictions of the poor date to the medium's inception, they had little impact until the development of high-speed printing and halftone technologies in the 1930s.[16] Acting in tandem with a burgeoning film industry, photographically illustrated magazines and newspapers fostered a new sensation of "media" and a voyeuristic hunger for realism.

In an era of advancing scientific technology, medical metaphors were deployed frequently. Drawing on terminology of germ theory and epidemiology, writers often spoke of "infections," "contagions," and "plague spots" within impoverished communities.[17] To Herbert Spencer, such sickness was a necessary part of social evolution:

> Having by unwise institutions brought into existence large numbers who are unadapted to the requirements of social life, and are consequently sources of misery to themselves and others, we cannot repress and gradually diminish this body of relatively worthless people without inflicting much pain. Evil has been done and the penalty must be paid. Cure can only come through affliction.[18]

Such attitudes became ingrained in welfare ideology. In his 1936 collaboration with Margaret Bourke-White, Erskine Caldwell described the internalized will to poverty commonly attributed to white sharecroppers as an illness. The tenant farmer, Caldwell wrote, has "not always been the lazy, slipshod, good-for-nothing person that he is frequently described as being. His shiftlessness, when apparent, is an occupational disease."[19]

Similar language persists in today's humanitarian literature, as evidenced in a recent ad from the Children's Defense Fund: "Poverty has become a bigger childhood disease than muscular dystrophy, diabetes, cystic fibrosis and cancer combined. And it's curable." This is the legacy through which causes and mitigating circumstances, from the profound to the superficial, are collapsed into a single text. These issues were most profoundly brought home in coverage of the Los Angeles riots, which a sensation-hungry media quickly framed in terms of social pathology. *Newsweek*'s Frank Washington spoke of what he called an epidemic of irrationality in which "violence became *contagious*" as it spread from block to block.[20] In addition to using metaphors of physical disease, writers cast the riots in terms of mental illness, with references to the insanity, craziness, and wildness of it all.

The events were further abstracted from the realm of human rationality in a racist vocabulary of savagery and natural (and thus unavoidable) cataclysm. From references on police radios to "gorillas in the mist" to commentaries in news magazines, rioting groups were dehumanized as marauding packs engaging in animalistic "orgies," or, in the words of *Time*'s Lance Morrow, "ritual sacrifices."[21] Other efforts to naturalize the events evoked a vocabulary of seismic eruption. According to Tom Mathews, "Now the big one has hit Los Angeles—not an earthquake as everyone feared, but a tectonic jolt in the nation's soul. It will take nerve and new ideas to ride through the aftershocks."[22]

For scores of sympathetic writers, there is only the "resilience" of the human spirit in the face of universalized suffering—a resilience, it is important to add, that is projected entirely by the commentators and viewers of the images. This message of spiritual transcendence further rationalizes the inevitability of failure. It suggests that because we cannot (or should not) eliminate hardship, we should try to understand it through observation. Writing about photography twenty years ago, John Szarkowski announced that "a new generation of photographers has directed the documentary approach toward more personal ends. Their aim has not been to reform life, but to know it."[23]

In recent decades these attitudes toward the poor emerge in the conservative definition of "the underclass" as an unrecuperable mass, permanently set apart from the rest of society. Historian Michael Katz dates this concept to the August 29, 1977, *Time* magazine feature story, "The American Underclass." In a now familiar vocabulary, the article states that "behind (the ghetto's) crumbling walls lives a large group of people who are more intractable, more socially alien and more hostile than almost anyone had imagined. They are the unreachables: the American underclass."[24] The author identifies this group as set apart from mainstream society:

> Their bleak environment nurtures values that are often at odds with those of the majority—even the majority of the poor. Thus the underclass produces a highly disproportionate number of the nation's juvenile delinquents, school dropouts, drug addicts and welfare mothers, and much of the adult crime, family disruption, urban decay and demand for social expenditures.[25]

The *Time* story typifies the conservative tendency to equate lack of social mobility with deviant values and behavioral pathology. Regrettably, such thinking also permeates the liberal Left. The willingness of well-meaning liberals to generalize about ghetto life, to speculate about conditions with which they have no experience, is evidenced in documentary photographic work of the 1970s and 1980s. In many of these pictures, the referential details of individual circumstance are collapsed into formal conventions and signature styles. As in the Swados essay, the work becomes more a manifestation of the image maker's subjectivity than any "real" conditions. Thus photographers such as Larry Burrows, Larry Clark, Bruce Davidson, Danny Lyon, and Donald McCullin juxtapose images of crime, decay, pregnancy, and malnutrition into a single "portrait" of a people that then becomes identified with *all* of those characteristics—both positive and negative.

The seeming inevitability of poverty is also part of traditions supporting the art world. The same voices that insist on the organic necessity of social hierarchies attribute essential characteristics of "quality" to selected cultural works. Ineffable definitions of quality are the cornerstone of an epistemological separation of the social from the aesthetic. Through this scheme of discursive fragmentation, cultural work is permitted no relationship to the omniscient mechanisms of social arrangements. The consequences of wealth and poverty are seen as inevitable.[26]

Similarly, the modernist championing of genius and originality parallels beliefs in individual freedom and personal charity. Such attitudes find their ultimate expression in the foster parent programs described earlier, in which donors are exhorted to save a "single" distant life. In one of the most cynical appeals to date, an ad placed in *Mother Jones* by the Plan International foster parents program suggests that "while world leaders hold peace talks, and spend billions on aid and arms, there's another way *you personally* can make a difference. By reaching out to a desperately poor child."[27]

Cultural activists can play an important role in correcting misperceptions of poverty and welfare. Yet the task is a difficult one, for in seeking to dramatize the problem, artists and writers often reinforce the very stereotypes that undermine their efforts—or they create new stereotypes. Many of today's better-known photojournalists still harbor misguided beliefs in the possibility of an "authentic" documentary practice that will persuade by virtue of its honesty. This disregards the fact that sign systems always function within specific power relations, historical moments, and cultural circumstances.

American Refugees (1991), by longtime homeless advocate Jim Hubbard, is a good case in point, although similar work is currently in circulation by Merry Alpern, Jim Goldberg, Abraham Menashe, Mary Ellen Mark, Eli Reed, and Eugene Richards, to name but a few. *American Refugees* argues that society permits people to become homeless because it fails to recognize their essential humanity.[28] As stated by Jonathan Kozol in the book's foreword, these are people "who, for no reason but the accidents of birth and circumstance, are left to wander in a darkness."[29] The volume depicts individuals and families in a variety of distressed circumstances: huddling over subway grates, standing in soup lines, being evicted from apartments. The selection and sequencing of images are clearly intended to dramatize the exceptional character of these hardships.

Preceding the images are brief texts by Kozol and Hubbard that attempt to frame the visual matter in empathetic terms. After expending half of his text on autobiography, Hubbard suggests that "as you look at these photographs, I urge you to see similarities between you and the people shown here. These people are our neighbors."[30] Later he adds, "If you look long and hard at the plight of the homeless it will change your life. These people are our brothers, our sisters, our children. These people are *us*."[31]

But this plea is as far as Hubbard goes in making the connection. The picture section is followed by a twenty-two-page listing of housing organizations that viewers presumably will be moved to contact. But nowhere is the reason for this discussed—much less an explanation of why the people in the pictures are in trouble. This logical gap undermines the book's coherence. No real effort is made to counter the exceptionalized visual portrait of the poor that Hubbard creates. There is no reason for a viewer to believe that "these people are us." Despite its intended purpose, documentary work that fetishizes difference in this way only increases the difficulty of understanding the dispossessed.[32]

Although formally similar to Hubbard's book, Stephen Shames's *Outside the Dream: Child Poverty in America* is more restrained in its romantic tendencies. Whereas Hubbard's pictures address challenges to daily existence (finding shelter, doing laundry), Shames's images evidence harsher realities (shooting drugs, beating a spouse).[33] In one of the most disturbing examples of this photographer's apparent acquiescence to criminal behavior, a thirteen-frame sequence entitled simply "Bucks County, Pennsylvania" (1987), shows a man menacing a woman in a bedroom, pursuing her into the street, striking her to the ground, carrying her over his shoulder, and then arguing again in the same bedroom.

Beyond this reportorial crassness, *Outside the Dream* is introduced by a statistically solid introduction (also by Kozol) and a politically well argued afterword by Children's Defense Fund president Marian Wright Edelman. Evidently practiced at speaking to prospective patrons without pulling punches, Edelman states, "Make no mistake. The nation *is* consciously sacrificing children. . . . Let what you see disturb you. Let it disturb you so much that it prompts you to act. Your action can, and should, come in many forms."[34] What follows is a provocative and useful list of strategies from role modeling to congressional lobbying. Although its images employ the same limited vocabulary as Hubbard's, *Outside the Dream* is considerably more coherent in its pitch for liberal reform. Its strength lies in the written grounding provided for Shames's photographs.

Kozol's participation in both of these projects is hardly coincidental, for over the past two decades he has emerged as a leading Left spokesperson on issues of poverty and education. In his own writing, public speaking , and frequent appearances on TV talk shows, Kozol has helped galvanize public sympathy for the disadvantaged as almost no one else. At the same time, Kozol's gestures of advocacy can be critiqued for the way the voices of oppressed people are appropriated into his own. Although Kozol is very careful to assemble the *contents* of his writings from texts and spoken testimony from many sources, ultimately he offers the *form* of master discourse that emanates from a central authoritarian source.

A former schoolteacher, Kozol gained public notoriety with the 1967 publication of his first book, *Death at an Early Age*, which won a National Book Award the following year. *Death at an Early Age* chronicled the inequities Kozol witnessed first-hand in the Boston public schools.[35] He maintained this fundamental concern with oppression through a succession of eight books, culminating with *Savage Inequalities: Children in America's Schools*.[36] As in his other works, Kozol's skill lies in his ability to combine within a highly evocative prose style detailed descriptions of events, analyses of financial data and legal proceedings, and interviews with teachers and students. More importantly, Kozol maintains a clear vision of the underlying discrimination and profiteering that create poverty and poor schools. And he criticizes other writers for ignoring these causes. As Kozol told one interviewer, "It's quite a trick to write an education story for a big-city newspaper in America and say everything except that these kids are victims of crushing racism and obliterating penury. But since you can't say that—since you can't say what's at the center—everything you write is out at the circumference. That's why it's dull."[37]

Clearly in an era in which neoliberals seem so timid about reforming social policy, populist progressive voices like Kozol's are desperately needed. At the same time, it is important to bear in mind the dangerous implications of such a "progressive" program if applied uncritically.[38] This is, after all, the same Enlightenment logic that motivates the imperial Western domination of the world. It is the unshakable belief that one party or nation has the knowledge to which all others should subscribe. It suggests that this knowledge originates exclusively in the consciousness of intellectuals, whose job it is to lead otherwise helpless people out of darkness.[39]

The prevalence of this condescending attitude has been troubling anthropologists and educational researchers for much of the past two decades. Indeed, how do social scientists grasp the limits of their own understandings? How do they come to recognize what they do not know? How can they come to accept that there are some things they may not be able to know?[40]

In his book *Culture and Truth*, Renato Rosaldo details the often paradoxical search for "appropriate" methods of description.[41] Quickly casting aside illusions of Weberian "distance" or "objectivity," Rosaldo examines the tricky territory of subjective analysis. If analysts accept the inevitability of asserting an interested position into the texts, if they accept the responsibility of changing the world rather than merely understanding it, how do they do so without romanticizing their objects? The most common approach is to become a "participant observer," an analyst who dances on the borderline between becoming one of the observed and remaining outside.[42] The difficulty with this is that observer and observed are invariably installed in unequal relations of power and knowledge. Not only are the power and knowledge of different quantities in the two parties, but they also are of different kinds.

The answer for Rosaldo lies in a moral commitment toward the studied community.[43] The observer not only becomes a part of the group to learn its ways, as Kozol did, but also assumes a stake in the group's interests. This has both negative and positive implications, inasmuch as people are constructed in multiple subjectivities and therefore belong to many groups. On one hand, try as one might, it is impossible to ever completely assimilate into another culture. On the other hand, this phenomenon of multiple membership in different groups can be seen as a unifying element among seemingly disparate communities. Without surrendering differences, groups can share members, affinities, and political strategies.[44]

A New Form of Address

Aside from matters of content and form lie the more significant issues of address. Besides limiting what can be said, coffee-table book or art-exhibition formats also preclude consideration of external voices. (The poor would not necessarily depict themselves differently than they have been depicted—although they might.) Such difficulties result from the implicit arrogance of cultural workers who fail to recognize problems in the act of speaking for others. This is not to say that activists should stop representing the disempowered altogether, but to suggest that responsible representation of one group by another requires more self-scrutiny than is commonly exercised. Clearly, ways must be found to connect the spheres of the poor with those of diverse audiences—otherwise learning and change will not occur.[45] More works are needed like those of artists Connie Hatch, Carrie Mae Weems, Greg Sholette, Lorna Simpson, and Krzystof Wodiczko, who challenge documentary conventions, signifying practices, and classification strata.

A common strategy is to acknowledge one's own speaking position. Such disclosure is an important element in the photographic work of Mel Rosenthal. In a recent project involving students from New York's Empire State College, a photographic exhibition depicting the South Bronx carried the following wall label:

> These photographs do not make any pretense of deep insight or trade on the neutral authority to convince us that we are being shown an intimate face of Long Island City. Rather they present themselves as photographs honestly taken by outsiders over a limited period of time. These conditions are, of course, exactly those under which most photojournalistic and documentary photographers are made, but many photographers—especially professionals—feel under pressure to deny it.[46]

By foregrounding this potentially exploitive relationship, Rosenthal destabilizes the privilege that photographers often carry. In this way the subjective character of representation is revealed, its fiction acknowledged, and its regressive authority (partially) neutralized. Practices such as Rosenthal's begin to erode the boundaries that separate photographers, audiences, and those photographed. Not unlike the cinema verité technique of an actor stepping out of character to speak personally into the camera, such explanatory messages fracture the hermetic closure of exhibition narrative. This impulse is extended in projects that yield authorship to those represented, such as the performances by homeless men and women presented by John Malpede's Los Angeles Poverty Department, or the photographs by homeless children in the "Shooting Back" exhibition in Washington, D.C.[47]

In educational discourse this process is the familiar "call to voice," in which those typically silenced are encouraged to speak. Much has been written by feminists about the overt and covert ways students and other subordinate groups are silenced. According to Michelle Fine, this process takes a number of forms, from the literal prohibitions against speaking or writing, to the exclusion of certain people's stories and histories from "official" texts and canonical curricula, to the more subtle "naturalization" of certain forms of academic speech and behavior.[48] bell hooks develops this notion further in discussing the importance of seeing oneself as an active subject rather than a passive object. As hooks explains, this process of a people assuming their own voice is an absolute prerequisite to revolutionary change.[49] Such a commitment to voice is all the more important at a time when European theorists are postulating the so-called death of the subject—the impossibility of any authentic speech.

On the other hand, as hooks and other commentators have pointed out, the positive lesson to be gained from postmodernism is that voice should not be overromanticized. First of all, there is no single "third world" voice or "feminist" voice.[50] It is exactly such narrow definitions of human difference that have allowed difference to be commodified and managed by the liberal establishment. Chandra Talpade Mohanty notes that "these practices often produce, codify, and even rewrite histories of race and colonialism."[51]

Second, romanticization of voice can cause uncritical attribution of validity to an essentialized position, which is actually constructed from social experiences. hooks characterizes the situation as follows:

> The unwillingness to critique essentialism on the part of many African-Americans is rooted in the fear that it will cause folks to lose sight of the specific history and experience of African-Americans and the unique sensibilities and cultures that arise from that experience. An adequate response to this concern is to critique essentialism while emphasizing the significance of "the authority of experience." There is a radical difference between a repudiation of the idea that there is a black "essence" and the recognition of the way black identity has been specifically constituted in the experience of exile and struggle.[52]

Thus in research or classroom practice, voice is valued and subjectivity respected, but no position is beyond critical scrutiny. Statements must be examined for the degree to which they both affirm identities and enhance the possibility of dialogue and democratic exchange.

Third, these essentialized positions of particular actors are not necessarily representative or progressive. This is well documented in Michael Susko's *Cry of the Invisible: Writings from the Homeless and Survivors of Psychiatric Hospitals*.[53] It might be expected that such a volume would resolve the problem of expert discourse posed by much of the work I have discussed. After all, wouldn't the actual writings of the homeless, speaking directly of their own experience, constitute a more powerful and authentic statement than that of a professional artist? The need for such a book is convincingly stated in its introduction: "The homeless are painfully seen, but with the averted gaze—by those who would prefer not to see. And if the homeless are 'seen,' more rarely does anyone listen to them."[54] Unfortunately, the rest of the book is an individualized and depoliticized assortment of reflections and confessions in the form of short essays, poems, and transcribed interviews. Although the phenomenological experience of homelessness, drug addiction, and mental illness is powerfully conveyed, the source of such problems emerges only through inference.

Take the story of Bruce Whitcomb, a homeless man with a series of psychiatric and physical problems. Whitcomb's narrative chronicles his seven-year passage from a secure life in Baltimore, to a period of unemployment and living on the streets, through several treatment programs, and ultimately to a return to middle-class existence. "If pressed to reflect," Whitcomb comments, "I would say a combination of factors led to my breakdown: too much drugs and too much work."[55] Typical of most contributors to the volume, Whitcomb declines to locate blame outside himself. Instead of identifying oppressive economic conditions or a failed social welfare system, he internalizes human shortfalls as psychological ills. Missing is the political project that might change the plight of these silenced voices.

This point is particularly important to address in light of the frequency with which voice has begun to appear on the agendas of activist artists and writers. Beyond simply increasing the number of women, people of color, lesbians, and gay men whose art is exhibited in galleries or who are hired for teaching positions, new efforts have been made to alter producer/audience relationships. In part this has represented an effort to overcome traditional high-/low-culture binarisms, while at the same time lending an immediacy to the artists' efforts. Increasingly artists are becoming frustrated by traditional categories of practice that bracket their work from the very conditions they describe.

For two decades San Diego artist Fred Lonidier has been producing exhibitions in art-world and non–art-world settings that address issues of poverty and work while incorporating the voices of those documented. From his well-known installation *The Health and Safety Game* (1976) to his more recent *Welfare Is Poor Relief* (1989–1992), Lonidier has striven to bridge gaps between audiences by mounting exhibitions in diverse locations such as government office buildings, union halls, and major museums. *The Health and Safety Game* combined photographs and written descriptions of job-related injuries with interview excerpts from workers and management in a way that yielded a uniquely multiperspectival image of the way accidents and disease are "handled" by corporate capitalism.[56]

On one level, by relying heavily on written texts, the work offered an implicit critique of romanticizing the descriptive capacities of "the purely visual." As Lonidier himself has pointed out, this fetishization of picture stories, particularly within union promotional and educational materials, has contributed to a subliterate view of workers.[57] On another level, the integration of texts from many sources permitted a decentered and contradictory contextualization of the images, which evoked the complex experiences of those pictured.

A panel entitled "Coke Oven Worker's Lung" juxtaposes a dispassionate chronology ("He decided he should be compensated for 'lung damage' and went to a lawyer recommended by the union. The lawyer seemed to believe that his client was damaged, but quickly accepted a low award at the hearing") with the subjective commentary for the stricken worker ("I was gassed three times out there, unconscious. Gassed with carbon monoxide . . . I feel sorry for the kids starting in there. They make good money and I tell them that your health comes first, but they don't listen"). The cumulative effect of reading the panels is a frustrating sensation of the complex relationship among the many players in the "game" of workers' lives. This type of artwork augurs against one-dimensional solutions or easily identified villains or victims. Clearly, profiteering and greed are producing conditions that threaten employees' well-being. But all involved—workers, unions, and managers—are partially implicated in the web of resistances and accords that comprise the universe of the workplace.

Beyond merely complicating what might otherwise be an oversimplified story, multiperspective projects begin to shift the emphasis from display to production. They begin to make the all-important shift away from a exclusively author-centered narrative. More significantly still, by moving the locus of display beyond the realm of convention, they transform both the experience of the exhibition ritual and the naturalizing tendencies of its enabling locales. In doing so it alters both text and context to be sure, but it also begins to interpellate a different viewing subject.

Instead of art being appreciated only as a commodity prepared for an assumed audience, inherent value is attributed to the act of making. Cultural work with such therapeutic dimensions is becoming increasingly prevalent, particularly as employment in the arts sector is diminished. Typical of such practice is the drop-in program at the Larkin Street Youth Center in San Francisco's Tenderloin District. At Larkin Street, artist-in-residence Peter Carpou provides an atmosphere in which homeless youth can engage the host institution on their own terms. In no-strings encounters in which nonviolence is the only rule, teens enter Larkin Street for sessions of drawing or collaging. The visits, which may be as brief as a few minutes, offer some of the young people their first positive experience with a social-service provider. Over time this can lead to a more formal relationship with a counseling program or group home.

In recent years the Larkin Street program has begun to exhibit collaborative youth art projects in Bay Area artists' spaces as a further validation of participants. Clearly, the display of such material entails a danger of conflating therapeutic and expositional intentions, particularly when the producers are outsiders to the art world. Also, art audiences tend to sentimentalize such work unless it is accompanied with sufficient contextualizing material. Therefore, as important as this participation by nonartists is, without a critical framework it can replicate the same narratives of oppression as conventional formats. As with *Cries of the Invisible*, simply naming a problem is not enough, no matter who is doing the naming. More useful are works that address the social and political circumstances in which they occur.

Homelessness and drug use are linked to broader issues of federal fiscal policy in a recent work by the Through Our Eyes History and Video Project, a collective composed of high-school students in the New York area. *Caught in the Middle: Of the Crisis* (1991) juxtaposes on-the-street testimony with in-class interviews to present the facts and fictions of urban problems. With intermittent barrages of statistical data, the tape compares government spending on domestic social programs to the defense budget. Following a report on real-estate rehabilitation programs in the Bronx, a student narrator turns the topic to Operation Desert Storm: "Do you know how many buildings could be renovated (for the homeless) on the $100 million the U.S. government is spending to keep our troops in Saudi Arabia?" Doubling its self-reflexivity, *Caught in the Middle* then segues to the issues of media representation. Standing beside a television image of a gesticulating George Bush, a student says, "At one point there was a belief that fifty percent of the population agreed with what Bush was doing. That is the side you get from the news. There is another side. It's called protesting." With this gesture *Caught in the Middle* takes the important step from offering a critique to promoting activism. Like *Outside the Dream*, the tape closes on a prescriptive note that binds the viewer to the work. *Caught in the Middle*'s final segments are shot at rallies and demonstrations in which students, parents, war veterans, and teachers join in objecting to government policy.

This rare confluence of dialogue, critique, and activism was central to the *If You Lived Here* project organized by Martha Rosler at New York's Dia Foundation and *Who's the Landlord?* coordinated by San Francisco's Artists' Television Access. Both projects took multidimensional approaches to issues of poverty and housing activism, combining eclectic group exhibitions or installations with publications and community forums. In doing so, they demonstrated the pedagogical potential of integrating documentary evidence, artistic interpretation, multiple viewpoints, and contextual grounding. By avoiding a single voice or formal strategy, the projects also pointed to the necessarily cooperative character of cultural/political alliance.

Of these two projects, *If You Lived Here* took a decidedly more theoretical bent. In her preface to the project's publication component (a 312-page art/theory book assembled by *Art in America* senior editor Brian Wallis), foundation consultant Yvonne Rainer stressed the noncommercial aspects of both the Rosler endeavor and a similar Dia project by Group Material:

> Needless to say, the governance of the art market was not in evidence here. And not unexpectedly, "pluralism," that ideological underside of market-value "one-of-a-kindness" and stanchion of cultural life in these United States, was not an operative factor despite the diversity of materials, styles, and origins of work shown. What surfaced again and again as one spent time in these shifting, seemingly chaotic installations was the conflict between official utterance and nonofficial representation of everyday life, between the exalted bromides of Western democracy, and their thinly disguised "free-doms:" to die of AIDS, to live in the street in a cardboard box, to not learn to read, to speak without being heard, to make art that will never be seen.[58]

The three exhibitions of *If You Lived Here* were crazy quilts of pamphlets, signage, videotapes, and works by both the famous and the unknown. A single room of an exhibition component entitled "Homeless: The Street and Other Venues" (1989) contained shelter beds, childrens' drawings, newspaper clippings, photocollages, and paintings. As Rainer suggests, the assemblage lent a powerful unity to a cacophony of dissenting voices generally heard separately—if at all. To name a few of the participants: Artists/Teachers Concerned, Border Art Workshop, Anton Van Dalen, Tami Gold, Julia Keydel, Nancy Linn, Louis Massiah, Marilyn Nance, Seth Tobocman, and the Urban Center for Photography.

Unlike *If You Lived Here*, which remained centered in a Dia Foundation building in Soho, the *Who's the Landlord?* project took place in numerous galleries, community centers, and housing projects throughout San Francisco. In its preparatory announcement, *Who's the Landlord?* stated its specifically local intentions: "White, middle-class artists and arts organizations have often been the primary tools and secondary victims in the displacement of ethnic and low income neighborhood residents.... This project specifically seeks to engender better relations between artists and their communities."[59] Assembled through open calls for work, the project featured contributions by such diverse producers as Peter Byrne, Stacey Evans, Eva Garcia, Ace Washington, and the St. Peter Housing Project.

Taking a more directly instrumental approach to publications, *Who's the Landlord?* drew upon the skills of artists such as cartoonist Spain Rodriguez and World War 3 Collective to produce supplements in neighborhood newspapers. One strip, entitled "Public Housing: Who's in Control?" (1990), presented an indictment of San Francisco Housing Authority executive director David Gilmore. Its narrative of corrupt city spending and discriminatory construction practices ends with housing-project tenants banding together to assume control of their homes and complexes. The final panel reads: "Why shouldn't we make management accountable to ourselves. Let's hang them out to dry. Who's in control? WE ARE! IF WE WANT!"[60]

Such declarative statements notwithstanding, the exhibits were deliberately framed as a series of questions—to which answers, in the form of new work, could be added over time. In one venue the artists gradually filled the walls with drawings done through the course of the exhibition by children from housing projects. In their multiple levels of articulation and discontinuous methods of address, both *Who's the Landlord?* and *If You Lived Here* avoided the sloganeering of conventional documentary practice. Together they involved hundreds of participants in creating multiple crossovers among producers and audiences, as well as art and nonart constituencies. With this polyvocal approach the projects showed that depictions are only as good as the contexts they inhabit. All images reproduce conventions and stereotypes of some kind. What is important to point out is the artifice of representations.

The projects also similarly questioned the implication of cultural workers in issues of gentrification and homelessness. Rather than appealing to a standard version of social critique that implicitly accepts the discursive subordination of the oppressed, these projects managed to frustrate conventional definitions or superficial solutions. Until public understanding of issues of poverty and homelessness is elevated above the discourse of one-liners, such problems will continue to be addressed as objects of political opportunism rather than as conditions in need of structural revision. If cultural work continues to be a form of representational charity, it will never do more than enable the regressive distribution of wealth. Its makers and audiences will forever wonder if they could "make a difference." The task ahead involves redefining more than methods of practice. To accomplish the political ends required to alleviate inequality will entail redefining the meaning of cultural work, the spaces in which it can occur, and the audiences to whom it is addressed.

FIVE

LOOK WHO'S TALKING

CONTESTED NARRATIVES OF FAMILY LIFE

> It occurs to me that much organizational grief could be avoided
> if people understood that partnership in misery does not
> necessarily provide for partnership in change: when we get the
> monsters off our backs all of us may want to run in
> very different directions.
>
> —June Jordan[1]

"**T**hank you for not talking about your relationship," reads the opening cartoon in John Callahan's book *Digesting the Child Within*.[2] In recent years, Callahan has achieved cult status for his cynical views of New Age introspection and twelve-step quests for "wellness." His favorite target is the family, as in his portrait of "The Dysfunctional Family Robinson,"[3] or his image of a politically correct marriage ceremony: "I now pronounce you man and wife, if you don't mind putting a label on it."[4]

Callahan's humor portrays an era in which the family, especially the conventional nuclear family, is an object of scrutiny and contest. This cynicism over the discourse of "codependency" and dysfunctional relationships reflects a growing resentment about the normative implications of contemporary therapeutic practice.[5] It points to a bitterness felt by families who increasingly find themselves beset by experts offering corrective regimens. Not only do such programs suggest a return to an oddly conservative-sounding set of values, they also depoliticize social ills by psychologizing them within a private sphere set apart from the "real" world. Human dilemmas are rationalized as personal shortcomings rather than considered as symptoms of broader, community problems. Any impulses for change or improvement are directed toward the self. In other words, the approach is good old Yankee individualism with a kinder, gentler face.[6]

This therapeutic solution creates an atmosphere in which political issues are consigned to the realm of personal perception. Impressions and rhetoric outweigh any actual social consequences in an era of image consultants and spin doctors. Within the struggle over what has been termed "the politics of meaning," no symbol has been fought over more than the family. And nowhere has it been more contested than in the ubiquitous medium of photography. In genres ranging from advertising and entertainment to journalism and art, professional image makers argue over what they perceive the family to be.

These debates are enmeshed in deep ideological conflicts. Although modern feminism deserves most of the credit for foregrounding the oppressive potentials of the traditional family, the rise of gay rights, Civil Rights, and labor movements helped legitimate alternative forms of it—single-parent families, communal families, interracial families, homosexual families. In this context it becomes clear that the national controversy over the well-being of the American family is actually about one highly specific definition of it.[7] Monolithic assertions of an idealized heterosexual union are pitted against claims for sexual and familial plurality. The growth of alternative models has eroded the primacy of patriarchal households to the point where traditional nuclear families no longer constitute a majority in the United States.[8] Not surprisingly, conservatives increasingly blame these "new" families for contributing to everything from rising crime statistics to declining national productivity.

In the cultural realm, the struggle over representations of the family has never been more intense, as religious fundamentalists and right-wing extremists have assaulted progressive filmmakers, writers, artists, and record producers. These tensions result from the recognition that attitudes toward personal relationships and sex are culturally influenced. Within this scheme families defined by so-called special interests are measured against the "traditional values" of the "mainstream." But what are the epistemological grounds on which such notions are constructed? We cannot exactly define this mythical American family, but we do know that it is not Asian, Latino, African American, or Native American. We know that it certainly is not gay, lesbian, or bisexual. We also know that it is not disabled, sick, old, young, abused, addicted, out of work, homeless, hungry, or poor. This is a family that, in fact, includes almost no one.

Nevertheless, such fantasized renderings are extremely useful in affective terms, because they claim to offer membership to all. A nostalgia for a fictional past is projected onto the future in such profamily themes as "the new morality," "the new abstinence," "the new femininity," "the new baby boom," and "the return of the good girl." This was the gist of the recent New Traditionalist advertising campaign developed by Hearst, Incorporated's *Good Housekeeping* magazine. To resuscitate a publication dedicated to a hopelessly outdated domestic ethos, *Good Housekeeping* reworked its image of the ideal mom. Accompanying portraits of well-dressed women flanked by children (never more than two) were blurbs like this one: "She's Monica Simon, New Traditionalist—and here she is right at the center of her world. She loves to cook. She loves family dinners. . . . She loves her job—because it lets her contribute to 'the family structure.' "[9]

That the photos for these ads were made by liberal activist Mary Ellen Mark adds a mild, though not inexplicable, irony to the New Traditionalist campaign. In the 1970s and 1980s Mark garnered considerable attention for her pictures of homeless children, psychiatric patients, and Indian prostitutes. Intended as liberal consciousness-raising devices, those sentimentalized compositions rarely addressed issues of structural cause or reform.[10] Mark's New Traditionalist images made a similar appeal to surface appearances (this time of affluence and well-being) while remaining equally shallow in their political dimensions. Rhetorically, the New Traditionalist images achieved a nostalgic effect by emulating the conventions of nineteenth-century pictorialism. Both literally and figuratively, a mystifying patina was employed to recuperate feminist self-determination within the primordial narrative of the double burden.[11] Even though a complete fiction, the New Traditionalist mother triggered a range of stories in the national media; similar ad campaigns by publications from the *New York Times* to *Country Living*; and comparable sales pitches by merchandisers from Ralph Lauren to Wedgwood. The *New York Times* even held up Barbara Bush as an example of the New Traditionalist trend, a case of a real woman living up to the standards of an image.

As the Barbara Bush instance suggests, these idealized images of women and families are frequently associated with patriotism and national pride. The New Traditionalist ethos of nostalgic Americana directly links the idealized working mother to the idealized motherland. Within this discourse the nation comes to signify a home and its citizens a giant family—all governed by benevolent patriarchs. Conversely, as Julia Hirsch has pointed out, the family often models itself as a ministate, a safe territory in a world of antagonisms.[12] Both the "official" diplomatic discourse among countries and family businesses in the public sphere are conducted by a controlling and protecting father.[13] Moreover, this metaphoric glorification of a national family is carefully scrutinized to exclude any nonreproductive aspects of sex. In the recent controversies over the National Endowment for the Arts, the transgressive sexualities of both homosexuals and aggressive straight women were quickly recognized by conservatives as anathema to the historically recognized norms.

Of course, complementing the positive stereotype of the New Traditionalist woman is the negative image of the woman who will not play along. In a recent *Time*/CNN survey more than 63 percent of women who participated stated that they would not classify themselves as feminists.[14] According to Susan Faludi, the reason for this is not that women are free and equal or (as some analysts have argued) that feminist leaders are out of touch with their constituencies, but that a "backlash" campaign has convincingly discredited the movement by distorting its goals and achievements.[15] The message has gone something like this: "Feminism is your worst enemy. All this freedom is making you miserable, unmarriageable, infertile, unstable. Go home, bake a cake, quit pounding on the doors of public life, and all your troubles will go away."[16] Witness the legions of journalistic accounts of the failure of career women to find mates, of the health problems associated with postponed childbearing, of abusive day care workers, and so on. Certainly the "domestication" of Hillary Rodham Clinton during the 1992 presidential campaign, in which she was transformed for the media from a snarling feminist to a happy cookie-baking mom, is another clear indication of this trend. Meanwhile, the entertainment media produce dichotomous stereotypes of neotraditional submission (*thirtysomething*) to monstrous aggression (*Fatal Attraction*).

The effectiveness of the backlash against women is evidenced in the continued implementation of conservative policies to force women back into the home.[17] During the Bush years, conservatives managed to legislate their version of the family by continuing to foreclose options of reproductive choice and devising regulations obliging poor women to get married.[18] As overall government economic conditions continue to worsen, more states are adopting such positions, often in the face of contradictory empirical evidence.

Needless to say, these discursive contests have provoked considerable activity in the arts community. Photographers in particular have turned to the home and family as subject matter for both documentary and artistic endeavors.[19] Along with politicians, preachers, and parents, cultural workers have recognized the importance of images in shaping identities and forging values. Unfortunately, artists have sometimes made the same mistakes as others in assuming a direct correspondence between what images say and how viewers interpret them. At the same time, as growing attention has turned to what artists, scholars, and media producers think about domestic life, very little notice has been given to cultural production generated by families themselves.

In this chapter I discuss some of the implications of these predicaments for cultural activists and their audiences, especially as they relate to the sorts of exhibitions, publications, and educational projects being produced by arts institutions and the mass media. Central to the discussion is the question of who speaks for the family and in what terms. Although artists, academics, and educators seem anxious to speculate about these matters, interest in what families actually say about themselves in snapshots, scrapbooks, diaries, and home movies produced for personal use has been almost nonexistent.

This suppression of family documentation in intellectual discourse depoliticizes the personal by rendering the home off-limits, insignificant, or not appropriate for serious academic "work." The representation of the family thus becomes a terrain of unchallenged male authority. In art world terms, the absence of attention to snapshots, home movies, and videos reflects the need to differentiate objects from the everyday and legitimate them as commodities. Collectible artifacts require identifiable authors and market-certified styles, both of which snapshots lack. More problematically, when homemade objects have been a site of scrutiny, it generally has been within extremely uncritical parameters. Very few projects have addressed structural inequities within the traditional nuclear family or provided support for possible alternatives.

DON'T TRY THIS AT HOME

When the family appears in artworks, it is almost always reduced to its simplest terms. In recent photographic history, this impulse can be traced to the 1974 publication of *The Snapshot* by Jonathan Green, a book celebrating the appropriation of the "amateur aesthetic" by the modernist canon. With pictures by Robert Frank, Lee Friedlander, Joel Meyerowitz, Todd Papageorge, and Nancy Rexroth, among others, the volume sought to examine "the vitality and ambiguity of the naive home snapshot and its bearing upon a variety of approaches used by contemporary photographers."[20] As Green's comment suggests, in the 1970s photographers unselfconsciously began to appropriate "nonartistic" genres such as the snapshot as the formal possibilities of photographic modernism gradually exhausted themselves. Owing to the formalist legacy of art photography, these forays into foreign semantic territory often were described in terms of strangeness or ambiguity. These romantic attitudes have maintained the myth of a photography that speaks without judging. Such a view denies not only the interests embedded in any representational act, but the essentializing character of language itself.[21] All signifying practices collapse meaning into sets of predetermined and reified codes.

Nowhere are such traditions more ossified than at New York's Museum of Modern Art (MOMA), as demonstrated in the landmark photographic exhibition *The Pleasures and Terrors of Domestic Comfort*.[22] The exhibition was curated by Peter Galassi, immediately following the retirement of John Szarkowski as MOMA's director of photography. Without a trace of irony, Galassi introduced the exhibition with a claim to reveal "the current state of the American dream," not as seen from the "detached viewpoint of the journalist or anthropologist, but from within. Moments that only an insider might notice are described with an intimacy only an insider can possess."[23]

Previously, such intimacy had been unattainable for two reasons, Galassi asserted: prior to the 1980s photographers tended to idealize family members in portraiture (Alfred Stieglitz, Harry Callahan, Emmet Gowin); or they photographed "other" types of families, typically poor or working-class ones, by stalking them on streets or in tenements (Larry Clark, Bruce Davidson, Garry Winogrand). By comparison, in the 1980s and 1990s, the new photography of domesticity would examine the "material culture" and lifestyles familiar to photographers themselves.

In passing by the harsh realities of those "other" families, these photographers seemed to beat a retreat to the realm of the personal. In his catalogue essay, Galassi dismissed the political altogether, along (not so coincidentally) with postmodern assaults on institutions such as MOMA: "To move beyond this rhetoric and the divisiveness it fed thus may be to see all varieties of current photography more clearly."[24] Thus, rather than focusing on critical themes or contentious viewpoints, Galassi scattered single images along the walls in vaguely arranged groupings: napping, births, embraces, and old people.

The result was a self-serving jumble of photographic conceits assembled for the rather dubious purpose of cataloguing the range of "current photography." In attempting to periodize an unwieldy sampling of styles into a field of unproblematic "variety," the exhibition could not help but reveal its connoisseuristic impulses. After all, shimmering, oversized prints and cibachromes clearly were not the "intimate" images suggested by Galassi's introduction, and one would hardly think of people like Lee Friedlander and Cindy Sherman as domestic "insiders."[25] A *New York Times* review entitled "Dark Domestic Visions? So What Else Is New?" quite accurately noted that in avoiding conventional stereotypes, the artists of *Pleasures and Terrors* typically replaced them with clichés of avant-garde cynicism. Consider Philip-Lorca diCorcia's *Mario* (1979), a view of an expressionless yuppie staring at the contents of his refrigerator, or Tina Barry's *The Landscape* (1988), in which a group of well-fed suburbanites ignore each other at a party.

"Inevitably and quite deliberately this survey assigns a level of generality to the pictures it includes that was not, or not necessarily, intended by their makers," writes Galassi.[26] And indeed, as a curated ensemble, *Pleasures and Terrors* reduced family histories and relationships to a homogeneous constellation of unrelated instances. The show smugly reinforced the dog-eared separation of the aesthetic from the social by forgoing any contextualizing material or written text to suggest that these pictures might have anything to do with actual families. Even the title, *Pleasures and Terrors*, attempted to dress routine activity in a rhetoric of drama. Why? Because the unadorned activities of daily life were deemed beneath the dignity of artistic rendering. As Galassi concluded, "What is ordinary depends upon who is speaking, and that is the point."[27] Certainly, that artists were doing the speaking *was* exactly the point.

The lapses of *Pleasures and Terrors* pale in comparison to the exhibition-cum-coffee-table book *The Circle of Life: Rituals from the Human Family*, assembled by David Cohen.[28] Explicitly marketed as a *Family of Man* for the 1990s, the book purports to document universal human impulses manifest in ceremonies of birthing, childhood, marriage, and death. "So it is, in different ways, for all of us," Cohen explains.[29] A team of picture editors from *Life*, *Fortune*, and the *London Sunday Times* culled the 151 pictures by well-known photojournalists from over forty thousand submissions.[30] Although the images are roughly grouped by type of ritual, the primary organizing principle is formal similarity. In a set of pictures of people holding babies, this logic enables such bizarre sequencing as a Dutch fraternity hazing next to an east Los Angeles gang fight next to a Masai circumcision ritual. On its most benign level, the volume offers a cross-cultural advertisement for family photography itself—a point hardly lost on the Eastman Kodak Company, which provided most of the funding for the project.

But beneath this facade lie more troubling ideologies, not the least of which is the incessant reassertion of global patriarchy. Scantily captioned and undated, the photography of *The Circle of Life* introduces difference only to smooth it over in an appeal to a unifying "human nature." Roland Barthes's comments on the *Family of Man* apply well in this context:

> Everything here, the content and appeal of the pictures, the discourse which justifies them, aims to suppress the determining weight of history: we are held back at the surface of an identity, prevented precisely by sentimentality from penetrating into this ulterior zone of human behavior where historical alienation introduces some "differences" which we shall here quite simply call "injustices."[31]

That *The Circle of Life* so perfectly mimics a project that emerged at the apex of 1950s cold war paranoia is hardly insignificant. Like the similarly corporate-sponsored *Family of Man*, *The Circle of Life* is being aggressively promoted internationally, with simultaneous publication in five nations; serialization in both *Life* and *Good Housekeeping*; and an advertising budget exceeding $200,000. This is much more than a New Age aesthetic enterprise. It constitutes, as Cohen describes it, an "ethical" project—one with multimillion-dollar support by a list of multinational corporations that includes Pan American, Federal Express, and Hilton International.[32] Once again the metaphor of the "utopian family album" has been recognized as a moral solvent for diluting international antagonisms.[33] Put more bluntly, the project can be read as part of a larger ideological enterprise to divert public attention from the very real atrocities perpetuated to maintain the imperialist marketplace of the "New World Order." Here the discourse of the world as family is deployed to silence any genuine discussion of such matters.

WHO'S TALKING NOW?

Whether in a corporation, a museum, or a government, an elaborate set of institutional mechanisms support the view that wisdom about domestic relationships derives from qualified experts, not families themselves. The same hegemonic apparatus that regulates family planning, legislates welfare eligibility, and declares the illegitimacy of alternative families insists that those photographed are incapable of articulating their own concerns. In this the Clinton administration is but a mild improvement over the Bush regime. Michel Foucault theorized this regulatory mechanism as a "social technology," developed by the bourgeois class to ensure its continued dominance. This governmentally sanctioned social technology focuses on the control of procreation, the sexualization of women and children, and the identification and stigmatization of anomalous sexual behavior.[34] Its discourses are conveyed through institutions such as education, medicine, and law for the explicit purpose of imposing order upon the family.[35] In the contemporary era photography figures prominently in all of these discourses of control: ordinary folks are not to represent their relationships; they are only to be represented, in this case in the precious vocabulary of the documentarian or other expert.

Criticism of this thinking has occupied much recent theoretical work in anthropology and sociology, as well as in the emergent discipline of cultural studies.[36] Such criticism is the impetus for *Family Snaps: The Meanings of Domestic Photography*, a book dedicated to the excavation of meaning from home imagery. The collection provides an important counterpoint to *Pleasures and Terrors*, *The Circle of Life*, and similar projects that reify the visual discourse on the family as the latest aesthetic movement or as part of a New Age utopia. More importantly, rather than neutralizing domestic imagery within the depoliticized realm of the private sphere, *Family Snaps* suggests that the snapshot marks a unique site of articulation between private and public.[37] When visual renderings are read within their original contexts, their highly charged psychic dramas *and* ideological innuendos become apparent.

The argument follows two lines: one addresses pictures made in the home; another examines the relationship between that imagery and more-public representations. Patricia Holland explains that "the compulsive smiles in the snapshots of today insist on the exclusive claim of the family group to provide satisfying and enduring relationships, just as the calm dignity of earlier pictures emphasized the formality of family ties."[38] Within this scheme, suggestions of family rupture or dysfunction are suppressed, along with any references to everyday routines such as work (either inside or outside the home). The family is idealized as a site of tenderness, safety, and common ethical values—a "haven in a heartless world," in Holland's words.

Historically, photography has played an important role in sustaining the identities of the poor and the working class. Until the development of the daguerreotype in 1839, only those with the money to commission paintings enjoyed the luxury of a visual family record. Photography permitted hitherto unknown access to new forms of family and community genealogy.[39] Nevertheless, in political terms, pictorial household histories can become a type of endorsement for paternal authority, produced by the family for its own consumption. The father is generally missing from the images because he is the one holding the camera, orchestrating the scene, and commanding everyone to address him and smile. This is not to say that other voices are absent, for the mother asserts her voice in the assembly and editing of the family album. Here further revisions are made as images are eliminated, sequences created, and written commentary added.

Even so, the vocabulary of the family snap operates within tight discursive parameters. As anyone who has ever used a Pocket Instamatic knows, these are matters of both content and form. In discussing the material evolution of amateur cameras and film, Don Slater associates snapshot photography with a range of interrelated consumer goods and services (washing machines, automobiles, "modern" kitchen appliances, bicycles) intended to redefine the "domestic" as a site of consumption. Within this logic of production and consumption, domestic photography received a new character. It was both *enabled* (the means of representation, of constructing meaning on a staggering scale were provided) and *limited*, structured (the means of representation were provided to a mass market of domestic, familial consumers)."[40]

A hobby once available only to well-to-do enthusiasts became both inexpensive and easy. But these benefits involved trade-offs. As the need for technical expertise was reduced, so was control over the process. Fixed-focus lenses with preset apertures ensured that pictures would be taken only from mid-distance (discouraging close-up scrutiny or long-view contextualization; encouraging pictures of small "family-sized" groups), and in appropriately lighted circumstances (in daylight or with a single direct flash). The ease of camera operation (from camera loading to exposure making) greatly mechanized the process. This loss of control translated into a diminished sense of authorship. Customers were further advised by illustrated instructional packaging about how, when, and what to photograph. Simply put, the very mechanics and operation of the device encouraged snapshooters to replicate the image of the family that Kodak was aggressively promoting in its advertising. Not so coincidentally, this was the same ubiquitous family that sold every other commodity of the "new" domesticity.

Beyond the material aspects of the snapshot lie its more complex implications in the production of identity. If the typical snapshot describes a conventional middle-class marriage-with-children, what about everyone else? If the snapshot's definition of the family foregrounds mainstream norms, how do those excluded situate themselves? What happens when children realize that they are not the same little boys or girls their parents envision in their snapshots? In such circumstances the idealized domestic portrait becomes a marker for a painful misrecognition, the resolution of which often lies later in life. As Simon Watney recounts, "The picture reveals nothing of the terrible secret that drove me so deeply into myself for so many long irrecoverable years—years that, without photographs, do not exist."[41]

Yet, if the family picture can invoke a regressive effect, it can also yield liberating ones. Under certain circumstances the family snap can produce power as it is redeployed in the service of personal insight and historical revision. In recent years such a notion of domestic portraiture has been extended in the phototherapy work of Rosy Martin and Jo Spence. The therapy process often begins with cocounseling sessions utilizing preexisting family photos as points of departure. Discussions of personal memories inform deconstructive readings of the pictures to locate, as Spence puts it, "the unspoken power struggles, the emotional double binds, the psychic and economic laws of family life."[42] This often leads to sessions in which participants photograph themselves or each other as they reenact or fantasize significant moments or relationships. Although such phototherapy appears to be a frequently painful process, the insights it provides help its participants to discover their own histories and received subjectivities as an important locus of strength.

As a pedagogical practice, phototherapy begins to suggest ways the oppressive logic of family pictures can be turned upon itself. Without question, family pictures operate within a tremendously overdetermined network of discourses and expected uses. Yet openings and alternatives do exist for resistance. This is where cultural workers can play a strategic role in helping to bring the personal domestic photograph to a broader social context. By rupturing the boundaries between public and private spheres, such images can yield significant insights, freeing meanings that have been bound or mystified within either the museum or the home.

School Gaze

Representations of family are not limited to the institutions of the museum and the mass media, but extend into other environments, including the classroom. Yet, due to their highly scrutinized and politicized position, schools rarely are permitted to stray far from the status quo in their depictions of the family. To Sigmund Freud, the regulation of sexuality for the maintenance of familial order was the central (although unacknowledged) function of school.[43] This is because adults recognize school to be an important dual gateway.[44] On one hand, it represents the child's physical passage from the protected private space of the home to the unpredictable public space outside. On the other, it constitutes a temporal gateway from childhood to adulthood. Unlike conservatives today, Freud acknowledged that young people possess sexualities even before their reproductive capacities mature. School denies them a sexual identity in which to locate their desires, instead imposing a set of prohibitions that limit sex to a certain age and a specific purpose. Schools teach young people about familial relationships in a number of ways: the contents of curricula and teaching materials, the forms of address teachers use, the gender politics that structure the school behaviors, and the students' own roles in the educational exchange.[45]

One of the purported gains of the multicultural-education movement has been the revision of standard texts and media material to reflect the demographics of a diverse population. Because multiculturalism has turned textbook editing into a tokenist numbers game, it is unusual to pick up a *new* textbook that does not have a racially proportioned number of illustrations.[46] Yet the written contents of such books rarely deviate from standard master narratives. More pertinent to this chapter is that although race (and to a lesser extent, disability) has at least superficially entered the picture, any deviance from traditional representations of the family has not. Every domestic scene of a brown, or black, or white home always portrays a stereotypical scene of mom, dad, and the kids. No single parents or same-sex couples here, and no poverty or excessive wealth, either. Only the illusion of the great All-American Family.

Attempts to redress this situation have been met with great resistance, as evidenced in the 1992–1993 controversy over the "Children of the Rainbow Curriculum" guide. Issued by the Office of the Chancellor of New York City public schools, "Children of the Rainbow" was a booklet produced to help students and teachers become more sensitive to cultural diversity. The booklet also contained a six-page section urging teachers to discuss different family structures, including gay- and lesbian-headed families, and to advocate to students the acceptance of sexual diversity. Reaction was swift from conservative parents, particularly in one Queens school district. Refusing the guide amid massive national publicity, the Queens district was able to inflict great damage on the New York City school system and contributed significantly to the removal of Chancellor Joseph Fernandez from office.[47]

Although normative images of the family appear throughout the curriculum, only in health or sex education (and to a limited extent in biology) are family and human sexuality addressed directly. Mariamne H. Whatley has discussed the ways such course materials reproduce status quo gender roles and definitions of family life.[48] They are conveyed through a positivist expert discourse of reproductive sex within the marriage contract—with no mention of desire and sexual pleasure, masturbation or nonpenetrative "outercourse," or lesbian or gay sex. According to Whatley, information is delivered in the context of distorted discussions of hormones and drives, focusing on passive-aggressive stereotypes of women and men. Not only do such essentialized renderings present reductive heterosexist analyses of human behavior, but they also make invisible any alternatives. This is especially disturbing in the age of AIDS.

This rigid control of texts and pictures derives from an amalgam of outdated transmission theories of learning and perversion theories of sexual behavior. Building on a belief that children uncritically internalize whatever they are shown, adherents of these theories assert that people are born with a natural heterosexuality and that homosexuality develops only as children are seduced and converted by older role models. Because this seduction can happen through texts and images, proponents of these views argue, it is of utmost importance to keep such materials out of children's hands. The same fundamental logic applies to such sexual "deviance" as masturbation or premarital intercourse.

Guarded attitudes toward sexuality and family values undergird the conservative tenor of school curricular materials. This ideology is upheld structurally through the narrow corporate control of production and by the specific markets for which materials are generated. With 90 percent of titles produced by the top twenty educational publishers, the top four publishers—Prentice Hall, McGraw-Hill, CBS Publishing, and Scott, Foresman—control 40 percent of all sales.[49] Because the cost of developing and producing an introductory text can run as high as $250,000, publishers are reluctant to do much boat rocking over issues such as sexuality and the family.[50] The editorial process is akin to that of a Hollywood film, with an endless cast of professional editors, executive consultants, and marketing analysts joining to orchestrate the "managed" text. Given that the commercial success of these books often hinges on bulk purchasing, their contents are often geared to the largest customers—the handful of states in the southern tier and the western Sun Belt that approve books on a statewide basis. Sales to California or Texas can account for 20 percent of the total distribution of many books. For this reason the commissioning, writing, editing, design, and promotion of books are often geared to ensuring a place on the list of state-approved material.[51] Thus, the political and ideological climate of these states often tempers the content of curricular materials offered to the rest of the nation.

Needless to say, texts are but one component of any pedagogical transaction. Free-thinking teachers have long devised ways to circumvent even the most oppressive schoolbooks—as have students. But textbooks constitute a considerable proportion of the basic material with which all teachers have to work, and their role in the classroom is increasing. As the conservative reform movement has intensified curricular controversies over sex education in the name of "traditional family values," teachers have come to rely more on the safety of prepackaged materials.

Exacerbating the problems of profamily curricula are the structures of schools themselves. Traditional gender roles are reproduced in personnel hierarchies, in which the majority of school administrators are men. In contrast, women account for 70 percent of all teachers in K–12 programs. This disparity is most pronounced in the lower grades, where women outnumber men in elementary schools five to one. Moreover, the vast majority of teachers are married (74 percent). This creates a teaching environment in which boys are treated like boys and girls as girls. Of course, students are hardly the passive receptacles of knowledge they were once thought to be. Not only do they alter or reject the official curriculum, but they also bring to it their own knowledge and expertise. However, as numerous feminist analysts have pointed out, this is not always a politically enlightened perspective. More often than not, students replicate the gender norms of their parents and their community, even in acts of resistance.[52]

Snapshots and Alternatives

Although the treatment of the family in mainstream cultural and educational institutions is anything but progressive, a serious critical discourse on the alternative family is quietly emerging in the margins. This work recognizes that the aestheti-cization of the family by the museum and its standardization in the school attempt to conceal the politics of familial relations to maintain existing power structures. At the same time, changing economic circumstances and attitudes toward work and sexuality have raised questions about the legitimacy of dominant family models.[53] The movement of women into the labor force (often as much a matter of necessity as of choice) has fostered an unprecedented skepticism among school-age girls about the standard domestic code. Unlike students of previous generations, many girls expect to enter the workforce on an equal (or nearly equal) footing with boys. Regrettably, schooling discourages such thinking by treating boys and girls differ-ently and by encouraging individualistic and private solutions to gender-based conflicts. For this reason it is important for cultural workers both inside and outside the classroom to recognize the need for collective discourses about family issues. If patriarchal power has been maintained through the isolation and silencing of women in the private sphere, then emancipatory potential lies in bringing that sphere into the open.

Outside the school, critical cultural producers are devising projects that trans-gress the lines between the public and private to deconstruct the interests embod-ied in the traditional family. Many of these projects bring the interests of artists and educators together to create pedagogical encounters in new contexts. Forums for public dialogue have functioned as central elements of several of the most powerful activist installations of the past few years. Group Material's *Democracy* installations and town meetings, The Kiss and Tell Collective's *Drawing the Line* exhibition, and Richard Bolton's *The Emperor's New Clothes* installation come to mind as works that ask viewers to participate in events. In some ways this gesture is reminiscent of par-ticipatory art of the 1960s and 1970s.[54] Yet unlike prior conceptual works, with their focus on "the event" as a formal occurrence, these new projects have a distinctly pedagogical character. The newer projects ask participants to join the action by tak-ing a stand on an issue, by making themselves heard on a collective concern, whether it is pornography, education, homelessness, or the family. In this respect, they incorporate the best elements of earlier participatory events in reversing tra-ditional roles of maker and viewer. But they take the next critical step by asking viewers to locate themselves politically in response to the issues raised by the cul-tural project. This involves a decision, a statement, an exercise of voice among other voices.

To this end New York's Snug Harbor Cultural Center in Staten Island offered a series of workshops to complement its multidisciplinary "Family Stories" project.[55] Far from being separate conventional "classes," the workshops (conducted by Celia Alvarez Muñoz, Pok-Chi Lau, Ann Fessler, Martha Madigan, and others) di-rectly involved audiences both as viewers and contributors to installations, read-ings, and performances.

Muñoz began preparing her installation *Stories your mother never told you* (1990) by visiting elementary, high school, and senior citizen groups in the Staten Island vicinity. Working within an oral tradition, Muñoz invited individuals to engage the theme of family with their own questions or concerns. "My aim was to search and find the proverbial questions we all start to ponder about our unique yet united existence—the roles gender plays to encourage or discourage a continuation of said roles," Muñoz stated.[56] Over time a broader question evolved from the community responses: "What constitutes the family?" Collected statements were placed inside a cabinet that became the installation's centerpiece. A wall covered with blank paper for commentary provided a means to continue the discussion.

Clearly, artists and arts organizations can be important resources in providing neutral spaces for communities to address their concerns or to bring those concerns to others. In the New York City area a program organized by the New Museum has recently begun a special initiative directed toward students in alternative schools, such as the Teen-Aid High School for pregnant teens in Fort Greene, Brooklyn. Coordinated by artist Zoya Kokur, the program offers a course examining the relationship between the self-image and the media image of the adolescent mother. In the first sessions, students critique the ways television programs and news coverage denigrate the pregnant teen; they contrast stereotypes of the "American family" with fictions such as "the welfare mother." In their analysis of this material, the students draw upon works such as Clarissa Sligh's book *Reading Dick and Jane with Me* (1989) and Branda Miller's *Birth of a Candy Bar* videotapes.[57]

Reading Dick and Jane with Me incorporates texts and images from the familiar children's reader, which are collaged with additional material provided by Sligh. A panel of a subsequently expanded section of the book entitled "See Me Jump" (1990) shows conventional Dick and Jane characters adjacent to a typeset text that reads: "See me jump Who can jump What can I do See me jump Who can jump . . ." Behind Dick and Jane are three black children and the handwritten statement, "Our parents want us to read this stuff we heard our teacher say we're not smart enough." This dialogue is then framed with dark blue drawing paper on which viewers are encouraged to write their responses. Implicit is the invitation by Sligh to "talk back" to texts, authority, and official pedagogy. When displayed in Minnesota, the piece collected the following responses:

Reminds me of my old home.

Don't take away my creativity before my childhood.

You might be able to learn vicariously, but you can't live that way.

You are smarter than they are.

Branda Miller's *Birth of a Candy Bar* tapes originated in the I-Eye-I Video Workshops for high-school youth at the Henry Street Settlement, a New York–area community center. The resultant series of video poems afforded participants an opportunity to utilize pop-cultural forms to speak openly and creatively about a topic typically suppressed by parents and other authorities: sex. The tapes were produced at a special summer workshop addressing teen parenting and pregnancy prevention as instructional aids for other young people. Although the students' treatment of their subject matter is often ironic, their discussions of dating and contraception convey a serious subtext. One seemingly whimsical *Birth of a Candy Bar* segment is a two-minute tape illustrated entirely by anthropomorphized candy bars. The spoken narrative borrows from a word game popular among East Coast urban youth:

> On Payday, Mr. Goodbar wanted a Bit-O-Honey, so he took Miss Hershey behind the Mars on the corner of Clark and Fifth Avenue. He began to feel her Mounds. That was pure Almond Joy and it made her Tootsie Roll. He let out a Snicker as his Butterfinger went up her Kit Kat and made a Milky Way. She screamed O' Henry as he squeezed his Twix and made a Nestles Crunch. Miss Hershey said you're better than the Three Musketeers.

This is not the type of exercise one encounters in a typical high-school English class, but perhaps it should be. With the onslaught of conservative educational reform movements, schools have increasingly become sites of moral regulation—with crackdowns on AIDS education, a return to traditional gender roles, and an enforcement of compulsory heterosexuality. In such a repressive environment, it is not surprising that sex and sexuality constitute areas of considerable anxiety for many young people, particularly as these topics are represented in movies, television, and magazine advertisements (not to mention the "instructional" media encountered in school itself). By providing a forum for humorously addressing their subject matter, *The Birth of a Candy Bar* tapes not only worked to reduce this anxiety, but also presented remarkable exercises in the exploration of figurative language through text/image juxtapositions.

More importantly, the tapes do something for the student viewers that conventional school does not. By suggesting that young people can use their own experience to create didactic material for others, it places them in positions of authority. This reverses the traditional student/teacher dialectic by positioning the teens as educators, implying a productive value in being a teenager, a student, and even a teen parent. It suggests that one's knowledge (even of painful experiences) can be useful to others.

Within the context of the Teen-Aid High School program, discussion of this material inevitably foregrounds not only the inaccuracy of mass media representations and canonical texts, but the systematic erasure of certain voices from those texts. From this gesture of critique, each Teen-Aid student begins to make a book about her own life, which counters the distortions seen elsewhere. The book is produced for an audience of one: the student's own unborn child. In this way the students embark on an important political project. By moving from a language of critique to a "language of possibility" the women are encouraged to value their own experiences and voices.[58] Yet of even greater importance is the way this program of self-actualization is linked to a project of antiracist and antisexist media critique. More than a class for managing "at-risk students," the New Museum program at Teen-Aid High School reinterpellates them as "of-value students."[59] In providing a means of reinscribing their identities in this way, the program encourages the type of positive agency so often foreclosed by schooling and the state.

Perhaps more than any other endeavor discussed in this chapter, the Teen-Aid program demonstrates the importance of restoring discursive authority to the family itself. By encouraging the young women to talk about and re-represent their lives and relationships, the project yields to their expertise. This is the type of work that cultural and educational institutions support all too infrequently. Rather than the family being viewed as subject matter for aesthetic contemplation or grounds for normative socialization, it becomes a site of reclamation and redefinition.

Artists and educators can help open such spaces for new articulations of family. Such efforts are already evident in the work of teachers who intervene into conventional curricula by challenging gender binarisms, stereotypes, and conventional definitions. Such pedagogy critiques the ways sex and gender are structured into school representations of family life. Often this analysis involves a deconstruction of the very roles of authority and address that structure subject/object asymmetries. It asks how the struggles surrounding these imbalances are related to other struggles. Without attempting to ameliorate alterity, it seeks to locate "common differences" that might bring people together across constituency lines while recognizing the human variability within groups.[60] All of these concerns are applied to an interrogation of the way the family is seemingly "naturally" inscribed in language, history, and the discipline of the body.

This is sorely needed work in political terms, for the family marks a crucial junction, where human desire and personal interconnectedness intersect with broader economic and societal forces. To deny the family's place in the "public sphere" is to ignore the way daily life emerges from social compacts. Indeed, the family is an open signifier that cannot be locked into simple definitions of authority, heterosexuality, or monogamy. This flexibility implies that we have not only the ability to "reframe" the family, but the mandate to reinvent the society that surrounds it as well.

SIX

READ MY LIPS

BUREAUCRATIC RHETORIC AND NARRATIVE AUTHORITY

> Quite simply, there is no "outside" to institutions in contemporary society; they fit together like the pieces of a jigsaw puzzle—to leave one institutional site is simply to enter another, which will have its own specific conditions and determinations. The artist who works for a trade union as an "artist" . . . simply exchanges the problematic of one institution for that of another; in so doing he or she risks abandoning a struggle to which they could bring some experience or expertise, for one to which they are novices.
>
> —Victor Burgin[1]

"**D**emocracy" is a relative term. Like any other expression, its meaning is a matter of interpretation, debate, and contest. In recent years it is a word we have heard a great deal—from the "democratic" reforms in Nicaragua, to the suppression of democratic protest in China's Tiananmen Square, to the democratic revolutions throughout Eastern Europe, to the democratic liberation of Kuwait. Yet despite such historic circumstances on the international front, the U.S. state of domestic democratic freedom could not be more in question.[2]

If freedom implies the enfranchisement of all voters, how is it that the majority of citizens do not participate in electoral politics?[3] If freedom means equal rights for all citizens, how can one explain the chronic disrepair of the social service network and the continued tolerance of predatory capitalism? If freedom means unmediated communication and access to information, what is one to make of the consolidation of media ownership in a handful of corporations? While totalitarian regimes and oppressive bureaucracies tumble across the globe, within the United States the tenets of justice and equality continue to weaken.

With the ascendancy of Bill Clinton to the White House, the nation's gradual shift to the Right has been slowed but not stopped. Corporate interests still set the tone for most national policy debates, as evidenced in the business-friendly orientation of Clinton's policies on tax revision, welfare reform, health care policy, military restructuring, and national "service." The result has been a series of compromises with conservative extremists, rationalized by neoliberals to promote national unity. The consequence of this may well be a further erosion of democratic principles, as less powerful groups—communities of color, the young, the aged, the poor—remain outside the neoliberal and conservative alliance.

That centrist policies are justified in the name of a national accord was demonstrated in the Clinton administration's early calls for "shared sacrifice" to support its regressive tax proposals on energy and Social Security. Such rhetoric evokes an unproblematic patriotism that conveniently sets aside differences between wealthy and poor, exploiter and exploited. But of course this is more than mere talk; it is in the realm of public policy that narratives about everyday existence begin to determine what life is like.[4]

Currently, considerable effort is being made by conservatives to reassert control over issues of authority, tradition, resistance, and difference. Artists, writers, and teachers can become instrumental in explicating the way ideologies and factions wield power through representations. After all, power, especially as deployed in contemporary capitalist democracies, is discontinuous and therefore open to subversion; it is only represented as uniform, unchanging, and invincible. When left unchallenged, images of virtual authority produce the impression that citizens are weak and ineffectual in the face of ruling regimes, and agency suffers as a consequence.

Many theories have emerged to explain how such representational power functions. These generally entail determinist theories of social reproduction, that foreground false consciousness. Throughout this book I have argued for what is often termed a "culturalist" extension of this critique, which construes readers of texts as partners in the making of political meaning. The contents of messages and the intentions of speakers are mediated by interpretive contexts and listener subjectivity. The limitation of this culturalist model is that social policy results from more than the simple exchange of information between government and citizenry. Transactions involving goods and services, the establishment of rights and entitlements—these are mediated in the structures of state bureaucracy. The problem is that, without the strictest critical oversight, bureaucracies tend to evolve undemocratically.[5] Even more insidious is the dependency of bureaucracies on expertise, especially that emanating from business interests. As Max Weber pointed out decades ago, "Only the expert knowledge of private economic interests in the field of 'business' is superior to the expert knowledge of the bureaucracy."[6]

This corporate skill is hardly politically neutral. It consistently operates to support the interests of business, and to direct government policies toward business. One way it does this is by deflecting blame for the consequences of economic inequity. As explained by David Tyack, schooling is a common target for finger pointers:

Reform periods in education are typically times when concerns about the state of the society or economy spill over into demands that the schools set things straight. The discovery of some problem—America losing in economic competition, the threat of Russian science, poverty, racial injustice, unassimilated immigrants—triggers such policy talk. Policy makers translate these anxieties and hopes into proposals for educational reform.[7]

In other words, business looks for someone to fault. During the last decade, reformers on both sides of the political aisle have followed suit, attributing the failure of public programs to their nonadherence to market principles. Again, Clinton emulates his predecessor in encouraging private-sector "partnerships" with government and in seeking the counsel of corporate advisers. This is only exacerbated by the way information travels through a bureaucratic hierarchy. The exercise of the authoritarian—or specialist—voice is but part of a larger strategy to frame issues and regulate communicative contexts. Making matters worse is the way citizens have been removed from decision-making processes. A complicated conduit system develops through which expert discourses operate outside public scrutiny. This is the speech of legal proceedings, legislative debates, official reports, and foundation studies—all of which employ technically encoded vocabularies and access privileged channels of communication. When they do reach the average citizen, it is usually in the telegraphic form of press accounts, truncated into the journalistic normativisms of "general interest." This process omits the level of detail necessary for critical scrutiny, and it creates a rhetoric that obscures and mystifies the realpolitik of government policy making.

Abstract ideologies, needs, and interests become textualized in this way. They are literally committed to print in the form of regulations, laws, and contracts that come to govern people's lives. This inegalitarian process promotes a privileged structure of communication that systematically excludes the voices of those discussed. Even more sinister is the establishment of a brand of knowledge that in a single gesture both defines and limits the rules of conduct for would-be speakers.[8] Operating in the guise of procedural rationality, this process silences such "irrational" voices as the homeless, the unemployed, single parents, and AIDS patients in "official" discussions of their rights and entitlements.

The bureaucratic forms of representation that I address in this chapter evolve from the historic conservative impulse within the United States to privatize public institutions and to remove issues of social need from political consideration. This discourse argues that all such matters are best addressed in the private sector. After all, it is in the politicizing of needs that they are opened to public debate, established as subjects of social policy, and even met through legislated entitlements.[9] Thus a dynamic emerges in which the forces of privatization and depoliticization are pitted against those of deprivatization and politicization. This reflexive relationship is cast within unequal power relationships that favor the former. Worse still, as civic concerns are removed from the realm of the political, they are recast typically in specialist language, a gesture that further guarantees their absence from popular discussion.[10]

In considering these matters, it is important to realize that constructions such as "the corporate sector" and "the state" cannot be discussed as either homogeneous or hermetic entities. Each consists of numerous overlapping competing/cooperating constituencies. Equally important is the acknowledgment that neither one exerts a virtual control over the citizenry, but instead constantly works to negotiate accords among competing interests. As reports, studies, and bulletins are produced by government agencies and private organizations, they usually present carefully tailored articulations of apparent consensus. Indeed, much contemporary management theory stresses the importance of negotiated agreement in the capitalist enterprise. This is manifest in the way recent educational-reform documents, beginning with the infamous *A Nation at Risk*, convey forms of accord between interests inside and outside schools. As education is pushed toward increasing levels of privatization, market interests need to build bridges to amicable parties at work within the system.[11] Therefore, recent policy papers advocating a free-market approach facilitate the expansion of spheres of control or profit by business people, efficiency experts, behavioral scientists, media producers, and computer developers.[12]

It is worth noting that tendencies to privatize and depoliticize are dynamic. Typically, then, hegemonic policy documents present arguments for change. In most cases, reports are written by outside contractors hired for the express purpose of reshaping an institution. Consequently, they are often hotly contested by those with long-standing experience (or interest) in the school program or cultural institution under review. Ironically, the documents usually are not directed to that constituency, but toward a legislative body invested with its fiscal or administrative oversight. Therefore, two groups are excluded from the dialogue: the institution and the broader public that it serves. In effect, this produces a closed conversation between one group of bureaucrats and the experts they have hired to express their combined viewpoints, and a second group of bureaucrats. As expert knowledge prepared for administrative consumption, complicated issues often are simplified into summary points that smooth over complexities and elide contradictions.

Language and address are carefully manipulated in bureaucratic reports. Issuing from government or foundation offices, such documents exude an aura of authority in their packaging, design, and vocabulary. In a style of scientific rationality and business efficiency, the writers frequently convey their arguments to pander to immediate (rather than long-term) needs. Beyond issues of public-relations appeal and rhetoric lies the more significant matter of address. Virtually all such reports

READ MY LIPS

assume the subject position of a universal "us"—a singular totality of agreement. As Philip Corrigan has observed, this is a strategy for establishing that

> *our* standpoint is the norm (the neutral, natural, universalizable, and obvious) and that this in and of itself is a violent abstraction, an illusory representation of where and whom we are, which represses, where it does not actually erase, the contradictory dialexis of authority and difference, the structures and relations of inequality, subordination, oppression, and exploitation in "our" standpoint, "our" point of view. Little pieces of our lexicon—words like "we" and "our"—replicate and thereby embolden a social grammar of normalcy.[13]

Differences are suppressed in the logic of a shared argument. Any notions of group diversity or divergent opinion are purged. This is in keeping with the concept of "corporate culture," a set of intersubjective arrangements that define employers and employees as members of a common enterprise. In the rhetoric of modern management, the construction of corporate culture is regarded as far more powerful a motivational instrument than economic coercion.[14]

The notion of the unified speaking subject is then deployed to frame issues and name the other parties. Externally motivated authorities often redraw the structure of the entity under review as it is appropriated into a paradigm supporting the patron's ideology. Consequently, those faced with revision often are obliged to respond in terms at odds with their immediate purpose or procedures. On an interpersonal level, the ultimate consequence of this process is a form of discursive violence with very real consequences for affected constituents. Nancy Fraser has described a two-stage process of textualization to which applicants for Aid to Families with Dependent Children (AFDC) must submit:

> To qualify to receive benefits, subjects must assume the stance of petitioners with respect to the administrative body; they must petition a bureaucratic institution empowered to decide their claims on the basis of administratively defined criteria. In the "masculine" subsystem, for example, claimants must prove the "cases" meet administratively defined criteria of entitlement; in the "feminine" subsystem, on the other hand, claimants must prove conformity to administratively defined criteria of need. The enormous qualitative differences between the two sets of procedures notwithstanding, both are variations on the same administrative moment. Both require claimants to translate their experienced situations and life problems into administrable needs, to present their predicaments as bona fide instances of specified generalized states of affairs that could in principle befall anyone.[15]

As Fraser's account demonstrates, bureaucratic administration both reduces lived circumstances to texts and creates narratives that dictate lived circumstances.

This double abstraction fragments social relations into atomized units of examination and control. It promotes a mentality in which unemployment, illiteracy, crime, drug abuse, and poverty are seen as isolated problems, each with its own differentiated set of agencies and departments. Within such an administrative structure, need claims must conform to the constraints of particular bureaucratic narratives, rather than the multiple and overlapping social contexts from which they emerged.

The subjective effects of this process are manifold. Claimants are interpellated into the role of respondent within a variety of bureaucratic discourses; they become, among other things, taxpayers, welfare recipients, food stamp users, Medicaid patients, grant applicants, and public housing tenants. Each of these categories inscribes the respondent as a solitary petitioner in a hierarchy of power and expertise. Far from being a neutral position, the role of respondent in many of these discourses is packed with procedural complexity and moral stigma. These are mechanisms of isolation and disempowerment.

I now critique a pair of federal policy documents: *America 2000: An Education Strategy*, released by the Bush administration, and *Report to Congress on the National Endowment for the Arts* (NEA), by the independent commission on that agency.[16] Although the extremism of these two documents illustrates a distinctly conservative pathology, they are instructive in the way their methods are currently being replicated by neoliberal policy makers. By combining these analyses I hope to illuminate the common tactics through which the bureaucratic interests of the corporate state articulate strategies of depoliticization and privatization. This is intended to dramatize the importance of viewing such individualized assaults as part of a broader political enterprise.

BACKGROUND ON THE DOCUMENTS

Ronald Reagan was an unapologetic ideologue with a brutally frank program of redistributive economics. His policies were applied throughout all government sectors, most definitely not sparing the educational realm. The 1983 Department of Education report *A Nation at Risk* used a militaristic rhetoric to recommend a wholesale dismantling of equity programs in favor of bureaucratic discipline and corporate management. ("If an unfriendly power had attempted to impose on America the mediocre educational performance that exists today, we might well have viewed it as an act of war.")[17]

Although *America 2000: An Educational Strategy* shared the same crude ideology, it was significantly understated. Its promotion of a standardized curriculum and a rigid program of scientific management came clothed in the kinder and gentler rhetoric of "excellence" and "common values." Yet these seemingly innocuous concepts masked a similar commitment to free-market competition and a disdain for cultural difference. The former would be promoted by a new series of tests and evaluations of students, teachers, and schools; the latter would be implemented through a national system of common standards for each level of measurement. While promising almost nothing in additional funding, President Bush listed the following general goals for the program:

> By 2000, we've got to, first, ensure that every child starts school ready to learn; second one, raise high school graduation rate to 90 percent; the third one, ensure that each American student leaving the 4th, 8th, and 12th grades can demonstrate competence in core subjects; four, make our students first in the world in math and science achievements; fifth, ensure that every American adult is literate and has the skills necessary to compete in a global economy and exercise the rights and responsibilities of citizenship; and sixth, liberate every American school from drugs and violence so that schools encourage learning.[18]

In a calculated effort to garner support outside the weakening conservative coalition (and to counter the claim that Bush had no domestic agenda), *America 2000* camouflaged its political mean-spiritedness by adopting a language of liberal concern and a strategy of claiming credit for existing reforms. The result was a document riddled with logical loopholes and ironic contradictions. One cannot, as *America 2000* pledged, provide prenatal care for all expectant mothers, food for all hungry children, preschool for anyone who asks, college scholarships for the poor, new schools, job training—and not spend an extra dime. And one certainly cannot resolve vastly different local education issues with a universal set of principles from the federal government.[19] While the suggestion of such a possibility revealed the crass cynicism at the heart of the Bush White House, it also showed some real savvy about the function of language and media. Factual honesty became irrelevant in an age of simulacra politics. More important was the ability to frame issues, define problems, and name players. Poststructuralists would call this *narrative authority*. More than the reality of circumstances, what matters are the stories told about them: the spectacle of a Desert Storm War, a world-class set of tests, or a thousand points of light.

These are persuasive fictions of the sort the business community has learned to exploit quite well. Corporate managers regularly deploy such narratives to defuse employee hostility toward authoritarian command structures. Typically, this involves the circulation of stories in which low-level employees solve difficult problems, advance quickly in the organization, or prevail in an exchange with a superior. As explained by organizational theorist Dennis K. Mumby, "Such stories highlight the possibility of advancement, while at the same time legitimizing the inequities that characterize work situations."[20]

Although somewhat less partisan in its political implications, the *Report to Con-*

gress on the National Endowment for the Arts shares many of the same characteristics. The report was generated by a group of specialists jointly appointed in 1990 by the White House and Congress to examine allegations of impropriety in the administration of the NEA. Initial complaints about the character of projects funded led later to criticisms of the processes through which submitted projects were evaluated. These challenges emerged shortly prior to congressional debate over the renewal of the agency's authorizing legislation, a period during which conservative lawmakers were petitioning the dismantling of the agency.

It is worth noting that such challenges have occurred at regular intervals since the NEA was founded in 1965, although they rarely approached the public notoriety of recent years. Headline-hungry legislators frequently would send their aides to scour documentation of agency grants. Not surprisingly, they would occasionally find an exotic-sounding project whose "discovery" could be announced at an opportune moment. However, throughout the NEA's history, not a single charge was ever taken seriously by Congress, and only a handful of grants were even challenged. To a large extent, the confluence of the massive publicity engines of a few fundamentalist groups launched the notorious censorship campaigns of the 1990s. Congressional attention to purportedly antireligious and obscene artworks was primed by organizations such as the Reverend Donald Wildmon's the American Family Association, which produces a monthly newsletter with a circulation of over 400,000, and the Coalition for Better Television, led by the Reverend Jerry Falwell.[21] As a consequence, temporary restraints were placed on the agency, strictures that were eventually lifted on constitutional grounds.

In an effort to defuse a debate that was increasingly a source of embarrassment to the Bush administration (which, early in the controversy, defended the NEA and its newly appointed chair John Frohnmayer), the White House acted jointly with congressional leaders to assemble the Independent Commission. The group was charged with investigating the agency and recommending required changes, if warranted. In its findings the group did, in fact, suggest changes in the agency's methods and standards of judgment. But it stopped short of investing the NEA with the authority to directly censor its applicants. Determinations of obscenity were left to the courts, although the agency was to be held to a "higher" standard than the private sector in its sponsorship of projects.

SHARED STRATEGIES OF ARGUMENT

In one respect, the production of official reports can be seen as part of any administration's drive for self-perpetuation. In modern Western societies this impulse is not acted out through direct coercion, but through sophisticated maneuvers that eliminate oppositional voice, discredit dissent, and discourage critique. Simply put, mechanisms are systematically put in place to undermine citizen participation in the democratic process. The structural elements of this program become apparent in comparisons of different government programs. In this respect, the two reports I am discussing reveal remarkable similarities.

Both *America 2000* and the *Report to Congress on the National Endowment for the Arts* were reformist documents that accused their objects of study of failure. Like *A Nation at Risk* and nearly every other education proposal issued during the past decade, *America 2000* blamed schools for a variety of societal ills.[22] "Think about every problem, every challenge we face. The solution starts with education," its preface proclaimed.[23] With respect to the NEA, the issue of "failure" similarly was deployed to mask another agenda. Although in nearly three decades of constant scrutiny only two dozen of the NEA's 100,000 grants were ever even questioned, the report stated that "the original system no longer works."[24] The report then challenged a system by which carefully scrutinized peer panels had reviewed grants, and replaced that system with procedures to centralize decision making in the hands of the politically appointed agency chair.

These assaults have been extremely effective in tactical terms. On one level they represent the brute exercise of power in the guise of investigatory procedure. As Michel Foucault has observed, "The examination combines the techniques of an observing hierarchy and those of a normalizing judgment. It is a normalizing gaze, a surveillance that makes it possible to qualify, to classify, and to punish."[25] The bureaucratic "study" becomes a form of ritualized domination that links the collection of data and the production of knowledge to a display of authority. This is the result of a process termed "symmetrization" by which parties with unequal power or authority are rendered as equal in a discursive context.[26] In this instance, the opinions of small groups of hired consultants become equivalent to entire fields of practitioners. By taking the initiative in making challenges to targeted groups, both educational and arts institutions are placed in defensive positions in which staying the same becomes a radical stance. A certain degree of change seems inevitable; any "compromise" becomes a partial victory for the opposition.

The virulence of the assaults proposed by the reports is attributable, at least in part, to the fact that they both were prepared by people with little or no direct involvement in the institutions under review. Like most recent school reform proposals from the White House, *America 2000* quite unself-consciously emphasized its reliance on business executives and private-sector advisers. The arguments framed educators as incapable of maintaining both quality control and sufficiently competitive atmospheres. In the words of Milbrey W. McLaughlin, "*America 2000*, for all of its localism, is a top-down strategy that makes schools the target for reform, but writes the key actors within them out of the action."[27] Likewise, not one member of the NEA examining commission was a practicing artist, critic, or historian in the field. Appointed by the president and leading members of Congress, the Independent Commission included university presidents, foundation directors, and government bureaucrats, but not a single person with direct experience of the types of enterprises funded by the agency.

An explicit element in the analyses of both education and the arts has been the assertion that those inside the field are incapable of objectively assessing their own activities. Here those "managed" by the external administration are deemed fragile, prone to irrationality, and in need of a more powerfully structuring discourse.[28] This further rationalizes monitoring and controlling these institutions. In his speech announcing the release of *America 2000*, Bush ridiculed educators and educational academics: "The time for all the reports and rankings, for all the studies and the surveys about what's wrong in our schools has passed. If we want to keep America competitive in the coming century, we must stop convening panels to report to ourselves. We must stop convening panels that report the obvious."[29] In the place of analysis by educators, *America 2000* advocated a radically new program "to set aside all traditional assumptions about schooling and all the constraints that conventional schools work under."[30] In short, "Sweeping, fundamental changes in our system must be made."[31] Rather than on theory and research, the replacement for the old program would be based on "common sense and common values."[32] Similar to the education report, the NEA plan reached the "judgment that the endowment is not, in setting policy and making grants, adequately meeting its public responsibilities at the present time."[33] This stemmed from the premise that review "procedures are less effective in guarding against apparent or actual conflicts of interests than procedures of other federal grant making agencies."[34]

As a consequence of these negative assessments, both documents suggested that field experts and professionals should be subservient to external managers. Based on the assertion that educators and arts professionals had failed to manage their own affairs adequately, the reports recommended the importation of professional managers in the name of "objectivity" and "efficiency." Management asserts itself as an imperial enterprise, the purpose of which is to rescue and impose order on an unruly Other. It constructs an aura of superiority premised on binary oppositions of order/chaos, right/wrong, sanity/madness, objectivity/bias, and, perhaps most importantly, politicized/depoliticized.[35] Not surprisingly, these are to be drawn almost exclusively from the corporate sector. As Weber prophetically put it:

> Only the expert knowledge of the private economic interest groups in the field of "business" is superior to the expert knowledge of the bureaucracy. This is so because the exact knowledge of facts in their field is vital to the economic existence of businessmen. Errors in official statistics do not have direct economic consequences for the guilty official, but errors in the calculations of a capitalist enterprise are paid by losses, perhaps by its existence.[36]

America 2000 advocated the establishment of a corporately managed entity called the New American Schools Development Corporation to attract private dollars to invest in schools. The report named the U.S. Chamber of Commerce and the Business Roundtable as the new movers and shakers in educational reform, not the American Federation of Teachers, the Parent-Teacher Association, or even the National Education Association. Similarly, within the arts, the NEA report recommended that the presidentially appointed chair (for the past decade these have been lawyers with little or no arts experience), not peer panels, should have total control over evaluating the artistic merit of proposals.

After discrediting education and arts institutions with claims of poor performance and mismanagement, and then suggesting installing external governing bodies, both reports recommended the implementation of "new" standards. These standards were specified most frequently in vague references to "excellence." In fact, the only way one can really deduce the meaning of "excellence" is through negative reasoning. In *America 2000*, it is not the tradition of liberal, student-centered, humanistic education. It is not a program based on equity. It is not a philosophy that tolerates diverse identities. What excellence implies, but never directly names, is a rationalist curriculum of Eurocentric patriarchy. Similarly, the *Report to Congress on the National Endowment for the Arts* stated that "the guiding standard for grant making at the NEA must be artistic excellence,"[37] that "Congress has, after all, enjoined the endowment to foster excellence,"[38] and so on. Again excellence was defined negatively, in examples of what does not constitute fundable art: projects by feminists, people of color, lesbians, or gay men; projects that address issues of sex, religion, or politics; projects that criticize conservative leaders.

Also common to the reports was a concern for "international competitiveness" and "world class standards." The usefulness of both schooling and art was conveyed strictly in terms of their applicability to foreign trade and global political domination. This is hardly new in education, an endeavor that historically has been rationalized according to its ability to prepare workers rather than citizens and to enhance material productivity rather than human values. As *America 2000* euphemistically put it, "Today, education determines not just which students will succeed, but also which nations will thrive in a world united in pursuit of freedom in enterprise."[39] By reducing education to its most instrumental functions, this strategy ignored its deeper roles in the formation of identities—identities, as indicated above, of a quite specific kind. In the NEA report was the same suggestion that "world leadership which has come to the U.S. cannot rest solely upon superior power, wealth, and technology, but must be solidly founded upon worldwide respect and admiration for the Nation's high qualities as a leader in the realm of ideas and of the spirit."[40]

More disturbing still is that, to reach these levels of achievement, differences among people were to be suppressed in favor of a common culture. *America 2000* was very direct about the need to administer uniform sets of knowledge to all students, regardless of race, class, gender, or ability to learn. Rather than developing programs to assist economically disadvantaged students or children from culturally diverse backgrounds, the reformers would subject them to standard curricula and national exams every four years. The NEA report was almost comical in its effort to draw guidelines for a type of expression that would never offend anyone. It stated that "to support art from public funds entails considerations that go beyond artistic excellence. Publicly funded art must take into account the conditions that traditionally govern the use of public money."[41] The commission then suggested the exclusion of conceptually difficult, intellectually disturbing, or constituency-specific works because "the arts belong to all the people of the United States and not only those who benefit from the agency."[42] At the same time all proposals should now "be sensitive to the nature of public sponsorship" and "the beliefs and values of all persons and groups."[43] That is, they should avoid saying anything that might displease anyone.

To ensure compliance with these new mandates, both reports recommended an increased emphasis on management hierarchies and "accountability." Pandering to populist suspicions of big government, the reports suggested that the public is duped by teachers, artists, and administrators. Indeed, as government fiscal crises continue to compound, it is true that taxpayers are getting less and less. But rather than questioning runaway federal spending, foreign debt, and structural corruption, the documents blamed workers. Consequently, *America 2000* had a fifteen-point plan for "accountability"—additional testing, report cards for schools, differential pay scales. At the NEA, more procedures were suggested (in addition to already extensive ones) checking conflicts of interest, monitoring adherence to rules, reclaiming grants, and legally prosecuting artists who deviate from agency guidelines.

Adding insult to injury, the reports suggested that all of this could be accomplished on less money through cost shifting to nonfederal sources. In both arts and education, the administration sought a two-stroke strategy of decreased funding with increased federal control. Specifically, *America 2000* recommended the adoption of an elaborate testing program within schools, the massive expansion of both child care and job training programs for adults, the construction of 535 new "model" schools, and the sharing of current public-school funding with private schools. The entire scheme was to be financed by already stressed state and local governments. The NEA report encouraged programs requiring more matching of grants with private dollars and with funds from local and state arts councils. Featured in both the education and arts plans, this emphasis on private and local funding has the retrograde effect of reinforcing economic inequities from community to community.

Luckily, neither of these government documents is law. Instead they are position papers intended to promote a particular viewpoint. That they emerged from the federal government is significant, because on a textual level such documents have a limited ability to persuade. I have discussed the ways that bureaucratic reports can convey an aura of authority and technorational inevitability. What has not been touched on is the context in which these studies are disseminated and promoted. This is accomplished through the public-relations engines of the White House and through the discursive support of the conservative intellectual apparatus.

One does not need a communications degree to recognize the role of hype and sloganeering in the promoting of such documents in the press. Few people ever actually see these reports, but many hear of them in news accounts and through thirdhand interpretations by policy analysts and spokespeople. In this way the conversation is removed from the polite precincts of governmentspeak and transported to the realm of media. This is where conservative hard-liners, religious fundamentalists, and other xenophobes pack the debate with reactionary interviews, essays, and books. Indeed, as commercial publishing has become consolidated in the hands of a few multinational corporations, its orientation has grown increasingly conservative and probusiness.

Meanwhile, another form of institution has gained prominence: the private foundations and think tanks funded by the conservative trust. Shortly following the release of the congressional NEA report, the Washington, D.C.–based Heritage Foundation issued its own scorching analysis of the agency. Turning the rhetorical tables in the freedom of expression debate, an article entitled "The National Endowment for the Arts: Misusing Taxpayers' Money" accused the NEA of censorship of canonical institutions and art practices:

> The NEA has become a platform for attacks on religion, traditional art
> forms, traditional families, and traditional values. In the name of tolerance it
> has shown increasing intolerance towards standards of any kind. Its peer re-
> view process has become a buddy system for awarding grants to colleagues,
> friends, and clients of panel members, who are almost uniformly avant-garde
> in orientation.[44]

This is an example of the bracketing of bureaucratic reports between more extreme publications. This positioning makes documents like *America 2000* and the *Report to Congress on the National Endowment for the Arts* seem like appeals to reason and moderation, rather than the deliberately conceived partisan statements that they are.

Throughout this chapter, I have focused on how administrative reports assert specific ideological narratives while purporting political neutrality and scientific rationality. They attempt this split in their contents, language, forms of address, and the circuitous channels of expert discourse peculiar to bureaucratic speech. Yet it is important to point out that, like all other texts, such documents never assert a virtual authority. Their meanings are constructed in communicative exchange, so they are always open to subversion or revision. Obviously, the initial step in confronting these documents is to reveal the ideologies they try to hide. Beyond this is the more complicated and difficult job of producing new texts and alternative interpretations of education and arts policy. In the next chapter, I discuss in more specific terms the way cultural policy has emerged in the mandates of the NEA. These developments indicate not only the tightening conservative grip on what can and cannot be considered a viable form of creative expression, but also the way earlier accords between conservatives and liberals are coming unraveled.

SEVEN

THE COLOR OF MONEY

CULTURAL POLICY AND THE PUBLIC INTEREST

> The fundamentalist attack on images and the art world must be
> recognized not as an improbable and silly outburst of
> Yahoo-ism, but as a systematic part of a right-wing political
> program to restore traditional social arrangements and reduce
> diversity. The right wing is deeply committed to symbolic
> politics, both in using symbols to mobilize public sentiment and
> in understanding that, because images do stand in for and
> motivate social change, the arena of representation
> is a real ground for struggle.
>
> —Carole S. Vance[1]

In the 1990s the arts have moved from the margins of public debate to the center, as politicians, journalists, and government bureaucrats have recognized art's importance in shaping human identities and forging values. Recent controversies over literary canons, school curricula, and arts censorship all reflect a growing awareness of the relationship of culture to public life. Unfortunately, this important relationship is often misunderstood and distorted by those who would exploit culture for political ends by blaming it for ills ranging from welfare dependence to car jacking.

Political opportunism aside, these misunderstandings have two sources. The first is the outdated view of ideological reproduction discussed throughout this book, which defines culture as a substance unproblematically conveyed from sender to receiver. The relational character of communication is ignored, as audiences are portrayed as lacking the capacity to contest, mediate, or even choose among cultural effects. The second source of misunderstanding emerges from this model, as competing groups seek to regulate cultural messages. To promote their own ideologies, both liberals and conservatives define culture in terms that exclude the interests of the other side.

For obvious reasons, these arguments get more heated when the topic turns to public money.[2] The National Endowment for the Arts is the single federal program exclusively dedicated to the living culture of the nation. As recent debates have demonstrated, despite its relatively small annual budget of $174 million, the NEA exerts a powerful influence in literature, media, visual arts, music, theater, and its other disciplines. Unfortunately, the contested character of culture has created an atmosphere of exclusion, in which the major players squeeze less powerful groups from full consideration. Thus people of color, lesbians, gay men, the aged, the young, and the poor have all received less than equitable treatment from the mainstream gatekeepers of culture. Statistics show that the majority of NEA grants are awarded to an educated, European-American elite of producers. In fact, within the agency, just two of fourteen programs, Expansion Arts and Arts in Education, have a specific mandate to reach beyond traditional art constituencies and delivery mechanisms. And in the past decade these "outreach" programs have experienced serious reductions. In part this situation was exacerbated by the Reagan and Bush administrations, which favored a cultural policy of rigid traditionalism; in part the elitism of the NEA is supported by avant-garde factions on the Left. These fundamental difficulties have remained largely unaddressed by the Clinton administration, which has become increasingly reluctant to expend political capital on marginalized populations. In this chapter I review the historical development of general funding policies at the NEA, as they have evolved in relation to conflicting social values. I begin with the way the agency was created and maintained as a series of legislative accords between conservatives and liberals. The analysis concludes with a series of recommendations for policy revisions to make the NEA become more equitable, accessible, and democratically responsive.

THE NAME GAME

Part of the difficulty in formulating a coherent public cultural policy comes from the slipperiness of words such as *art* and *culture*. Raymond Williams was one of the first to address the way terms change in different circumstances and historical contexts by distinguishing between a general view of culture as "a particular way of life, whether of a people, a period, or a group" and a more specific definition of culture as "works and practices of intellectual and especially artistic activity."[3] Williams notes that this distinction emerged in the late eighteenth century with the development of Western nation-state capitalism and the resultant emergence of modern class divisions. Rather than acknowledging artistic creativity as a necessity of both work and leisure, the reified category of "the aesthetic" evolved as a component of the new modernist subjectivity.[4] In material terms this separation of "art" from the everyday emerged as an abstract exchange value was artificially substituted for a concrete use value. In other words, the aesthetic is a myth.

Terry Eagleton further elaborates on the distinction that the term *aesthetic* initially enforced; it is not simply one "between 'art' and 'life,' but between the material and the immaterial: between things and thoughts, sensations, and ideas."[5] To

Eagleton, the metaphysical roots of this split can be traced to that between ortho-dox and reformist elements, which have come to characterize broader divisions be-tween conservatives and liberals. In the orthodox view, culture is seen as the em-bodiment of timeless values, not the reflection of everyday life. Orthodox culture manifests itself in a chosen list of "great books" and masterpiece artworks housed in special preserves of aesthetic contemplation. Separated from the exigencies of daily life, art is devoid of political content or implication. Culture is seen as a means of social improvement, as a way that the poor and undereducated can learn to emu-late the more fortunate. It is also a method by which traditions can be reinforced.[6]

In historical terms this orthodox view reflects a reverence for the aesthetic "tastes" of the European aristocracy. Throughout early U.S. history, claims of a dis-tinctly "American" voice were undermined by insecurities about the ultimate inferi-ority of U.S. art. Despite the intellectual nationalism of writers such as Ralph Waldo Emerson ("Our day of dependence, our long apprenticeship to the learning of other lands, draws to a close"), a fundamental disbelief in frontier culture persisted throughout much of the nineteenth century.[7] These attitudes began to change after 1900 with the increased migration of European artists to the United States and with the development of regional artistic styles. But the elitist legacy remained of a highly evolved, perhaps inborn, sense of artistic value.

This racially coded and class-bound concept of taste has sustained itself as a means to stratify people of different economic and educational levels.[8] It constitutes a symbolic indicator of privilege and authority, embodied in types of art specifically abstracted from the harsh realities of work and from the "easy" pleasures of mass entertainment. As Max Weber wrote, the arts offer "a way in which men who are wealthy and powerful may legislate their superiority and assert themselves as wor-thy, marking themselves off as a deserving elite from those who are merely wealthy and powerful."[9] Hence, art is identified as a categorically nonutilitarian activity that becomes a ritualized exercise of wealth and power.[10]

In contrast to this view, reformists see truth emerging from the lived experiences of human beings. Realists recognize that values develop differently from culture to culture, but need to be evaluated in the context of changing social needs. Similarly, because culture and art are manifestations of the daily encounters people have with one another, they can be used to educate citizens and improve their living condi-tions. To reformists, culture is found in many places—from the gallery to the class-room to the street. Often related to this view of culture is the claim that art is a route to political activism, even a means of critical empowerment. Herbert Marcuse wrote of the importance of raising public consciousness to create the conditions for revolutionary change.[11] In this sense art has a twofold function: it can provide in-sights about oppressive social conditions, and it can facilitate people "coming to voice" in response to those conditions.[12] Ultimately, this practice of instilling political literacy is the bedrock of a functioning democracy in which all citizens partici-pate.[13]

PASSING THE BUCKS

Exactly how these theories play out in public policy has been the topic of wide-spread debate. In *The Democratic Muse*, Edward Banfield argues against govern-ment intervention in the cultural marketplace, asserting that the "sole legitimate function of the state is the protection of its citizens against force and fraud."[14] In other words, government must ensure citizens a "negative freedom" by shielding them from harm, but it should do little to promote their well-being or to redistribute resources. Such matters are best left to the consequences of individual competition and will. Within this general framework, Banfield constructs a view of culture as the natural province of the privileged:

> The art public is now, as it has always been, overwhelmingly middle and
> upper class and above average in income—relatively prosperous people who
> would probably enjoy art about as much as in the absence of subsidies. In-
> deed, they might enjoy it more, for subsidies tend to create and perpetuate
> institutions that are relatively unresponsive to the tastes of those they exist
> to serve.[15]

Simply put, art exists for an elevated economic class that all others should emulate. When government interferes in this process—by creating, for example, art pro-grams for the elderly or the disadvantaged—it only serves to divert arts organiza-tions from their true purposes. As Banfield suggests, this use of public funding en-courages "activities that have little or nothing to do with art properly understood."[16] These activities transform art into "entertainment, psychotherapy, material for his-torical studies, and so on. By misrepresenting the nature of art, they contribute to widespread public confusion."[17] This view of art is narrowed further by *New Crite-rion* publisher Samuel Lipman, who condemns current institutions for practicing what he views as a debilitating pluralism:

> From the idea that everything is art has developed an unwillingness to make
> necessary distinctions between arts and crafts, and between high and popu-
> lar culture; from the idea that art can improve everything has evolved a will-
> ingness to see art as improving the amenities of everyday life and reclaim-
> ing whole neighborhoods from the blight of urban decay.[18]

Along with their fellow conservatives, Banfield and Lipman conclude that agen-cies like the NEA allow government to intrude into yet another precinct of public life. There should no more be a National Endowment for the Arts, Banfield claims, than a National Endowment for Religion. Furthermore, the government already subsidizes entities such as museums and churches by releasing them from property levies and state sales taxes.[19] Add to that the tax-deductible contributions from foundations, corporations, and wealthy individuals and it becomes clear that the vast majority of arts support comes from indirect government subsidies. In fact, by some estimates direct federal arts support constitutes less than 5 percent of total public and private cultural giving.[20]

Taking an opposing viewpoint, Dick Netzer argues the benefits of market intervention and resource redistribution in his classic book *The Subsidized Muse*.[21] According to Netzer, market forces favor a mass-produced culture that is antithetical to what he terms a "merit good." Because so few people are willing to pay for art forms such as poetry, government has a legitimate role in offering subsidies for it. Moreover, Netzer asserts, because artistic production tends to be individualized, decentralized, and of a small scale, without government help art becomes affordable only by the rich. In contrast to Banfield's trickle-down private philanthropy position, Netzer argues that indirect subsidies offered by tax deductions tend to support the interests and ideologies of those giving them. Therefore, the state has a responsibility to make culture accessible to the general public and to preserve the best of the nation's art for future generations.

A further redistributive point to which Netzer alludes, but which he does not develop, is the need to compensate for the way majority cultures suppress minorities. Increasingly in recent years, this movement toward larger, more monopolistic cultural forms has been rationalized by the Right. The now familiar call for a "common culture" for all citizens implicitly devalues difference. When attached to government subsidy programs, such a call becomes a mechanism for silencing those outside the prevailing regime. There is no place for a singular definition of culture in a democratic society. Instead, public subsidies should be directed to the kinds of expression that the majority culture cannot or will not support.

In *Art, Culture, and Enterprise*, Justin Lewis addresses just such a redistributive role for government.[22] From the simple proposition that "it is generally more profitable to produce a small range of goods for a lot of people than a diverse range for a number of small groups," Lewis concludes that those "with limits on their disposable income, such as the unemployed, or with restrictions on ways of spending it, the disabled for example, will be more or less ignored by the process of cultural production."[23] It is worth stressing that Lewis suggests a government role in making the *production* of culture a part of people's lives. He advocates the broadening of cultural participation in such areas as education as both a means and a metaphor for more active civic life. Lewis is not alone in perceiving that cultural elitism and exclusion have contributed to public alienation from social institutions. In a recent survey less than 6 percent of people polled considered the arts a leisure activity in which they could participate.[24] Needed are forms of culture in which art becomes a way that common citizens can respond to an expert discourse that tells them their ideas do not matter.

Negotiated Accords and Government Patronage

From the arguments surrounding its enabling legislation in 1965 to the recent controversies surrounding artistic censorship, partisan disputes have remained unresolved over whether federally subsidized art should serve realist *social purposes* (education, employment, therapy) or whether it should serve idealist *aesthetic purposes* (exemplar, moral guide, inspiration). Legislative policy about cultural funding has been the product of a series of carefully negotiated accords. These have produced limits on the role of both government bureaucrats and policies in matters of cultural funding—limits that have been tampered with in the recent debates about freedom of expression. As a consequence, long-held cultural accords are coming undone.

The history of these arrangements is significant. With the collapse of Europe and the subsequent emergence of the United States as an international superpower following World War II, domestic cultural products came to be regarded as symbols of American might. During the cold war years, Washington politicians and bureaucrats recognized the publicity value of U.S. art as evidence of the benefits of a free society. The formal interventions of abstract expressionism were championed as stemming from the democratic ethos. Yet despite this mood of enthusiasm, there was also considerable nervousness about government stepping into the art business. Conservative legislators feared that federal subsidy would lessen the competitive spirit among artists, whereas their liberal counterparts believed that the NEA would become a "ministry of culture" mandating the production of official art.[25] For that reason a balance had to be struck, at least on paper, that would insulate the agency from partisan influence.[26] The NEA's enabling legislation, the National Foundation on the Arts and Humanities (NFAH) Act, states: "In implementing its mission the endowment must exercise care to preserve and improve the environment in which the arts have flourished. It must not, under any circumstances, impose a single aesthetic standard or attempt to direct artistic content."[27] The NFAH Act further limited the role of government by forbidding NEA staff to participate directly in funded activities. Grants were to be made to external entities only, as indicated in Section 4 (c) of the authorization law:

> In the administration of this Act, no department, agency, officer or employee of the United States shall exercise any direction, supervision, or control over the policy determination, personnel, or curriculum, or the administrations or operations of any school or other non-federal agency, institution, organization or association.[28]

The NFAH Act directed the endowment to focus on "projects that will encourage and support artists" to "achieve standards of professional excellence."[29] But in a similar spirit of political compromise, the terms of this excellence intentionally were never defined. Instead, interpretation of these policies was left to the endowment's rotating "peer panels" of art consultants. Besides keeping government out of the decision-making process, this reflected the widely held view that arts professionals were best equipped to direct cultural policy. Such an attitude is consonant with the structure of specialist discourse that characterizes bureaucratic organization both inside and outside government.[30]

This had a variety of effects, not the least of which was the perception of conflict of interest in the peer process. Hilton Kramer, among numerous others, accused the agency of becoming a "kind of private club," in which panelists swapped favors by awarding each other grants.[31] Others accused the process of ethnocentrism. According to former NEA deputy chair Michael Straight, the peer panel system often "refused to fund minority projects on ethnic grounds alone" and "resisted the introduction of quotas into its funding of artists and arts organizations."[32] Peer recommendations usually were not questioned, but were rubber-stamped by the National Council on the Arts (the NEA's presidentially appointed board of directors) and subsequently approved by the NEA chair. Despite these facts, in twenty-seven years of service the NEA has achieved a near-spotless management record, with complaints having been raised over only a handful of grants awarded—that is, until recently.[33] As the grant-making judgment of the NEA has been challenged by conservative groups, this deference to the authority of artist-peers has eroded, as discussed in chapter 6.

THE ROAD LESS TRAVELED

Although the NEA has received relatively few complaints over the years, one cannot automatically conclude that its programs have been completely fair or just. The lack of discord merely indicates that those who would complain are rarely heard, and that the constituencies served well by the NEA are among the nation's most powerful and vocal. As suggested in the previous section, growth among traditional cultural entities has been exponential, but the same cannot be said about more marginal or politically troublesome groups. Funding by the NEA for museums and for theaters is more than triple that for the socially oriented Expansion Arts and Arts in Education programs and double that for less traditional categories such as Design and Visual Arts.[34]

In analyzing less powerful "mass constituency" programs such as Architecture, Expansion Arts, Education, Jazz, and Folk Arts (as opposed to "elite constituency" programs such as Opera and Dance), Edward Arian recorded radical cutbacks enacted by the Reagan administration. Reagan's 1981 *Mandate for Leadership* transition document prepared by the Heritage Foundation argued that the NEA had grown "more concerned with the politically calculated goals of social policy than with the arts it was created to support. To accomplish goals of social intervention and change . . . the Endowment . . . serve[s] audiences rather than art, vocal constituencies rather than individually motivated artistic impulses."[35] In the name of "depoliticizing" the nonprofit sector, the administration restructured funding with a conservative vengeance, purportedly to increase the proportion of private philanthropy. As a result, from 1978 to 1981 funding for mass constituency programs was reduced from 27 percent to 14 percent of total grants.[36] In later years, those numbers dropped even further. By 1987, the Expansion Arts program for "minority" constituencies received but 2.3 percent of NEA funding, with Arts in Education doing just slightly better at 3.9 percent.[37]

More recent efforts (and political pressures) have brought those numbers back up considerably. In terms of overall NEA funding, the amount of money spent on communities of color (including individual grants, awards to organizations, and "minority outreach" programs at mainstream institutions) rose from 11.8 percent in 1987 to 15.2 percent in 1991.[38] During that period, grants to minority groups exceeded 22 percent. To make that progress, the NEA enlisted more people of color as panelists—from 22 percent of panelists in 1987 to 33 percent in 1991. The only catch is that these grant statistics purportedly indicating support to minority groups are inflated by the awards to "outreach" programs sponsored by institutions such as the Lincoln Center and the Metropolitan Museum of Art. Funding minority outreach programs at large museums and symphony halls is not the same thing as directly supporting ethnic cultural organizations. More often than not, such outreach campaigns amount to little more than efforts at force-feeding dominant aesthetics to people perceived as having no legitimate culture of their own. Moreover, this diverts funding from organizations run by people of color. One need only look to the pages of *Arts*, *Artforum*, or any of the glossy magazines these days to see how equitable and diverse the cultural universe has actually become.

Because the lion's share of NEA support goes to mainstream art forms and large institutions, ambivalent attitudes toward multiculturalism are entrenched in the endowment's operations. More significantly, the favoritism extended to the cultural mainstream has become intrinsic to the agency's legislative longevity. Some even argue that funneling most of the money to rich and highly visible groups is necessary because it draws public attention from more politically troublesome or marginal projects.

Interestingly, when the NEA was formed in 1965, it had a relatively unorganized political constituency. In the five years following the creation of the NEA, thirty-three states established arts agencies. At the same time, a new breed of national advocacy and lobbying organizations developed, such as the American Association of Museums, the National Association of State Arts Agencies, and the American

Council on the Arts. Though lacking the financial resources of for-profit political action committees, these entities have become increasingly visible and vocal. They ensure that the interests of major museums and symphony orchestras are always represented in congressional debates. Most have offices in Washington, substantial publicity budgets, and staffs of paid lobbyists, who organize constituents, convene conferences, and draft legislative memoranda.

This is not to suggest that the NEA is a monolith or that progressive alternatives have been totally lacking. Particularly among visual arts organizations, recent decades have witnessed numerous movements to democratize culture within the frameworks of existing agencies and policies. One such effort was the "alternative space" movement of small government-sponsored artists organizations, most of which were founded in the 1970s. In the analysis of Ruby Lerner, a consultant for the National Association of Artists' Organizations, this phenomenon occurred within a broader social movement "to break the tutelage of the larger bureaucratic institutions that dominated American political and economic life."[39]

Yet as Grant Kester has recently pointed out, the artistic avant-garde is tainted by its own brand of professionalized ethnocentrism. Conveniently overlooking questions of audience demographics and its own class identity, the largely white artists' space movement cast the cultural worker "as the universal subject, able to embody (or at least speak for) any number of subject positions and identities, simply by virtue of being an artist."[40] The avant-garde allowed itself to make "an unlimited range of moral judgments on the surrounding social order without having to account for its own cultural position, and privilege."[41]

The consequences of this attitude have become painfully clear in recent years. As with mass constituency programs, the "conservative mandate" of the 1980s produced a philosophical reorientation toward established definitions of culture. The result was a disproportionate reduction of support to alternative spaces with "fringe" activities such as installation and performance art programs, community art initiatives, and artist employment services. Not so coincidentally, it was exactly these transgressive alternative spaces that were the primary targets of the conservative censorship campaigns of the 1990s.

BACK TO SCHOOL: ART AND EDUCATION

"And so I think we come to some idea of a proper role for the National Endowment for the Arts. It should be educational, an attempt to teach rather than to beguile."[42] As suggested in these comments by Samuel Lipman, there is a glimmer of hope in the agency's new emphasis on education. Despite the gradual shift of NEA policy to the Right, one sees in this "Endowment Priority" the promise of cultural philanthropy addressing the consuming public in potentially progressive ways. Of course, to government bureaucrats, art education generally has meant the rote mastery of predetermined skills. And the agency has yet to significantly increase its Arts in Education budget. Yet in making education an overall agency priority the NEA has acknowledged the fundamental, interconnected relationship between culture and pedagogy. The mandate for all programs to begin considering the issue of education opens the door for definitions of art that counter the agency's current drift toward reified idealism.

Not that the task will be easy. One indication of the endowment's pedagogical bent is found in its former Artists in Education program, renamed Arts in Education near the close of the Reagan years. The name change was significant, for it signaled a structural shift long sought by conservative policy makers. The bulk of the $5.5-million Artists in Education budget had supported state and regionally administered artist-in-residence programs, primarily in school districts. Begun in 1969, Artists in Education brought more than forty thousand professional artists to an audience of some 20 million schoolchildren. In many areas the program provided the only government funding individual artists could receive. Even more significantly, in California and other states that have largely eliminated art from the K–12 curriculum, residencies enabled by NEA support represented the only contact young people had with working artists.

Under the revised plan, residencies came to compete with programs in curriculum development, teacher training, informational services, and testing. Although the NEA's previous evaluation of its residency program, contained in *The National Endowment for the Arts: Five Year Plan, 1986–1990*, indicated that it "has proven enormously popular" with artists, parents, and state agencies, advocates for educational constituencies argued that teaching was best done by those trained to do it.[43] Moreover, the growing popularity of artist-in-residence programs was seen as a potential threat to teachers' jobs. Writing in *Design for Arts Education*, David B. Pankratz stated that "Artists in Education is actually more a policy to provide employment for artists than an education policy."[44] Pankratz added that, although it was never the intention of such programs to replace teachers with artists, many schools were continuing their collaborations with artists after initial residencies. "This would seem to suggest a growing dependence on or orientation to outside resources is a more frequent consequence of Artists in Education than the development of sequential K–12 in-school programs."[45]

Aside from such practical exigencies, it is also important to consider the threat artists sometimes represent to school districts. Increasingly under pressure to maintain order, enforce discipline, and produce quantifiable results, many administrators are less than enthusiastic about potentially disruptive or critical projects by artists from the "outside." Thus, most schools in the United States have little time, money, and patience for experiments in activating student voice. The Bush and Clinton administrations have incrementally shifted the burden of school financing to the state and local level, and the resulting budget squeeze has encouraged a narrow back-to-basics pragmatism. During the equally parsimonious Reagan years the former NEA Artists in Education program played an important role in leveraging local money for the arts and artists. Now matters have changed dramatically.

Initial funding for the nonresidency components of Arts in Education were modest, with grants totaling $2.1 million. However, in NEA terms these are hardly trifling sums; the total disbursed for all visual artists fellowships is typically less than $2.5 million. Some observers have questioned the logic of reducing already minimal NEA funding for artists in order to supplement the billions spent annually on elementary and secondary education. In response, NEA officials stress the strategic importance of demonstrating the government's commitment to art education. A similar argument was made in assigning $1.9 million of NEA money, primarily from the NEA Media Arts program budget, to a children's arts television series cosponsored by the J. Paul Getty Center for Education in the Arts. Other awards of up to $650,000 have been made through the NEA's Challenge Grant Program to institutions such as the Exploratorium in San Francisco and Boston's Cultural Education Collaborative. More modest projects have been initiated within the Design Arts, Folk Arts, Inter-Arts, Literature, Museum, and Opera-Musical Theater programs.

Given these proclivities, it should come as no surprise that the NEA continues to promise a more educational orientation, and in its 1993–1994 guidelines education was listed as an Endowment Priority. As these plans progress it is important to keep in mind that in directing the arts and humanities along a more pedagogical course, conservative bureaucrats have seized the political high ground. The precise character of this agenda reveals itself in the NEA's *Toward Civilization: A Report on Art Education*, discussed in chapter 2 in the context of media education. Not surprisingly, the report focuses on the same brand of ethnocentric hagiography that conservatives have been promoting in other disciplines. *Toward Civilization* borrows liberally from ideas developed in the Getty Center's 1985 *Beyond Creating: The Place for Art in America's Schools*, the book that introduced the concept of Discipline-Based Art Education (DBAE).[46] Since the late 1980s, DBAE has provoked significant controversy in both art and education circles. The stated aim of DBAE is to secure academic credibility for the arts within the nation's schools by attaching art to four fundamental "disciplines": art production, art history, art criticism, and aesthetics. As explained by Elliot Eisner,

> [DBAE] ought to engage youngsters in the making of art, it ought to help them learn how to see visual qualities in both art and the environment, it ought to help them understand something about the relationship of art to culture over time, and it ought to engage them in conversations about the nature of art itself.[47]

These objectives have been implemented through a variety of strategies to quantify and measure the curriculum that, along with DBAE's emphasis on art as a "cognitive" endeavor, have made progressive educators quite nervous. Indeed, most of the debates over DBAE have resulted from fears that the program would somehow deaden the creative impulses of young people or that DBAE would enforce a particular brand of culture. As Eisner is quick to point out, however, DBAE was originally designed more as a structural model than a content-specific prescription.

Nevertheless, the problem that most DBAE advocates fail to acknowledge adequately is the extent to which the program is influenced by the politics of the curricular environments in which it is used. The ideas of DBAE come wrapped in issues of cultural elitism, ethnocentrism, and testability. Perhaps most disturbingly, the plan inherently devalues the everyday cultural production of young people by limiting notions of creativity to the sphere of "art."[48] Within this scheme, the worlds of work and leisure are discredited as inherently artless, as are other areas of academic inquiry. There can be no joy or spiritual fulfillment in areas such as science, mechanics, or sports. This program becomes particularly disturbing when endorsed in a government publication like *Toward Civilization*.

At the same time, both the Getty Center and the NEA plans emphasize the production of audiences over the production of objects, a position consonant with the Reagan and Bush administrations' repeated efforts to dismantle programs of federal support to artists. Throughout the 1980s, government advisers led by NEA council member and *New Criterion* publisher Samuel Lipman urged the agency to leave the fortunes of painters to the laws of supply and demand. This may be explained by noting that *Toward Civilization* identifies only two of its twenty-nine advisory committee members as practicing artists.

Like the Getty report, *Toward Civilization* asserts that artistic study should entail more than mere practice for it to have scholastic merit. The study recommends sequential K–12 art instruction within the broader contexts of criticism and history. Unfortunately, these admirable goals are embedded within the report's overriding concern for high culture and artistic genius. Statistically speaking, the brand of expression promoted in *Toward Civilization* corresponds to the narrow spectrum of artists, which is 88 percent male, 96 percent white, and 99 percent U.S. or European. Advocates of this standardized curriculum argue that in addition to making the arts more academically viable, the program will provide more equity. Mandatory art history courses would extend culture beyond the domain of the privileged. Of course, this also means force-feeding privileged-class values to everyone. It erroneously assumes that the same materials, pedagogies, and methods of evaluation are appropriate for all students regardless of their varying interests, histories, languages, and skills.

As evidence of the national decline in cultural literacy, *Toward Civilization* points out (without apparent irony) that nearly "half of 17-year-old high school students could not identify Rembrandt's *Night Watch* as the work in comparison to three ordinary works."[49] To obviate such occurrences, the report suggests uniform standards for art appreciation. The rationale comes from the U.S. Department of Education publication *The Nation's Report Card*, prepared for former education secretary William Bennett, in which the redesign of standardized tests is recommended as a means of curriculum manipulation. "What is assessed tends to become what the community values," the report states.[50] But which community is this? The NEA program's emphasis on historical masterworks discourages students from seeing themselves in artworks or seeing artworks in themselves. For this reason it is constantly fighting an uphill battle of imposing a worldview that seems dated and irrelevant.

Rather than insisting on idealist models of "great art" delivered through transmission models of mastery learning, NEA policy makers would do well to emphasize the inherently pedagogical value of *all* programs the agency funds. This notion is implied already in the elevation of education to the status of an Endowment Priority, but it has not yet been implemented in progressive ways. Rather than focusing on aesthetic achievement as the product of expert "professional" discourse, the agency should turn its attention to the everyday practices of cultural production that exist so richly in the lives of ordinary citizens. In the rest of this chapter, I discuss a variety of historical and hypothetical applications of such cultural pedagogy, as a means of forging a democracy in which citizens write, sing, paint, and participate equally.

HISTORY AND POSSIBILITY

No discussion of future cultural policy would be complete without reviewing the rise and fall of two other historic federal forays into arts funding: the depression-era Works Progress Administration (WPA) and the Comprehensive Employment and Training Act (CETA) of the 1970s. At its peak in 1936, WPA arts projects employed more than forty thousand artists and constituted a hitherto unknown government legitimization of the role of artists in society. Not only did it support artists as never before, but the WPA enjoyed considerable popularity in its initial phases. Unfortunately, as Steven Dubin points out, there historically has been a problem in the United States whenever government has made culture *too* accessible.[51] As art projects are held up to broad public scrutiny, they are invariably criticized from some quarters as offensive or frivolous. This is attributable partly to politics and partly to views of artistic nonutilitarianism.

Hence, despite the wide popularity of WPA cultural projects, they were gradually looked upon with suspicion. In particular, conservative legislators criticized as antipatriotic plays and exhibitions dealing with social issues such as poverty and crime. Before long the WPA Federal Writers Project was under investigation by the

House Un-American Activities Committee, as lawmakers including J. Parnell Thomas branded the agency "a hotbed of communism."[52] In 1939 the Writers Project and all other arts programs were terminated by Congress.

A similar fate befell CETA. Enacted in 1973, CETA's initial goal was to end structural unemployment by improving the skills of relatively untrained workers. Nonprofit art galleries and theater companies could hire artists for jobs ranging from administration to the actual creation of artworks. The scope of the program was such that by 1979 CETA arts funding had surpassed that of the NEA. Unfortunately, CETA itself came under fire well before its dismantling by the Reagan government. The program was accused of mismanagement and poor supervision. Worse still, a perception spread that political patronage often usurped economic need in determining who got CETA jobs. This was exacerbated by public skepticism over the employability of artists, fed in part by stereotypes of artists as deviants, mystics, or individuals somehow beyond the realm of material concern. As a consequence, CETA arts projects were held up as prime examples of government waste by articles in the popular press with headlines such as "While You're Up, Get Me a Grant" and "Artist Rakes in Your Tax $$ with Weird Sculptures." Ironically, due to such negative publicity, arts projects have been credited with a significant role in CETA's downfall.

The histories of the WPA and CETA, as well as the ongoing NEA controversies, demonstrate the need to formulate a cultural policy that can withstand political assault. Until 1990, the NEA had kept out of harm's way by offering a service widely considered to be in the public interest but utilized (and scrutinized) by a rather narrow and homogeneous constituency. Unfortunately, the distance of the NEA from a broader public has made it vulnerable to recent incursions by attention-seeking politicians. In fact, a recent study conducted by People for the American Way found that 93 percent of the population opposed arts censorship, but most people did not care enough about the NEA to do anything about it.[53] As columnist Jack Germond recently quipped on NBC's *The McLaughlin Group*, "Most people are too sensible to take the arts lobby seriously."[54]

The remedies for this situation lie in returning to the basic policy objectives of the NEA: to serve the broad diversity of the nation's cultural producers, and to make that culture available to the widest possible audience. But to achieve these objectives will entail major departures from the idealist definition of "art" that guides the majority of NEA programs and that supports the NEA's more politically powerful constituents. Justin Lewis argues that the appropriate function of government within a capitalist economy is to act as a corrective to market forces.[55] Consequently, the policy alternatives to be described here would support cultural activities that are untenable in commercial terms, either because they serve small constituencies or because they do not result in a salable product.

By far the most important change is to increase the NEA's commitment to cultural diversity, to make it the central objective of the agency. As W. McNeil Lowery has pointed out, private arts philanthropy is radically biased in favor of traditional European standards of culture and the institutions that support them.[56] There is little need, if any, for government to contribute further to this imbalance. Nor is there a need to continue regressive practices by large mainstream institutions geared toward "outreach." Such programs function only to promote an oppressive assimilation to a common culture, implicitly offered as superior to others.

Mechanisms are needed to preserve and further develop the many other cultures that make up the nation. Defining art in multicultural terms means recognizing different definitions and applications of art itself, as much as the varying traditions of many peoples. It means acknowledging that art has many roles in everyday life beyond mere acts of aesthetic contemplation. It can constitute pedagogy, therapy, or social work.[57] The NEA would begin by redesigning program categories such as Opera that intrinsically exclude diverse groups. But beyond this, the change would mean hiring staff and peer panel judges from communities outside the traditional pool of professional experts. Thus, the panel reviewing applications for Dance would not just represent choreographers from the classical ballet and avant-garde communities, but would be drawn from the multiplicity of international and vernacular dance styles.

Currently, except within the special Expansion Arts and Arts in Education categories, projects that originate from community groups, amateur clubs, social welfare agencies, and education are excluded from consideration because they do not qualify as professional-level activities. Here is where the contradiction becomes evident between the NEA's mandate to enhance the quality of art in the United States and to serve the general public. If endowment grant makers can recognize programmatically that avant-gardism and aesthetic traditionalism are but two of many legitimate cultural categories, then the agency will be obliged to acknowledge that what can be defined as art exists across a spectrum of art and nonart disciplines. It is found in institutions other than museums, galleries, and symphony halls. As suggested earlier, the alternative space movement of the 1970s made some positive efforts to broaden institutional definitions of art, but it suffered in the conservative reform movement. To rekindle this alternative spirit, the NEA should fund entities such as schools and community centers. Its legislation should be used to ensure this. If the NEA is serious about making culture available to the widest possible audience, it must sponsor culture in the places ordinary people frequent rather than funding institutions alien to them.

A number of groups are already moving in this direction. Beyond the now familiar efforts to colonize new constituencies through minority outreach or marketing-oriented education programs, some arts organizations and museums have begun to seriously rethink the very definition of the cultural space. New York's Exit Art recently announced plans to diversify its former gallery programs by adding a café and a home furnishing store—not as adjunct activities, but as integral programming components. The café will function as a public meeting place and community forum to promote informal discussion in a relaxed and inviting atmosphere. It specifically seeks to soften the distinction between art and recreation. According to Exit Art cofounder Jeanette Ingberman, "We are expanding the cultural, aesthetic, and social possibilities for a new reading of our culture."[58] Similarly, the home furnishing store will offer purportedly "useful" original objects made by artists. Examples include a queen-size bed made by David Sandlin, dishes by Ida Applebroog, and clocks by Richard Artschwager. Not only does this gesture imply a reexamination of the art versus craft distinction, but it also introduces a previously forbidden commercialism in a not-for-profit atmosphere. In effect, the new project admits merchandising and consumption as acceptable components of the cultural process. Efforts similar to the Exit Art redesign are under way at a variety of other organizations including Art in General in Manhattan, Randolph Street Gallery in Chicago, and Southern Exposure in San Francisco.

DEMOCRATS AND DEMOCRACY

The Clinton administration has indicated that it may move to popularize the government cultural agenda by reviving the now dormant Federal Council on the Arts and Humanities. That entity existed before the founding of the NEA and was sustained through the Carter years to make policy recommendations about federal cultural initiatives. The Federal Council was dismantled by the Reagan administration in the interest of "privatizing" cultural philanthropy. The reconstitution of the Federal Council would serve two important functions, according to Theodore Striggles, a former executive director of the New York Council on the Arts. Interviewed in the *New York Times*, Striggles explained that by executive order the president could immediately install a director of the Federal Council to lead congressional debates over the NEA.[59] More significantly, the Federal Council could be given a charge to look into arguments for expanding arts spending beyond a single federal agency.

In this way the Federal Council might help broaden the role of the arts throughout the federal government. During the Carter administration the Federal Council was used by Joan Mondale to sponsor arts projects through CETA. In addition to helping provide employment for artists, Mondale worked with the Department of Transportation to turn unused railroad stations into small community cultural centers. Such efforts were reminiscent of the New Deal–era Federal Art Project, the Federal Writers Project, and the Federal Theater Project developed by Franklin Roosevelt's administration to help counter domestic economic stagnation.

As governor of Arkansas, Clinton employed a model inspired by the work of the Federal Council. Recognizing that only limited moneys could be earmarked to cultural programs though the state arts council, Clinton pressed for the expansion of projects such as the annual blues festival in Helena, using other state agencies. The festival is operated from the Delta Cultural Center, housed in a restored Union Pacific railroad depot and primarily financed through the Department of Arkansas Heritage. As further evidence of his commitment to public art programs, Clinton has stated his interest in art education and in making the arts available to larger audiences. Moreover, Clinton's affinity for a socially integrated approach to cultural spending would seem to imply a place for the arts within public works programs.

It is worth reiterating that these ideas are not particularly new, and although they have not been tried for a while, they have been proposed regularly over the past two decades by proponents of the "cultural democracy" movement. Don Adams and Arlene Goldbard, among others, have advocated a return to a WPA-style "Federal One" model of multifaceted arts support across a variety of national agencies.[60] Adams and Goldbard point out that the expansion of arts sponsorship and employment beyond the precincts of the NEA will allow both practitioners and consumers to get beyond reified display conceptions of cultural production. Rather than a static product that only exists in specialized contexts, art becomes a more integrated process of learning, experimentation, and critical evaluation. Ultimately, art becomes a means by which audiences engage issues and become part of cultural experience. Also, the broadening of federal cultural patronage is an important means of expanding constituency support for such funding. It can help build the political support to protect agencies such as the NEA from reactionary assaults.

Beyond this level of constituency organizing, a commitment to cultural diversity is an obvious prerequisite for social equity. In a democratic culture, people are encouraged to express their views rather than rely on those of experts. For an agency like the NEA, the encouragement of such "voice" is in part a pedagogical endeavor. The NEA should encourage critical consciousness by favoring through its evaluative criteria projects that bring forward the concerns of specific constituencies. Paulo Freire writes that this is a process by which citizens "not as recipients, but as knowing subjects, achieve a deepening awareness both of the socio-cultural reality which shapes their lives and of their capacity to shape that reality."[61] On an organizational level, the NEA might encourage the development of "free spaces" for community debates, exhibits, and performances that provide forums for democratic dialogue.[62] For the first time in decades, the potential exists for this sort of movement. As I suggest in the next chapter, the political implications of such a cultural reorganization could be enormous.

EIGHT

Rethinking Media Activism

Why the Left Is Losing the Culture War

> The epic scale of the United States global power and the
> corresponding power of the national domestic consensus
> created by the electronic media have no precedents. Never has
> there been a consensus so difficult to oppose nor so easy and
> logical to capitulate to unconsciously.
>
> —Edward Said[1]

At the height of the recent arts censorship controversies, conservative columnist Patrick Buchanan wrote a column entitled, "In the War for America's Culture, Is the 'Right' Side Losing?"[2] In this frequently quoted piece Buchanan claimed that while conservatives had been busy defending democracy around the globe, leftists had been infiltrating schools, the media, and the art world at home. It is no secret what happened next, as numerous legislators, religious figures, and journalists cashed in on the publicity of the ensuing "culture war."[3] It also should go without saying that the Left has never held "all the commanding heights of art and culture," as Buchanan asserted.[4]

Nevertheless, the myth of a radical juggernaut took hold, as manifest in countless outcries over arts funding, multiculturalism, political correctness, and school curricula. But close examination of the outcomes of these controversies demonstrates that they hardly represent progressive victories in a broad-based war. Instead they constitute a few highly publicized skirmishes (that the Left has actually lost) generated by ideology-driven politicians with little interest in movies or schools, but with great interest in diverting public attention from failing social policies.

Unfortunately, the scheme seems to be working. If the Left is winning the so-called culture war, why are musicians and record store owners now routinely arrested for playing concerts or selling CDs? If the Left is winning the culture war, why are museums and art galleries closed for showing "unpatriotic" art?[5] If the Left is winning the culture war, how can the reactionary figure Rush Limbaugh top the best-seller list? The nation's cultural sphere (both its "low" and "high" ends) has always been dominated by the wealthy conservatives. This is not to say that *liberalism* has not made its mark in education, communications, or the art world; it is only to point out that these areas are strongly influenced by the moneyed interests that support them.[6]

Many conservatives now admit that the Left offers little real threat in the academy. As free-market apologist David Rieff wrote recently in *Harper's*, "Radicals on campus are no more dangerous than a display of Mao caps and jackets would be in Bloomingdales."[7] Statistics bear this out. In a recent survey of college professors conducted by the Carnegie Foundation for the Advancement of Teaching, when given a choice of five labels to describe themselves (Left, liberal, middle-of-the-road, moderately conservative, and strongly conservative) a mere 5.8 percent described themselves as "Left" and only 33.8 percent as "liberal."[8]

Turning to communications, the near complete control of the U.S. communications industry by a handful of multinational conglomerates has been dramatized in numerous statistical analyses.[9] Not surprisingly, these very same commercial media firms continue to hype the threat purportedly posed by the Clinton-friendly "Hollywood Left." Yet as Elayne Rapping asserts, this is another false alarm sounded by conservatives:

> The myth that these people have, in fact, any power at all over the content of Hollywood films is ludicrous and serves to obfuscate, for an already confused public, the actual economic and political workings of the movie industry. . . . Racism, sexism, and the glorification of violence in the service of illegitimate power are thriving in Hollywood as never before. And the Hollywood Left has absolutely no inclination or power to do anything about it.[10]

In the arts the story is the same, particularly when public money is involved. The now all-too-common practice of censoring politically troublesome artists can be traced to the Reagan administration's 1981 *Mandate for Leadership* transition document prepared by the Heritage Foundation. The publication provided both a rationale and a plan for the systematic defunding of the cultural Left. As a result, the 1980s saw a dramatic decline of funding to activist media and arts groups, which drove many out of business. Despite campaign promises to the contrary, Bill Clinton has given every indication that he plans to continue supporting only uncontroversial arts projects.

Historically, there have been as many approaches to cracking this conservative hegemony as there have been "Lefts"—almost all of them failing for one reason or another. In this chapter I review a range of such efforts during the past sixty years, with specific emphasis on the role of "alternative" or "independent" photography, film, and video. From its inception, photography promised to play an important part in progressive politics, as a means both of recording the putative "truth" of social circumstance and of circulating this message to a mass audience. Because of the accessibility of photographic equipment and the reproducibility of prints and films, photography was touted as the most "democratic" of media.[11] Regrettably, much of the Left has failed in its efforts to capitalize on this utopian promise. Besides ignoring media altogether, Left activists often have unintentionally replicated relations of class privilege and ethnocentrism in practices that ignore issues of diversity and dialogue. For this reason the difficulties of many radical groups in the culture war have emerged as much from their own attitudes as from the material domination of the Right. These attitudinal problems fall into three general categories. The first and most familiar is the seemingly unresolvable antagonism between "textualist" and "materialist" camps discussed in chapter 3, which perpetuates a debilitating separatism. Despite years of discussions about multiple subject positions and the need to build coalitions, this rigid division persists. The second type of problem centers on debates over identity, and similarly results in a tendency of progressive groups to discount the efforts of "others." This critique of identity politics stems from the absence of a political imaginary capable of containing the very diversity that has been the Left's strength. Socialists in particular often still cling to a crude economism that dismisses issues such as race or sexuality. The third category involves viewing issues of media and culture as apolitical and somehow harmless. As a consequence, many groups on the Left simply ignore the politics of representation.

In part, the resuscitation of the archaic textualist/materialist division results from the perception of a boom in cultural studies.[12] Proponents of this view minimize the importance of media by asserting that the culture war diverts activists from more immediate concerns such as poverty or unemployment. As Teresa Ebert has recently argued, "Politics, in this sense, then is a process without a product; it is a mode of semiotic activism."[13] Ebert's arguments typify that particular strain of Marxist reasoning in which words and images are seen as reflections of a preexisting economic base, rather than as factors that actually shape it. Besides promoting a shallow all-or-nothing binarism, these arguments weaken the Left by limiting the terrain of activism. Political work is seen as taking place either in the library or in the street, but never both.[14]

When this critique of cultural activism turns specifically to identity, the assertion is commonly made that such issues matter only to people who cannot gain access to genuine power.[15] Not so coincidentally, these arguments are surfacing at exactly the time when oppressed people's stories are being heard for the first time. This privileging of material instrumentality over the politics of representation further forecloses access by women, people of color, lesbians, and gay men to suppressed histories and narratives of emancipation. From the Right, this claim is typically used to suggest that cultural organizations are now overrun by formerly oppressed groups—most typically women, people of color, lesbians, and gay men—an assertion contradicted by the facts. Although some small (and hard-won) advances have been made, the same groups that suffer discrimination and economic violence in society at large are victimized in the media and cultural realms. Mable Haddock and Chiquita Mullins of the National Black Programming Consortium explain that "the rumor of institutional privilege for people of color is propelled by those outside communities of color," adding that "white producers who get no money or less than they want propagate this myth most fiercely."[16]

Still, it is not unusual to find members of the Left establishment criticizing activists concerned with issues of racial or sexual identity by either trivializing their efforts (as irrelevant) or condemning them (as selfish). This typifies a disturbing historical tendency of radicals not to listen carefully to those they believe they represent. In more strategic terms, by narrowly defining politics as economics, the Left also has allowed conservatives to take the initiative in battles over schools, libraries, arts, and even the language spoken in certain regions of the country. These are major reasons that the Left has been losing not only the culture war, but the broader struggle over U.S. politics. By assuming that politics exists outside talk, images, and writing about social issues, the power of information has been ceded to AT&T and the Pentagon. Moreover, this failure to effectively engage the mass media has contributed to the perception that the Left, particularly its academic quarters, is out of touch with "mainstream" concerns. As Michael Berubé has recently pointed out, the Left's inability to know whether to deploy a sound bite or a five-thousand-word essay has allowed the Right to define the terms of many public issues.[17]

Certainly, when the Bush government blacked out journalistic access to the Persian Gulf War, it was not underestimating the politics of representation. This is something the neoliberal Clinton administration also grasps.[18] One needs to look no further than the nearest bookstore to see that media and culture have been the focus of endless recent tirades by the likes of Lynne Cheney, Hilton Kramer, Samuel Lipman, Diane Ravitch, and Dinesh D'Sousa, to name but a few. As Buchanan excoriates, "The hour is late. America needs a cultural revolution in the '90s as sweeping as the political revolution in the '80s."[19] The Right recognizes the potential danger that the diverse groups of the progressive coalition pose if they ever gain the collective agency to organize, vote, and legislate social policy. Conservatives also see that if people can be convinced to trust the status quo and to believe that they are powerless against its authority, they will be less likely to question its agenda or act against it. Unless the Left begins in earnest to rethink both the subject and object of its works, it will continue to inhabit a position of marginality. Effecting this change will involve more than picking up the latest camcorders and satellite technology. It will mean redefining the very territory and terms of activism. It will involve changes in the definition of political intervention and in where it can occur.

THE PRICE OF A FANCY ADDRESS

One of the funniest subplots of the 1992 presidential campaign was Dan Quayle's attempt to salvage his public image by attacking what he termed a "cultural elite." Like Buchanan, Quayle sought to align himself with "average" citizens whose media environment supposedly had been overrun by progressives. Ironically, Quayle's scheme paid off. It soon became clear that the vice president had capitalized on the perceived distance of activist cultural producers from the "mainstream." Pandering to familiar stereotypes of writers, musicians, and filmmakers as somehow different from "normal" citizens, Quayle and others lumped both Hollywood liberals and radical activists together as prime examples of the many "special interest" groups unfairly claiming governmental perks. The Reverend Donald Wildmon of the American Family Association conveyed these sentiments well when he said that artists see themselves as

> an elite group of people, superior in talent to the working masses, who deserve to be supported by . . . tax dollars . . . imposed on the working people of America. . . . We ask that the Senate stop all funding to the National Endowment for the Arts, or provide equal funding for all other groups of artists—carpenters, brick masons, truck drivers, sales clerks, etc.[20]

Rather than dismissing such statements as rabid extremism, cultural activists might ask why people believe them. A recent survey sponsored by the NEA determined that the audience for visual arts organizations constitutes just 2 to 4 percent of the population, a group predominantly identified as educated, affluent, and white.[21] Turning to media, another study revealed that the prime-time audience for Public Broadcasting Service (PBS) programming was an alarmingly low 4 percent.[22]

This failure to connect with "the public" results in large part from a genuine lack of contact with it. Despite much rhetoric about group process and democratic decision making, most Left media-producing entities have evolved around single individuals whose "drive" or "vision" motivates the enterprise. This auteurist focus on the maker fosters an emphasis on personality that frequently overshadows the topic examined: the heroic social documentarian is an outsider entering the picket line, the riot, or the tenement to bring back evidence for a similarly distanced public. In the media world, the activist producer must compete with others for grants or journalistic assignments in an atmosphere that requires as much attention to career building and publicity as it does to political causes. Along the way, personal notoriety is frequently mistaken for political achievement.

This emphasis on individual rather than collective voice is part of a long history of intellectual conceit in which self-selected activist authorities presume to tell the masses what to think. It reflects a lingering vanguardism in certain segments of the

Left, a Leninist legacy of the professional intellectual revolutionary who creates an oppositional public sphere separate from what exists.[23] The affinity for and frequent coinvolvement of U.S. political activists in the 1920s and 1930s with immigrant artists and filmmakers from the European avant-garde partially explain this vanguardism. Indeed, one of the first proponents of media as a means of public manipulation was Lenin himself. "Of the arts," he stated in 1922, "film is for us the most important."[24] The tendency among leftist media activists to discount the critical abilities of ordinary people was further extended by the elitist Frankfurt School notions of a "false consciousness." To their credit, these arguments fostered a realization of the need to enhance public understanding of the conditions required for revolutionary change.[25] But implicit in the intellectualism of the Frankfurt School was the necessity of a visionary intelligentsia to provide a compensating "true consciousness." Many of these scholars fled Europe during World War II and assumed jobs in American universities, and their condescending views of media held sway well into the 1970s.

Often motivating this elitism was a solipsistic moralism, licensing educated white activists to speak about and on behalf of all other "oppressed" groups.[26] Again, this tendency can be traced to the early twentieth century, as in the theatrical documentaries of Robert Flaherty and Basil Wright. While explicitly anticolonialist in their intention to present native cultures "untouched" by Western culture, Flaherty's *Nanook of the North* (1922) and subsequent *Moana* (1926) now stand as benchmarks in the commodification and sale of otherness to mass audiences.

Extensively critiqued in anthropological circles, this penchant for turning disempowered people into spectacles for liberal sympathy is practiced even today in the work of photographers and filmmakers such as Larry Clark, Bruce Davidson, David Douglas Duncan, Jim Goldberg, Jim Hubbard, Susan Meiseles, and Mary Ellen Mark. Despite its claims of "consciousness-raising," documentary work that exploits difference in this way often only increases the distance between viewers and those viewed. As Martha Rosler has put it, "Documentary is a little like horror movies, putting a face on fear and transforming threat into fantasy, into imagery. One can handle imagery by leaving it behind. (*It is them, not us.*)"[27]

LIVING IN THE MATERIAL WORLD

The Left's cultural elitism is more than a matter of attitude; it also results from the way media practices have evolved in material terms—most significantly in the split between commercial and noncommercial production. Although this bifurcation of "low" and "high" culture contradicts the populist goals of both Right and Left, it is most damaging to the latter. Although a figure like Dan Quayle might decry the disregard of common citizens by a cultural elite, the Right's political agenda is actually enhanced by a belief in social stratification, inherited values, and adherence to tradition. Within this reasoning, a politically loaded high culture (claiming to be non-political, of course) is the standard to which all people should aspire, but that only a select few will achieve. On the other hand, the Left's program of social equity and respect for difference is at odds with rigid notions of cultural authoritarianism. The Left would be expected to favor a more grassroots view. Instead, many activists have subscribed to the same regressive cultural attitudes as the Right. In doing so they have replicated forms of address that reinforce social hierarchies and inequities, while draining the cultural realm of political possibility.

This process began in the 1930s, when Hollywood's willingness to finance documentary features declined in the face of a steadily growing studio system. Social analysis became subservient to melodrama or comedy, as documentary was consigned to the superficial realm of entertainment newsreels. By the time of the depression, films addressing political controversy were all but eliminated by a film industry bent on lifting the nation's spirits. This left documentary sponsorship in corporate and government hands, where production budgets would be lower and audiences more narrowly defined. Over time, the nonfiction film would all but disappear from the arena of popular culture. As a consequence, despite its historical commitment to notions of working-class entertainment, Left media would pursue a more esoteric course.

Such a shift had already taken place in England, where government bureaucrats early on recognized film's potential for documenting the nation's colonial legacy. In the late 1920s and 1930s the Empire Marketing Board (EMB) began underwriting productions intended to illustrate the benefits of British influence worldwide. John Grierson's *Drifters* (1929), about the international fishing industry, and the EMB's *Housing Problems* (1935) exemplify this genre. By 1939 the Canadian government had begun to produce similar material. Because filmmakers had to answer to political bureaucrats in both Britain and Canada, the status quo was rarely criticized.

In the United States, two related types of activity emerged in this period: the first was the government-sponsored documentary programs of the Works Progress Administration (WPA), discussed in the preceding chapter.[28] A remarkable number of photo essays and films were produced through such employment programs that both recorded the poverty of the depression and functioned as publicity for the Roosevelt administration. Artists involved included Walker Evans, Dorothea Lange, Carl Mydans, and Ben Shahn. At the same time, the rise in socialist movements in the United States fostered the launching of the Workers Film and Photo League in 1930, whose members included activists such as Berenice Abbott, Margaret Bourke-White, Pare Lorentz, Ralph Steiner, Paul Strand, and Willard Van Dyke.

The Film and Photo League (as it was later renamed) differed from the WPA programs in that it at least paid lip service to the development of a grassroots radical vision. Rather than simply hiring professional propagandists to produce media materials, the league offered film and photography classes so that working people could become the authors of their own stories. Due to this commitment to the collective process, the Film and Photo League periodically was able to rise above the proselytizing that characterized (and still characterizes) much activist media. Regrettably, its time and influence were limited.

With the exception of a few anomalies, such as Lorentz's Dust Bowl documentary *The Plow That Broke the Plains* (1936) and his later *The River* (1938), the work of the New York City–centered league rarely reached mass audiences. Explicitly seeking to counter the slick finish of Hollywood films, most Film and Photo League productions never made it into commercial theaters, and were shown instead at league meetings. By the outbreak of World War II and the subsequent decline of the U.S. Communist Party in the Stalinist era, the activity of the league had all but ceased. Increasingly preoccupied with international conflicts, Roosevelt allowed the U.S. Film Service, the last vestige of the depression-era programs, to go out of business.

Activist media practically disappeared during the 1940s and 1950s. In 1947, the U.S. House of Representatives opened its committee hearings on "un-American activities," which successfully put an end to the work of groups like the Film and Photo League, while also persecuting much of the Hollywood liberal Left. The industry responded somewhat later, when CBS journalist Edward R. Murrow began a series of critiques of the McCarthy-era witch-hunt in his "See It Now" series, which ran through the late 1950s.

In the 1960s the confluence of civil rights struggles, antiwar protest movements, and New Left activism—particularly among college students—created an atmosphere of renewed resistance to ruling-class values and institutions. In fact, the lack of radical activism in the prior two decades gave many youthful proponents of the New Left the brash belief they had invented the movement.[29] But while seeking to forge a new political imaginary, new leftists often alienated more people than they persuaded. Just as the Right had oversimplified issues into convenient clichés, many groups on the Left similarly collapsed all activist causes into a single category of dissent.

This presumption of an undifferentiated New Left failed to acknowledge the many factors of identity and interest that motivate people to act politically. As described by film historian Michael Renov, the activities of the 1960s journalistic collective Newsreel in many ways typified this reactionary radical practice. Newsreel provided documentation of Left activism (demonstrations, marches, and sit-ins) through grainy, jerky films that took viewers behind the lines of protests, into occupied school administration buildings, and face-to-face with sometimes brutal police. But in focusing on the performative aspects of protest, the films often dramatized responses to inequity and injustice without offering explanations of their underlying causes. The publication *Rat* covered a 1969 evening presentation of a Newsreel film at the State University of New York at Buffalo:

> At the end of the film, with no discussion, five hundred members of the audience arose and made their way to the University ROTC building. They proceeded to smash windows, tear up furniture and destroy machines until the office was a total wreck; and then they burned the remaining paper and flammable parts of the structure to charcoal.[30]

Despite the motivational value of the screening, the result was not entirely a productive application of political power. Although useful in promoting camaraderie and inspiring enthusiasm, much early work of groups such as Newsreel offered little besides superficial sloganeering and knee-jerk iconoclasm. Like much activism of the 1960s counterculture, Newsreel did not account for the exceedingly complex ways that alliances are negotiated, as well as the often partial and contradictory construction of civic subjectivity on both the Left and the Right. Most importantly, by focusing strictly on direct action, Newsreel overlooked the interconnected ways that political subjects are seen *both* as bodies and representations.

This affinity for vanguardist polemic still characterizes much film production in the 1990s. Indeed, it is a recurrent problem for many Leftist media groups that even the most critically sophisticated among them fail to convey their radical critiques with an equally radical attitude toward the viewing subject. These are deeply political issues in that they involve the ability of citizens to speak—or not speak. But unfortunately, the Left has rarely been able to capitalize on the potential of popular voice. As Andrew Kopkind has put it:

> The natural left—as opposed to small groups of self-conscious leftists—comprises an overwhelming majority of the world's population. It can't be that this force has no power to change things for itself, and for the better. For too long, however, the "talking" leftists have been telling the natural left (what used to be called the "masses") what to do and how to do it.[31]

No Popularity Contest

By placing itself in opposition to the Hollywood monolith, the activist Left historically has foreclosed the possibility of intervention within that system. This attitude correctly assumes that most mainstream films or TV shows will be cleansed of radical content in the current realm of "managed" production. But at the same time it incorrectly assumes that the commercial sector is devoid of political contradiction or subversive potential. The Right certainly did not share this view when it launched the Hollywood blacklist in the 1950s. Then, as in the culture wars of the early 1990s, any interventions that did manage to get produced were seized upon as anti-American.

By viewing every Hollywood production as part of a capitalist conspiracy, activists have distanced themselves from the affective pleasures that people often want. Indeed, due to this reluctance to engage commercial aesthetics, one generally does not expect much humor, sensuality, or visual excitement from activist media productions. Yet these qualities draw millions to politically reactionary films such as *Basic Instinct* (1992) and *Falling Down* (1993). Here again, it is the Right that has been winning the culture war. Consider the appeal of Rush Limbaugh. In just four years, the pudgy talk-radio reactionary has built a small empire, with a radio show boasting 15 million listeners, a late-night television program, a newsletter read by 300,000, and books topping the best-seller charts. More than his counterparts, Limbaugh uses satire to make his points. "If conservatism is out of fashion," Limbaugh recently quipped, "why do liberals think I'm the most dangerous man in America?" His performance evolves into an ironic self-parody intended to excuse his periodic attacks on the disabled, homeless, and unemployed—even as it taunts his critics. More importantly, Limbaugh casts liberals as snobs who act as though "the average American is an idiot—stupid, ignorant, uninformed, unintelligent." "With talent on loan from God," Limbaugh reassuringly jokes that these grumpy ideologues try to distort the world for their own ends—a world that would be just fine if left in the hands of jolly Republicans.

What is so worrisome is that all of this "talk" is beginning to have an effect on actual politics, which underscores the uncomfortable truth that despite its populist posturing, the cultural Left has always had an Achilles heel when it comes to engaging mass audiences. Limbaugh, who now appears regularly as a guest on news and variety shows, is credited with the ability to instantly shift public opinion polls—for instance, the ones conducted around the Zoë Baird nomination. In part, Limbaugh's success demonstrates that even in an age of presumed public willingness to "sacrifice," the nation is still looking for people to blame for its problems. But more importantly, it shows the effectiveness of a cultural activism that embraces popular entertainment and everyday life.

In contrast to Limbaugh's mass-cultural politics, one need only look at the pages of publications such as the *Nation* and *In These Times* to find a view of culture as a rarefied substance set apart from political reality. As acknowledged by *In These Times* senior editor Pat Aufderheide, "Although there is widespread consensus on the Left that cultural expression is empowering, the notion that art offers a way to envision other ways of being is less common than the notion that art is something pleasant and extra at the end of a hard day."[32] The apolitical and exclusionary view of culture among educated leftists that Aufderheide describes has been a major stumbling block in the formation of a broader progressive coalition. It was a significant contributor to the failure of Left media activism for much of the twentieth century.

MISUNDERSTANDING MEDIA

Television and the critical activity around it have offered encouraging possibilities for restructuring relationships between media activists and their audiences. After more than a decade of commercial development, video came to the activist agenda in the 1960s, with the introduction of the low-cost ($1,500–$2,000) porta-pak. This technology was immediately seized upon as a way to decentralize TV and invert production hierarchies. Although it became apparent over time that small-format video alone could not democratize the television industry, the idea of independent production encouraged the founding of scores of nonprofit media organizations nationwide. Paralleling this material decentralization was an intellectual shift in the way media were understood. With the application of literary reader response theories to media, it became apparent that although people may watch the same television programs, they often draw radically different, and quite culturally specific, conclusions about them.[33] (This view of media consumption would develop even further during the 1980s in the cultural studies movement. Rooted in Gramscian populism, cultural studies proponents regard communities as capable of formulating revolutionary sensibilities without the guidance of an intellectual vanguard.)[34]

By the end of the 1960s, two basic camps had emerged, both of which stressed decentralized media production: "guerrilla" television and community television. Associated with the guerrilla TV movement were entities such as Ant Farm, the Videofreex, Top Value Television, and Global Village.[35] Stridently iconoclastic, these groups eschewed any clear ideological identification with the New Left. Working on the street, from roving "media buses," or in schools, guerrilla media groups tended to be more enamored with the apolitical utopianism of the period. As Raindance founder Michael Shamberg wrote, "Power grows from computer print-outs, not the power of a gun."[36] In this spirit the guerrilla television movement— along with the installation and conceptual art movement in the art world—was among the first efforts to put video cameras in the hands of poor people, children, people of color, and the elderly.

Nevertheless, the guerrilla TV movement lacked the political focus to effect broad-based social change. Its outreach efforts to disenfranchised groups occurred only occasionally, and as a consequence guerrilla TV failed to garner much of a following outside the student legions of the counterculture. As described by media historian Martha Gever, "All revolutionary allusions aside, the prominent figures among the first generation of video activists were almost all white, middle-class, and male, with most women, Blacks, Latinos, Asian-Americans, etc. playing supporting roles."[37]

Setting the standard for more concrete political work with video was the Canadian National Film Board (NFB). During the 1960s the NFB initiated a series of experimental programs that had profound implications for media activism. As part of the NFB's "Challenge for Change" program, producers used film and video to enable local groups to communicate to government leaders with minimal third-party mediation. Based on earlier cinema verité and "consent film" efforts by producers such as John Adair, Colin Low, George Stoney, and Sol Worth, NFB units confronted the paternalistic notion that filmmakers can make objective statements about those photographed. They did this by engaging community members in the process of their own documentation, much in the way anthropologists conduct "participatory research." Dorothy Hénaut and Bonnie Klein applied these principles in a series entitled *VTR-St. Jacques* (1969) that involved a French-speaking community near Montreal. St. Jacques residents scripted, acted, shot, and critiqued a series of programs describing the issues facing their neighborhood. Hénaut and Klein found that citizens quickly gravitated to the idea of producing a tape about their civic concerns.

As the project moved to other Canadian towns it repeatedly demonstrated the enormous potential in creating new forums for popular speech. In group after group, it became apparent that vast storehouses of ideas and expression had been waiting for release.[38] Speaking of similar efforts, bell hooks has suggested that this process of "coming to voice" can be an important initial step in instilling political agency. If, as hooks puts it, people can "talk back" to the media, they may be moved to challenge other forms of authority.[39]

In a nation dominated by a corporate media monopoly, the idea of decentralized production has clear political implications. For this reason the development of an alternative media infrastructure in the United States has been fraught with difficulty, especially when government money has been involved. During the 1970s, two new institutional forms came into existence: local cable access facilities, and regional media arts centers in a nationwide network.

GETTING WIRED

Long before the promise of a "wired nation" was realized, counterculture advocates of cable television predicted yet another democratization of the media. Not only would cable increase the number of channels tenfold, but it would also, more importantly, give local communities the capacity to select and produce their own television. Federal Communications Commission (FCC) regulations enacted during the 1970s required cable operators to provide channels dedicated to local use. Beyond this, many towns bargained with cable companies to build free community access studios as part of their municipal franchise contracts.

The actual gains of the cable access movement proved more modest than initially speculated. Although many local cable outlets did indeed permit community organizations, labor unions, and youth groups to gain spots on the television dial, the audiences of such programming proved to be minimal. This is partly attributable to the inherent "narrowcasting" of programs intended for specialized audiences. But it also results from the inability of cable producers to replicate the visual pyrotechnics of commercial studios and, in most cases, from the failure of program-listing services to publicize access programs.

Despite these shortcomings, a range of successful models have emerged in the past decade, many of which focus on the use of media for educational purposes. One highly regarded cable access collective, the shoestring Paper Tiger Television, which produces a cable series in Manhattan, critiques magazines and newspapers in its weekly programs. With makeshift sets and a comical wraparound, each episode opens with the question, "It's 8:30. Do you know where your brains are?"—a spoof on a local Group W news program that asks, "It's 10 PM: Do you know where your kids are?" Paper Tiger episodes feature scholars or artists (commentators have included Myra Bain, Brian Winston, Serafina Bathrick, Joan Braderman, Alexander Cockburn, Herbert Schiller, and Ynestra King) deconstructing periodicals from *Cosmopolitan* to the *New York Times*. Consider this excerpt from Murray Bookchin's reading of *Time* magazine:

> *Time* makes time disappear. Everything is the same. There is no
> history. . . . The essence of *Time* is that it destroys the present, the past, and
> the future. Just like the hands of a clock keep turning around and around
> and give you no message, no perspective, no coordinates, no sense of direction. What *Time* does is relax you in time.[40]

In addition to discussing the contents of the periodicals, Paper Tiger programs also provide information about the economic structure of the publication, its reader demographics, the composition of its board of directors, and so on. In this way Paper Tiger Television explicitly addresses issues of viewer interpretation and the ability of people to make informed decisions about the media. Their productions suggest that the meaning of a media text is not a stable substance that flows unproblematically from message sender to receivers, but something that emerges in the relationship between them. Because meaning is made in this fashion, audiences can assert a degree of autonomy in viewing.

Beyond specific projects such as Paper Tiger Television, a broader level of collective strategizing is needed to effect large-scale political reform. This must entail establishing or strengthening alliances among those groups that have always been the backbone of progressive politics: trade unions, student groups, churches, ethnic coalitions, peace and justice collectives, and environmental organizations. Models for large-scale media organizing are relatively few, particularly when funding agencies encourage only the most bureaucratic and politically ineffectual of such systems. Yet one entity developing from the cable access movement seems to hold promise.

The Deep Dish cable satellite network was developed to structurally correct the stumbling block of narrowcasting that plagued cable access from the beginning. The project began in 1986, when members of Paper Tiger in New York City and Boston began renting time on the Westar Galaxy 1 television satellite (which also carried services such as the Nashville Network and the Disney Channel). With grant support to help publicize the initial hour of programming, Deep Dish suddenly put community access, in the form of thematic programs gathered from producers nationwide, onto scores of cable networks and into the homes of over 11 million satellite-dish owners. In offering a program of subsidized transponder time, Deep Dish has provided activist videomakers and community groups with a national system for cable access and home dish reception.[41] Although the impact of its current one hour of weekly programming should not be overstated, the effort offers an important model of intercommunity exchange outside the realm of corporate authorization.

MEDIA INDEPENDENTS

Multipurpose media arts centers were established to provide shared pools of equipment, distribution resources, and noncommercial screening facilities. Beginning in the late 1960s with start-up money from the National Endowment for the Arts and the Rockefeller and Ford foundations, such facilities grew in number to two hundred within a decade. Regrettably, the legislative mandate of the NEA to stay out of politics by supporting "professional" artists (as opposed to amateurs, students, or community groups) limited the populist potential of such centers. It also tended to skew their programming toward the fine arts.

Despite these difficulties, the network of regionally based media organizations has remained intact and remarkably politically active, due in large part to the activist commitment of the independent film and video producers they serve. In most cases, these entities have survived because they offer specific communities the means to produce, exhibit, or distribute media. Such groups include Appalshop in Kentucky, New York City's Women Make Movies, the Rocky Mountain Film Center in Colorado, the Southern California Asian American Studies Center in Los Angeles, and the San Francisco International Lesbian and Gay Film Festival. Lobbying under the umbrella of the Association for Independent Video and Filmmakers (AIVF), media centers and their members have repeatedly pressured the stodgy PBS and the Corporation for Public Broadcasting into more diverse and politically pointed programming.

It is worth reiterating that these advances have occurred in an atmosphere of inconsistent (and frequently antagonistic) sponsorship. The strength of these media centers demonstrates the potential of an activism that embraces cultural inclusion and genuine constituency involvement. By enabling diverse peoples to gain access to the tools of video and film, media centers have made a politically important departure from the monolithic and one-directional address of prior producers on the Left. In this dialogic approach to audiences, the regional–media center movement has proven its centrality in the future of political activism.

The strength of the movement was demonstrated in the establishment of the Independent Television Service (ITVS). In 1988, Congress responded to complaints from independent producers about the commercialized and unrepresentative character of public television. Lawmakers created the ITVS to receive $6 million of funds formerly administered by the Corporation for Public Broadcasting. Now quietly functioning, this entity has been specifically designed to create alternative models of media discourse. This means working as much on the development of audiences as on the production of new programs. As described by ITVS board member Lawrence Daressa, the entity is an endowment for viewers who do not yet exist: "Instead of naturalizing a single point of view, it makes point of view its overt subject matter."[42] Daressa's statement succinctly articulates the responsibility facing activist media artists: to create an environment in which diversity and contest are encouraged rather than suppressed. Obviously, this is not a new task, for progressive culture has always entailed a struggle by the disenfranchised to gain voice. But what is often overlooked in contemporary media work is the power of those voices when drawn together. That the ITVS could be brought into being is evidence that such structural revision is indeed possible.[43]

The need for models like Deep Dish and the ITVS is becoming all the more important as the nation embraces fiber optics cable (carrying up to five hundred channels), direct broadcasting satellites (transmitting straight into homes), and the Internet communications system. One need not be a technophile to understand that the way information is distributed is again about to change dramatically. As in the past, commercial interests are anxious to maintain their hegemony, media activists Jeffrey Chester and Katherine Montgomery assert:

> Technological innovation has triggered a power struggle of unprecedented proportions. The country's giant communications industries are locked in battle over which will control telecommunications in the 21st Century. . . . These developments will have a significant impact on the future of independent video and filmmaking. Depending on the outcome, independents would either have new opportunities for access and funding or find themselves pushed further to the edges of the electronic media system.[44]

The future of media activism lies in the unified efforts of progressive cultural workers to band together, across the boundaries of individual struggles, to meet its challenges head-on. These issues assume a heightened urgency in an era in which public gatherings and social rituals are increasingly undermined by the isolation of home-based culture. They take on even greater importance at a time when cultural difference advances to the front of the political agenda. Progressive activism can no longer limit itself to exclusionary and hierarchical forms of one-directional address. Groups on the Left can no longer afford to insist that issues of identity and representation have no place in material struggles. Overcoming these attitudinal problems will mean recognizing the reciprocal role of media as both reflective and constitutive of social formations. The Left is not doomed to lose the culture war, but it will continue to do so if it clings to old definitions of activism and politics.[45]

NINE

Pedagogy and Ethics

Notes for a Radical Democracy

> If the task of radical democracy is indeed to deepen the democratic revolution and to link together diverse democratic struggles, such a task requires the creation of new subject positions that would allow the common articulation, for example, of antiracism, antisexism, and anticapitalism. These struggles do not spontaneously converge, and in order to establish democratic equivalences, a new "common sense" is necessary, which would transform the identity of different groups so that the demands of each group could be articulated with those of others according to the principle of democratic equivalence.
>
> —Chantal Mouffe[1]

Much of this book has been devoted to an analysis of the culture wars and of the strategies both Right and Left have used in the struggle over civic subjectivity. Without a doubt, conservatives are seeking to regain their grip on U.S. politics by targeting cultural issues. With a rhetoric of ethical foundationalism, the Right has seized on popular symbols to put both liberals and radicals on the defensive. This has included an appropriation of the very vocabulary of "morality" and "community" once thought to be the province of the Left. As a result the leftist coalition finds itself in a reactive position in which the very terms of its antagonisms seem to be defined by the other side. In a continual battle against this or that conservative motion to silence or defund, a positive agenda has become difficult to formulate.

As the centrist government in the White House has shifted from Republican to Democratic hands, there is little indication that meaningful social change will arrive in the near future. For this reason it is more important than ever for radical activists to seize the initiative rather than wait for others to act. Ernesto Laclau and Chantal Mouffe argue that "if the demands of a subordinated group are presented purely as negative demands subversive of a certain order, without being linked to any viable project for the reconstruction of specific areas of society, their capacity to act hegemonically will be excluded from the outset."[2] Framed in this manner, the solipsistic nihilism of much postmodern theorizing is both defensive and counterproductive. We need a positive plan.

This new initiative must combine a politics and an ethics of a sort not typically drawn upon by radical activists. These entail types of practice that eschew both foundational closure and free-floating relativism. Such seemingly paradoxical practices respect differences, oppose oppressions, and permit the contingencies of provisional spaces of experiment with new social forms. Given such a challenge, it is incumbent upon radical cultural workers to reassert their roles in civic life. This calls for new subject positions and new forums for civic dialogue.[3] It will involve promoting notions of shared responsibility for community life, along with the belief that change is indeed possible.[4] This is a profoundly pedagogical endeavor in that it is an act of political education. Such a pedagogy convinces people that individual acts of citizenship (such as voting) can make a difference—that they themselves can command the authority to make community decisions.

At the heart of the struggle must stand a set of competencies through which cultural activists can dismantle structures that dictate societal norms and decide what issues can be considered political. At the same time it is necessary to connect a pair of concepts that conservatism seems unable to reconcile: *difference* and *egalitarianism*. To those on the Right, differing needs or interests are to be overcome or suppressed because they frustrate the will to systemization, standardization, and normalization.[5] Implicit in this view is a hierarchy of subject positions supporting an idealized "national" identity that is impossible for most citizens to attain. The ethos of this new mandarin class is discursively constructed in the texts of culture, high and low, to be sure. But it is also learned through the myriad of institutionalized roles and naturalized rituals through which human actors are cast as either winners or losers. Moreover, it is profoundly inscribed in the production, exchange, and consumption of commodities in daily routines of work and play.

Challenging this on a representational level will mean reclaiming many icons and rituals that conservatives have appropriated. If deconstruction has demonstrated anything, it is that the meanings of cultural signs are unstable. After all, it was through the false recontextualization of Robert Mapplethorpe and Andres Serrano as negative symbols that the Right succeeded in limiting artistic expression.[6] Cultural activists can work to unmask such methods of image manipulation while also forging a positive iconography. Yet in approaching this endeavor, care must be taken to avoid replicating universalizing models.

An important metaphor of this new iconography is democracy itself—not the idealized democracy of unproblematic civic verisimilitude so favored by the Right, but instead a democracy defined by continual struggle, change, and critical revision. This is not to suggest a return to nostalgic origins, but to propose a democratic imaginary yet unrealized in human history. The task has both political and ethical dimensions. In political terms, the common shortcoming of all hegemonic regimes (including utopian ones) is their implication of totalizing ideology or subjectivity. This problem becomes particularly evident within conventional liberalism. Although frequently presented as a pathway to emancipation, the neoliberal ethos of the Clinton administration perpetuates distinctions between historical subjects and objects: those who act and those who are acted upon. It seeks to make surface corrections to a structurally flawed system without interrogating its underlying inequities.[7] Lamentably, this is the pitfall of much avant-garde artistic and intellectual practice, which commits the additional sin of claiming vanguardist wisdom only for its own members. Such condescending logic has also been attributed to the prescriptive exhortations of "empowerment" associated with certain forms of emancipatory pedagogy. In contrast, a radical democracy defines itself on all levels in pluralistic terms. There is no single set of attitudes nor social group to which all others must conform, because an acknowledgment is made of the impossibility of any one perspective satisfying diverse needs. Instead, the unifying ethos is one of decentered authority. Owing to this latter principle, such a political program resists the vacuous amoralities of relativism and unexamined pluralism. For obvious reasons, such a scheme seems dangerously unstable to many neoconservatives who warn of the "threat" of uncontained difference.

This is where the ethical dimension of radical democracy comes in. Beyond a utilitarian program based on simply what works, and beyond an aesthetic attachment to transcendental ideals, lies a commitment among the members of the democracy to their mutual project. This is hardly a new idea, but it raises questions that resist easy resolution. Richard Rorty seeks to address the issue in *The Consequences of Pragmatism* by postulating a coexistence of pragmatism and romanticism.[8] Rorty sees bloodless pragmatism as a prerequisite for a democratic system unsullied by subjective interests, and thus relegates all political affairs to a rulebound "public" realm of rationalism. This is his prescription for communal existence. Turning to the sphere of the individual, Rorty constructs a nonpolitical realm of the "private" in which human actors can express selfishness, elitism, and creativity. Although the private is necessary for the development of innovative or transgressive ideas, it must be held in check and structured by the public. Otherwise, democracy will devolve into fascism.

The difficulties with this position are manifold. Many feminists have argued that it is impossible ever to separate the public from the private. Attempts to do so (for example, by relegating wage labor to the former and child rearing to the latter) typically create social relations that encourage the domination of certain groups.[9] Even more problematic is the difficulty of determining exactly "what works" in the pragmatic scheme. Indeed, the entire adaptive program of pragmatic ethics is thrown into dispute by the poststructuralist questioning of "according to whom?" and "in whose interests?"[10]

Needed is a way to integrate public and private realms without succumbing to a universalizing reason. A first step in this process is recognizing the importance of identity-based social movements and constituency groupings in the organization of politics. Again, the notion of radical democracy is useful in envisioning a series of continually evolving accords among such groups. Perhaps John Rawls comes closest to seeing the need for reciprocity among historical actors in arguing for a distributive ethic that tempers individual liberty with a firm commitment to equality.[11] In striving to reconcile these often mutually exclusive domains, Rawls expects social agents to pursue their own interests within limits set by the rights of others. Regrettably, as with Rorty, what is lacking in this formulation is any acknowledgment of the cultural identities and subject positions by which people develop affinities, form associations, and act in their collective interest. This dilemma is addressed in the profoundly cultural (in the anthropological sense) aspect of radical democracy that defines constituencies that then must establish among groups an ethics of behavior. This necessarily dynamic process of collective agency becomes the new democratic compact.

To put these theories into practice, activists must develop the mutually supportive character of their struggles. This presents a challenge to the cooperative tolerances and communicative capacities of the interests involved. Groups defined by gender, sexuality, ethnicity, nationality, or occupation need to recognize their imbrication in the social totality. To encourage a degree of coalescence, boundaries (and the hierarchies often implied) must be softened, especially distinctions that separate groups such as amateur/professional or mass/elite. Here it is necessary to work toward a worldview that is horizontal rather than vertical. The emotional dimensions of this struggle cannot be overstated. The concept of guaranteed equal rights carries enormous popular appeal, as revealed during 1988 in the advances of the Rainbow Coalition and more recently in battles over national health care reform. Both phenomena demonstrated the willingness of large numbers of people with different interests to come together around the issue of their common estrangement from power. Similarly, the world has witnessed remarkable progress in recent years in the reforms of Eastern Europe. The popular revolutions in Poland, Romania, and the former Czechoslovakia, East Germany, and Soviet Union, have demonstrated the ability of ordinary people to topple massive bureaucracies without resorting to violence.

It bears reiteration that in seeking to establish linkages among constituency groups, care must be taken to avoid merging one identity into another. This requires a form of ethics premised on a moral "respect" for the other in the face of totalizing impulses. Suspicious of how the concept of ethics can be deployed as a means of ideological control, Emmanuel Levinas discusses the cautions necessary in forging the relationship of ethics and egalitarian politics.[12] According to Levinas, the key is a form of respectful *dialogue* that allows the other to retain an external alterity. Again, this can be a tricky process, because parties rarely enter dialogues on an even footing. Without denying that such asymmetries exist, Levinas suggests a moral attitude toward the civic subjectivity. It is not an attribute of autonomous egos, but a substance fashioned in a relationship of mutual dependence.[13] More specifically, "Ethics redefines subjectivity as heteronomous responsibility in contrast to autonomous freedom."[14] When the Left begins to articulate this message, it will start regaining the popular backing it needs.

COMPETING NARRATIVES OF DEMOCRACY AND COMMUNITY

The construction of an ethos of interdependency will involve a redefinition of existing concepts of citizenship, duty, and community. As suggested by Stuart Hall and David Held,

> It seems to be the case that citizenship belongs exclusively to neither Right nor Left, not indeed to the middle-ground. Like all the key contested political concepts of our time, it can be appropriated within different political positions—as its recuperation by the New Right clearly shows. The concept can only mean something decisive for the Left if we are prepared to do some theoretical and political work around it, actively integrating it within a whole set of related political ideas.[15]

Certainly the centrist alliance has been busily at work attempting to claim such terms for its own, at the same time promoting a myth of mutual benefit through self-interest. A decade ago, Margaret Thatcher put it this way: "There is no such thing as society, only individual men and women and their families."[16] Through such atomized relationships personal desires are purportedly balanced with moral commitments to the common good, as wealth is equated with virtue in a "trickle-down" vision of civic responsibility. Sadly, Bill Clinton's exhortations about civic "sacrifice" suggest little in the way of genuine social reform. Instead, they ask the less fortunate to accept their plight until business reaps the full benefits of neoliberal economic policies. With a rhetoric of corporate self-righteousness, the current president echoes George Bush in equating the welfare state with liberal weakness. The collapse of economies in Eastern Europe similarly is characterized as a triumph for the American system, which promises all citizens the opportunity to rise above their neighbors.

Achieving the level of community activism required for change will mean activating mechanisms of collective agency that encourage people to act politically. This is what tells people that their actions have an impact in the face of governments and corporate bureaucracies. It is a deeply pedagogical task in that it requires an express disavowal of old habits and diminished expectations. To approach this task one must first examine in more detail the structures that hold such apathy and indifference to political involvement in place. The most damaging impediments to

PEDAGOGY AND ETHICS

radical democracy can be summarized in three words: objectification, rationalization, and commodification.[17]

Objectification is the process through which people come to be seen as passive and manipulable objects rather than as active and autonomous subjects. Objectification perpetuates a fatalism that tells people they can do little to alter the course of history or their own lives. This ideology of passive spectatorship is deployed in many forms, including the mass media. Movies, television, magazines, and newspapers suggest that the production of ideas and images is something that is always done by someone else. This message is perhaps most powerfully transmitted through traditional educational practices that stress a distant, immovable body of official knowledge that can be verified and delivered only by a certified teacher. It is the regressive embodiment of the Hegelian master/servant dialectic that is tragically repeated in even such "progressive" theoretical practices as Marxism and psychoanalysis.[18]

Rationalization, often associated with modernism, structuralism, and functionalism, is the imposition of bureaucratic regulation, surveillance, and measurement to human activity for the purpose of increasing efficiency. In a rationalizing society, people submit to larger structures in the presumed interest of social progress. What often gets lost in the process is any sense of accountability or any ability of the individual or group to challenge the common order. Beyond being told that they cannot make a difference, citizens are implicitly warned that they should not rock the boat, cause trouble, upset the system. Disagreement becomes a function of individual anomaly, maladjustment, perversion, inadequacy, lack of will, or genetic defect.

Commodification foregrounds valuation and exchange as elements of objectification and rationalization. It encourages acquisition and consumption as means of personal satisfaction, while on a structural level promoting hierarchies of production and distribution. On a broader scale, commodification frustrates community ethos by encouraging competitive acquisition. Debilitating fictions of "making it" and "the good life" are defined in terms of solitary consumption rather than civic concern. The first strategy of progressive cultural workers is to raise the question of how well off the average citizen is, posing this question to those who have suffered the consequences of economic violence. Given the glaring lack of equality in the United States, one cannot help asking why more people are not clamoring for radical change. Maybe the reason is the perception that the task is so overwhelming. Or perhaps it results from the lack of a meaningful program from the Left. At the very least, cultural workers can encourage the growing rage of all citizens silenced by the illusion of unproblematic patriotism. As Kobena Mercer has pointed out, for every idealized scene of flag-waving jubilation, there is an nonidealized scene of lived oppression, discrimination, and economic violence.[19] With each passing year the distance between the dream and the reality widens. The reckoning that is coming holds both possibilities and potential difficulties for pedagogical cultural workers.

One of the most important cautions to be observed involves the tendency to slip into moralizing dogma. For political activists this means beginning with a reconsideration of the very notions of address and reception embodied in the articulation of struggle. As suggested in chapter 8, it means a reexamination of the concept of audience. Exactly who is the presumed public for the radical cultural workers? Does a singularly defined constituency even exist? If not, how can any speaker address the interests of a multifaceted collectivity? These issues of authority and address must be resolved to effect a strategy for radical democracy.

The battle lines are clearly drawn on two fronts in the contest to reconfigure public life and political involvement. First, on a discursive level, cultural activists need to confront efforts to depoliticize and dehistoricize social forms. All too often conservatives have been permitted to label selected territories off-limits to political debate and thereby silence or discredit oppositional work. Therefore, the first gesture of cultural radicals is to bring to public light underexamined regions of oppression. Second, at the more crucial level of institutional practice, the job entails seizing means (or inventing new means) to encourage diverse identities, to promote the development of communities, and to foster forms of respectful solidarity—whatever it takes to win the argument, get the job, or organize the boycott to make material change happen.

History has demonstrated that power is rarely yielded willingly. As Paulo Freire so insightfully pointed out two decades ago, it is the responsibility of the oppressed to teach their oppressors a new way of organizing society.[20] This is not always a comfortable process. A radical democracy admits the necessity of struggle and of various communities making different entitlement claims. These are exactly the programs that the Right so vigilantly seeks to dismantle in the name of a purportedly "colorless" society, which is predicated on outmoded views of identity as monolithic and static. The conservative position fails to recognize the partial, overlapping, and indeterminate character of certain communities in relation to intersections of race, age, sexual orientation, class position, nationality, occupation, geography, and so on.

In contrast, a radical democracy acknowledges that just as an individual can belong to many different communities simultaneously and to various degrees, it is equally important to avoid generalizing about communities that have dramatic internal subdivisions. There are no single definitions of feminists, rappers, religious fundamentalists, business executives, or hospital patients—only singular *representations* of these groups. Through such representations difference is managed and contained, both by external forces and in the linguistic complicity of those who use hegemonic icons, symbols, and texts.[21]

In this way language commits a form of violence on its objects of depiction.[22] Representational convention is deployed to simplify definitions, thereby stripping the contours from multiple subjectivities. This is what produces stereotypes, as mainstream discourses both mediate and discredit diversity. For this reason the politics of representation constitutes a profound ground of struggle. Difference is rendered negative or irrational by institutions with the authority to determine such communicative forms as "official" versus "unofficial" speech, high and low culture, canonical and noncanonical books, political and nonpolitical issues.[23] Activists on the Left should oppose the vocabulary and syntax of this representational violence, because the Right is already hard at work attempting to ossify cultural meanings and narrow the field of democratic possibility.

ETHICS AND IDENTITIES

As asserted repeatedly in these pages, one of the most powerful affective tools in political organizing is the appeal to civic solidarity on a national level. But it seems that only recently have groups on the Left begun to recognize their stake in the battle over national subjective identity.[24] Certainly this fact has not been missed by conservatives. By deceptively cashing in on the alluring prospect of a national accord, the Right exerts an exclusionary effect on virtually every speaking subject. Instead of encouraging citizen participation and criticism, the concept of unproblematic solidarity and unity suppresses all opposition, in its casting of dissent as unpatriotic. By ignoring the repressive elements of social conformity, the Right has promoted the idea as a necessity for civic coherence. In this way, the xenophobic, conservative "cultural literacy" movement is perversely equated with democratic consensus.[25]

The parameters of the conservative case are framed well by Samuel Lipman: "What is necessary are definitions of culture and democracy based less on the muddling of definitions and more on their clarification, less on inclusions and more on exclusions, less on finding similarities between conflicting realities, concepts, and goals and more on recognizing the differences between them."[26] Within this argument the Right advances its program of eternal truths and all-American values as a populist crusade. Although the citizenry is nowhere near a moral consensus on such issues as reproductive choice, capital punishment, cohabitation, and gay rights, the illusion of agreement has tremendous appeal in the collective consciousness.

Much of the contemporary discourse of ethics supports this universalizing position by holding up the promise of foundational truths or rational structures of analysis. Consistent within utilitarianism, consequentialism, pragmatism, and perfectionism are efforts to establish generalized means to persuade "reasonable" people to act or think in particular ways.[27] In keeping with the formulation of a democratic constellation of competing/cooperating interests, it is important to rethink ethical arguments based on moral validity, ethical objectivity, or even human justice. Needed is an approach to ethics that acknowledges both the constructed character of meaning and the viability of cultural difference as positive elements in social organizations. Cornel West describes a "radical historicist" approach to ethics that seems to satisfy both criteria:

> First, the radical historicist sees the dynamic historical processes as subjecting all criteria, grounds, and foundations to revision and modification. . . . By rejecting these notions, the radical historicist is precluding the possibility of either timeless criteria, necessary grounds, or universal foundations for ethics. Second, for the radical historicist, the only plausible candidates for the criteria, grounds, or foundations in question would be contingent, community-specific agreements people make in relation to particular norms, aims, goals, and objectives.[28]

In this formulation the task of ethics is not so much to establish irrefutable platforms from which to establish rules and norms, as it is to develop larger commitments to communal exchange. At the same time, the multiplicity of this goal makes it difficult to formulate in conventional ethical terms.[29] Care should be taken to assure that the very concept of moral judgment, while appealing to transcendental virtue and reason, is recoded in each circumstance of ethical argument.[30] Moral judgment entails an appeal to justice, but not a commitment to any one justice. It is a compact of rights, but not a single definition of rights. A single viewpoint can never satisfy the needs of all people. Such solipsistic thinking is what blinds colonial powers to the tyrannies they project. At the same time, however, radical historicism should not be confused with moral relativism. Again, the distinction between the two has a poststructuralist character. Moral relativism, as a reaction against hard objectivism, allows itself to be defined in negative terms. Radical historicism refuses to get bound up in such binary arguments by acknowledging the situated usefulness of relativism and objectivism. These are issues for semiautonomous communities to work out in their own contexts.

In advocating a more adaptive pragmatism or a critical ethics that refuses to go by a single name, the Left runs the risk of losing whatever "movement" appeal it still has. Here again the model of the Rainbow Coalition has demonstrated the possibility of linking struggles without surrendering difference. Yes, people can get confused by what appears to be a fragmented and directionless message. But by stressing the moral elements of the plan, it is afforded a coherence. Chelda Sandoval has used the metaphor of an automobile transmission to describe a "differential" mode of activist strategizing.[31] Rather than permanently foregrounding one agenda, a differential strategy operates like the gears of a car, using what tactically makes sense in any given situation.

How will this program be implemented? Probably not through the forms of Enlightenment vanguardism typically associated with messianic leadership or rationalist definitions of "progress."[32] Instead, the first step in laying the groundwork for a radical democracy is to establish an environment in which a democracy is possible. In conceptual terms, this is another pedagogical issue of unlearning privilege, control, and singular definitions of worth.[33] It is no simple task. Suitably reconstructed, the new nonvanguardist cultural activists have their work cut out for them. They need to address the issue of community by celebrating difference rather than denying it. This constitutes the distinction between the radical democracy of the Left and the conformist democracy of the Right. To achieve this radical vision, a unified counterpractice is needed that reaches beyond the androcentric realm of binary power relationships. This will entail both theoretical and practical reformulations of the roles of cultural producers and consumers. Cultural workers can address the difficult task of developing coalitions in an era in which the Left has become particularly suspicious of normative ethics and universalizing agendas. They can introduce a program of moral thinking, without insisting on the idealist mandates of a "common culture."

Activist writers, artists, and teachers have a vital role to play in opening a public space where the lessons of participatory democracy can be relearned and its history reexamined. Eminently pedagogical in character, this project constructs human subjectivity along a continuum that connects the recipient of knowledge with its production. Within this context schooling is both a practical instrumentality and a metaphoric construction for locating individuals on that continuum. Education is the powerful mechanism of socialization that citizens all encounter for the better part of their early lives, as well as a process of growth that citizens carry with them ever after. Wherever it is encountered, schooling is a primary apparatus through which people understand how to be in the world. It is also how they learn to make the world, and to change it if they wish. In short, schooling is a model through which notions of public life, ethical responsibility, and citizenship are acquired.

Democracy is a process that depends on participation—the willingness to believe that the actions, voices, and votes of individuals can have an effect on the collective totality. In part this constitutes an exercise in political imagination; in part it is a consequence of an active citizenry convinced that its constituents are their own rulers. To a large extent, what makes democracy work is a faith in its fairness, a conviction that participation is unstymied by inequity and injustice. This is what gives the practice of democracy its moral character—not a reliance on a common culture that supplants all others, not a confidence in an unproblematic form of patriotism that unthinkingly follows symbols, not a reverence for a dehistoricized heritage.

Democracy achieves its ethical dimension in its invitation for participation from all quarters, and by necessity through its resistance to racism, homophobia, commodification, sexism, and all other forms of objectifying, colonizing, and dehumanizing behavior. In a democracy, citizens are bound by the responsibility to act on their beliefs, rather than waiting for others to do so for them.[34] Within this moral environment pedagogy has a dual function. It is both the means by which the oppressed come to know their oppression and the vehicle through which they struggle to find methods for change.

1. THE CRISIS OF MEANING IN CULTURE AND EDUCATION

1. Stuart Hall, "Cultural Identity and Diaspora," in Jonathan Rutherford, ed., *Identity, Community, Culture, Difference* (London: Lawrence and Wishart, 1990), 225.
2. Daniel Hellinger, "Empire Strikes Back," *In These Times* 17, no. 18 (July 28, 1993): 26–27.
3. Etienne Balibar, "Racism and Nationalism," in Etienne Balibar and Immanuel Wallerstein, eds., *Race, Nation, Class: Ambiguous Identities* (London and New York: Verso, 1991), 37–67.
4. Henry A. Giroux, "Living Dangerously: Identity and Cultural Politics; Toward a Critical Pedagogy of Representation," in *Living Dangerously: Multiculturalism and the Politics of Difference* (New York: Peter Lang, 1993), 59–88.
5. Patrick Buchanan, "In the War for America's Culture, Is the 'Right' Side Losing?" *Richmond News Leader*, June 24, 1989. See also Richard Bolton, *Culture Wars: Documents from the Recent Controversies in the Arts* (New York: New Press, 1992); James Davison Hunter, *Culture Wars: The Struggle to Define America* (New York: Basic Books, 1992); Ira Schor, *Culture Wars: School and Society in the Conservative Restoration, 1969–1985* (London and New York: Routledge, 1986); William J. Bennett, *The De-Valuing of America: The Fight for Our Culture and Our Children* (New York: Summit Books, 1992).
6. Antonio Gramsci, *Selections from the Prison Notebooks*, ed. and trans. Quintin Hoare and Geoffrey Nowell Smith (New York: International Publishers, 1972). Particularly in recent years, the all-encompassing aspects of Gramscian principles have been overstated in pedagogical theory. Clearly the institutional matrix in which schools reside exerts an influence upon the individual that is partial, at best. However, as one of the last great totalizers, Gramsci provides an important means of bridging gaps among disparate fields.
7. Stanley Aronowitz and Henry A. Giroux, *Education under Siege: The Conservative Liberal and Radical Debate over Schooling* (South Hadley, Mass.: Bergin and Garvey, 1985).
8. Russell Ferguson, "The Invisible Center," in Russell Ferguson, Martha Gever, Trinh T. Minh-ha, and Cornell West, eds., *Out There: Marginalization and Contemporary Cultures* (Cambridge, Mass.: MIT Press, 1991), 9.
9. Quoted in Phil Mariani and Jonathan Crary, "In the Shadow of the West: An Interview with Edward Said," in Russell Ferguson, William Olander, Marcia Tucker, and Karen Fiss, eds., *Discourses: Conversations in Postmodern Art and Culture* (Cambridge, Mass.: MIT Press, 1990), 94.
10. Michel Foucault, *Discipline and Punish: The Birth of the Prison*, trans. Alan Sheridan (New York: Vintage, 1979), 225.
11. Henry A. Giroux and Roger I. Simon, "Popular Culture as a Pedagogy of Pleasure and Meaning: Decolonizing the Body," in Henry A. Giroux, *Border Crossings: Cultural Workers and the Politics of Education* (London and New York: Routledge, 1992), 180–206.
12. Ernesto Laclau, *New Reflections on the Revolution of Our Time* (London and New York: Verso, 1990), 39
13. The dialectic of critique and possibility was first developed in Henry A. Giroux, *Teachers as Intellectuals* (New York: Bergin and Garvey, 1988).
14. Michel Foucault, "The Subject and Power," in Hubert Dreyfus and Paul Rabinow, eds., *Michel*

Foucault: Beyond Structuralism and Hermeneutics (Brighton: Harvester Press, 1982). For an earlier discussion of this principle, see Michel Foucault, *Discipline and Punish.*

15. Michel de Certeau, *The Practice of Everyday Life* (Berkeley: University of California Press, 1984). This work elaborates in depth on the productive character of culture.

16. Dennis Carlson, "Constructing the Margins of Multicultural Education and Curriculum Accords," unpublished paper delivered at the American Educational Research Association Conference, San Francisco, April 24, 1992.

17. James Davison Hunter, *Culture Wars*, 135–58.

18. These issues are taken up at length in Stanley Aronowitz, *Roll over Beethoven: The Return of Cultural Struggle* (Hanover, N.H., and London: Wesleyan University Press, 1993).

19. Jeffrey Escoffier, "The Limits of Multiculturalism," *Socialist Review* (Spring 1992): 61–73.

20. Chandra Talpade Mohanty, "On Race and Voice: Challenges for Liberal Education in the 1990s," *Cultural Critique* (Winter 1988/89): 179–208.

21. Samuel P. Huntington, *The Crisis of Democracy: A Report on the Governability of Democracies to the Trilateral Commission* (New York: New York University Press, 1975).

22. Allan Bloom, *The Closing of the American Mind* (New York: Simon and Schuster, 1987), 246–47

23. Ibid., 247.

24. U.S. Department of Education, *America 2000: An Education Strategy* (Washington, D.C.: U.S. Government Printing Office, 1991).

25. Samuel Lipman, "Redefining Culture and Democracy," *New Criterion* 8 (December 1989): 11.

26. People for the American Way, *The American Public's Perspective on Federal Support for the Arts and the Controversy over Funding for the National Endowment for the Arts* (Washington, D.C.: People for the American Way, 1990).

27. Perhaps the best-known example of this work is Ernesto Laclau and Chantal Mouffe, *Hegemony and Socialist Strategy: Towards a Radical Democratic Politics*, trans. Winston Moore and Paul Cammack (London: Verso, 1985). A variety of additional perspectives are assembled in Chantal Mouffe, ed., *Dimensions of Radical Democracy: Pluralism, Citizenship, and Community* (London: Verso, 1992).

28. Stanley Fish, *Is There a Text in This Class? The Authority of Interpretive Communities* (Cambridge, Mass.: Harvard University Press, 1980).

29. Sara M. Evans and Harry C. Boyte, *Free Spaces: The Sources of Democratic Change in America* (New York: Harper and Row, 1986). This book provides a thorough historical account of the free space concept across a range of political movements. It also contrasts the notion of a democratic free space with authoritarian spheres of restricted discourse.

30. The implications of the "free space" in the cultural community are discussed at length in David Trend, *Cultural Pedagogy: Art/Education/Politics* (New York: Bergin and Garvey, 1992), 105–59.

31. Timothy W. Luke, *Shows of Force: Power, Politics, and Ideology in Art Exhibitions* (Durham, N.C., and London: Duke University Press, 1992).

32. Steven Watts, "Academe's Leftists Are Something of a Fraud," *Chronicle of Higher Education*, April 29, 1992, A40.

33. William F. Pinar and C. A. Bowers, "Politics of Curriculum: Origins, Controversies, and Significance of Critical Perspectives," *Review of Research in Education* 18 (1992): 163–90.

34. Robert Young, *White Mythologies: Writing History and the West* (London and New York: Routledge, 1990), 11.

35. See Barbara Christian-Smith, "The Race for Theory," *Cultural Critique* 6 (1987): 51–63. These ideas are taken up in an educational context in Peter McLaren, "Multiculturalism and the Postmodern Critique: Towards a Pedagogy of Resistance and Transformation," *Cultural Studies* 7, no. 1 (January 1993): 89–107.

36. Louis Althusser, "Ideology and Ideological State Apparatuses (Notes Toward an Investigation)," in *Lenin and Philosophy and Other Essays*, trans. Benjamin Brewster (London: NLB, 1971), 121–73.

37. Herbert Marcuse, *An Essay on Liberation* (Boston: Beacon Press, 1969), 21.

38. Hans Magnus Enzenberger, "Constituents of a Theory of the Media," in *The Consciousness Industry*, trans. Stuart Hood (New York: Seabury Press, 1974).

39. Samuel Bowles and Herbert Gintis, *Schooling in Capitalist America: Educational Reform and the Contradictions of Economic Life* (New York: Basic Books, 1976).

40. Michael Apple, *Education and Power* (New York: Routledge and Kegan Paul, 1982).

41. Paul Willis, *Learning to Labour: How Working Class Kids Get Working Class Jobs* (Aldershot, U.K.: Gower, 1981).

42. Paulo Freire, *Pedagogy of the Oppressed* (New York: Seabury Press, 1970); Paulo Freire, *Cultural Action for Freedom* (New York: Penguin, 1972); Paulo Freire, *The Politics of Education* (South Hadley, Mass.: Bergin and Garvey, 1985). Freire's significance is discussed in Peter McLaren and Peter Leonard, eds., *Paulo Freire: A Critical Encounter* (New York and London: Routledge, 1993), and Henry A. Giroux and Donaldo Macedo, *Paulo Freire: History, Pedagogy, and Struggle* (Minneapolis: University of Minnesota Press, forthcoming).

43. Michael Apple, *Ideology and Curriculum* (New York: Routledge, 1979); Michael Apple, *Teachers and Texts* (New York: Routledge, 1987); Henry A. Giroux, *Ideology, Culture, and the Process of Schooling* (Philadelphia, Pa.: Temple University Press, 1981); Henry A. Giroux, *Theory and Resistance in Education* (South Hadley, Mass.: Bergin and Garvey, 1983); Henry A. Giroux, *Schooling and the Struggle for Public Life* (Minneapolis: University of Minnesota Press, 1988); Peter McLaren, *Life in Schools: An Introduction to Critical Pedagogy in the Social Foundations of Education* (New York: Longman, 1988); Peter McLaren, *Schooling as a Ritual Performance: Towards a Political Economy of Educational Symbols and Gestures* (London: Routledge, 1986); Ira Schor, *Culture Wars*.

44. See Patti Lather, *Getting Smart: Feminist Research and Pedagogy with/in the Postmodern* (New York and London: Routledge, 1991); Carmen Luke and Jennifer Gore, eds., *Feminisms and Critical Pedagogy* (New York and London: Routledge, 1993); Jennifer Gore, *The Struggle for Pedagogies: Critical and Feminist Discourses as Regimes of Truth* (New York: Routledge, 1993); Cameron McCarthy, *Race and Curriculum* (Philadelphia, Pa.: Falmer Press, 1990); Christine Sleeter, ed., *Empowerment through Multicultural Education* (Albany: SUNY Press, 1991).

45. Paul Willis, *Learning to Labor*, 50.

46. Henry A. Giroux and Roger I. Simon, "Popular Culture as a Pedagogy of Pleasure and Meaing," 202.

47. Mica Nava, "Consumerism Reconsidered: Buying and Power," *Cultural Studies* 5, no. 1 (January 1991): 157–73.

48. Susan Willis, *A Primer for Daily Life* (London and New York: Routledge, 1991).

49. Paul Willis, *Common Culture: Symbolic Work at Play in the Everyday Cultures of the Young* (Boulder and San Francisco: Westview Press, 1990).

50. Homi K. Bhabha, "DissemiNation: Time, Narrative, and the Margins of the Modern Nation," in Homi K. Bhabha, ed., *Nation and Narration* (London and New York: Routledge, 1990), 310.

51. Eve Kosofsky Sedgwick, "The Age of Wilde," in Andrew Parker, Mary Russo, Doris Sommer, and Patricia Yeager, eds., *Nationalisms and Sexualities* (New York and London: Routledge, 1992), 241.

52. Andrew Parker et al., introduction to *Nationalisms and Sexualities*, 6.

53. Fredric Jameson, "Postmodernism and Consumer Society," in Hal Foster, ed., *The Anti-Aesthetic: Essays on Postmodern Culture* (Port Townsend, Wash.: Bay Press, 1983), 111–25.

54. Gayatri Chakravorty Spivak, *The Post-Colonial Critic: Interviews, Strategies, Dialogues*, ed. Sarah Harasym (London and New York: Routledge, 1990), 9.

55. See Henry A. Giroux, *Teachers as Intellectuals*.

56. Jennifer Gore, *The Struggle for Pedagogies*, 120.

57. Thomas Popkewitz, "The Problem of Change and Educational Sciences: Notes on the Relations of Knowledge, Intellectuals, and Social Movements," in *A Political Economy of Sociology of Educational Reform: Power/Knowledge in Teaching, Teacher Education, and Research* (New York: Teachers College Press, 1991), 217–56.

58. Ibid., 235.

59. Quoted in Henry A. Giroux, *Border Crossings*, 173.

2. WHAT'S IN A NAME? NATIONAL IDENTITY AND MEDIA LITERACY

1. Homi K. Bhabha, "Introduction: Narrating the Nation," in Homi K. Bhabha, ed., *Nation and Narration* (London and New York: Routledge, 1990), 2.

2. Homi K. Bhabha, *Nation and Narration*, 1.

3. David Lusted, introduction to Lusted, ed., *The Media Studies Book* (London and New York: Routledge, 1991), 5.

4. Benedict Anderson, *Imagined Communities: Reflections on the Origin and Spread of Nationalism* (London: Verso, 1983).

5. Ibid., 22.

6. David Morley and Kevin Robins, "Spaces of Identity: Communications Technologies and the Refiguration of Europe," *Screen* 30, no. 4 (Autumn 1989): 12.

7. David Buckingham, "Teaching about the Media," in David Lusted, ed., *The Media Studies Book*, 12.

8. Quoted in Herbert I. Schiller, *Mass Communications and American Empire* (New York: Beacon Press, 1969), 1.

9. Quoted in Herbert I. Schiller, *Communication and Cultural Domination* (White Plains, N.Y.: International Arts and Sciences Press, 1970), 25–26.

10. Quoted in ibid., 44

11. Benedict Anderson, *Imagined Communities*, 14–15.

12. Quoted in Herbert Schiller, *Communication and Cultural Domination*, 40.

13. UNESCO, International Commission for the Study of Communication Problems, *Many Voices One World* (London: Kogan Page, 1980).

14. John Tomlinson, *Cultural Imperialism: A Critical Introduction* (Baltimore: Johns Hopkins University Press, 1991), 71.

15. Jody Bertrand, "Angels Dancing: Cultural Technologies and the Production of Space," in Lawrence Grossberg, Cary Nelson, and Paula Treichler, eds., *Cultural Studies* (London and New York: Routledge, 1992), 38–51.

16. Quoted in David Morley and Kevin Robins, "Spaces of Identity," 20.

17. Quoted in ibid., 22.

18. See Benedict Anderson, "Patriotism and Racism," in *Imagined Communities*, 129–41.

19. The racist underpinninings of nationalistic impulses is explored in depth in Etienne Balibar and Immanuel Wallerstein, *Race, Nation, Class: Ambiguous Identities* (London and New York: Verso, 1991). In separate essays, both authors link racism to the capitalist nation-state in antagonisms among people over monetary competition and national origin.

20. John Tomlinson, *Cultural Imperialism*, 68–99.

21. These points are elaborated in David Buckingham, "Teaching about the Media," 13–17.

22. See Paul Mattick, Jr., "Art and the State: The NEA Debate in Perspective," *Nation* 251, no. 10 (Oct. 1, 1990): 354.

23. Homi K. Bhabha, "DissemiNation: Time, Narrative, and the Margins of the Modern Nation," in *Nation and Narration*, 310.

24. This error of technological determinism is most eloquently made in the much celebrated essay by Walter Benjamin, "The Work of Art in the Age of Mechanical Reproduction," in *Illuminations*, trans. Harry Zohn (New York: Schocken Books, 1969), 198–231.

25. Ben J. Bagdikian, *The Media Monopoly*, 3rd ed. (Boston: Beacon Press, 1990).

26. These four points of national and international communication are summarized in Noel King and Thomas Rowse, "'Typical Aussies': Television and Populism in Australia," in Manual Alvarado and John. O Thompson, eds., *The Media Reader* (London: British Film Institute, 1990),

36–49. In elaborating this typology, the authors borrow the concept of "flow" introduced by Raymond Williams in *Television: Technology and Cultural Form* (New York: Schocken Books, 1975).

27. Ernesto Laclau, *New Reflections on the Revolution of Our Time* (London: Verso, 1991).

28. A lengthy discussion of films glorifying the expansion of American capitalism is found in Judith Williamson, "Up Where You Belong: Hollywood Images of Big Business in the 1980s," in John Corner and Sylvia Harvey, eds., *Enterprise and Heritage: Crosscurrents of National Culture* (London and New York: Routledge, 1991), 151–61.

29. Sharon D. Welch, *A Feminist Ethic of Risk* (Minneapolis, Minn.: Fortress Press, 1990), 33. Welch cites James Chace and Caleb Carr in her development of this typology of U.S. foreign policy.

30. Quoted in ibid., 34.

31. Robert M. Diamond, "Single Room Television," in Robert M. Diamond, ed., *A Guide to Instructional Media* (New York: McGraw-Hill, 1964), 3.

32. John M. Hofstrand, "Television and Classroom Observation," in Robert M. Diamond, ed., *A Guide to Instructional Media*, 149.

33. Marshall McLuhan, *Understanding Media: Extensions of Man* (New York: McGraw-Hill, 1964), 23.

34. John M. Culkin, "Films Deliver," in John M. Culkin and Anthony Schillaci, eds., *Films Deliver* (New York: Citation Press, 1970), 28.

35. The terms *visual literacy* and *media literacy* have been employed in a variety of differing contexts during the past two decades. The formalist media literacy of the 1970s should not be confused with the critical media literacy movement of the 1980s and 1990s.

36. Linda R. Burnett and Frederick Goldman, *Need Johnny Read? Practical Methods to Enrich Humanities Courses Using Films and Film Studies* (Dayton, Ohio: Pflaum, 1971), xv.

37. These issues are taken up in depth in Elizabeth Ellsworth and Mariamne H. Whatley, eds., *The Ideology of Images in Educational Media: Hidden Curriculums in the Classroom* (New York: Teachers College Press, 1990).

38. Benedict Anderson, *Imagined Communities*, 14–16.

39. This expression was coined by Juan Bautista Alberti in his *Bases* (1952) for the Argentine constitution.

40. Andrew Parker, Mary Russo, Doris Sommer, and Patricia Yeager, introduction to Andrew Parker et al., eds., *Nationalisms and Sexualities* (New York and London: Routledge, 1992), 5.

41. Lorraine Kenny, "The Birds and the Bees: Teen Pregnancy and the Media," *Afterimage* 16, no. 1 (Summer 1988): 6–8.

42. Ibid., 6.

43. Ibid.

44. Quoted in N. R. Kleinfield, "What Is Chris Whittle Teaching Our Children?" *New York Times Magazine*, May 19, 1991, 79.

45. See Nadine McGann, "Consuming Passions: Feminist Video and the Home Market," *Afterimage* 16, no. 1 (Summer 1988): 14–16.

46. Margaret Cooper, "Final Report and Documentation: Arts in Education Project," unpublished manuscript, Women Make Movies, 1987.

47. This banality of culture is taken up at length in the often quoted Raymond Williams essay, "Culture Is Ordinary," in *Resources of Hope* (London: Verso, 1989).

48. A representative sampling of recent texts on critical pedagogy: Michael Apple, *Teachers and Texts* (New York: Routledge, 1989); Stanley Aronowitz and Henry A. Giroux, *Postmodern Education: Politics, Culture, and Social Criticism* (Minneapolis: University of Minnesota Press, 1990); Henry A. Giroux, *Border Crossings: Cultural Workers and the Politics of Education* (New York: Routledge, 1992); Peter McLaren, *Life in Schools: An Introduction to Critical Pedagogy in the Foundations of Education* (New York and London: Longman, 1989); Peter McLaren, ed., *Postmodernism, Post-colonialism, and Pedagogy* (Albert Park, Australia: James Nicholas Publishers, 1992); Chandra Talpade Mohanty, "On Race and Voice," *Cultural Critique* 14 (Winter

1989): 179–208; Roger I. Simon, *Teaching against the Grain* (New York: Bergin and Garvey, 1992).

49. Quoted in Ben Moore, "Media Education," in David Lusted, ed., *The Media Studies Book*, 172.

50. Stanley Fish, *Is There a Text in This Class? The Authority of Interpretive Communities* (Cambridge, Mass.: Harvard University Press, 1980).

51. Donna Lloyd-Kolkin and Kathleen Tyner, *Media and You: An Elementary Media Literacy Curriculum* (San Francisco: Strategies for Media Literacy, 1991).

52. John Fiske, "Cultural Studies and the Culture of Everyday Life," in Lawrence Grossberg, Cary Nelson, and Paula Treichler, eds., *Cultural Studies*, 156.

53. National Endowment for the Arts, *Toward Civilization: A Report on Arts Education* (Washington, D.C.: NEA, 1988), 18.

54. Len Masterman, "British View: Achieving an Impossible Task," *Mediacy* 11, no. 3 (Fall 1989): 3.

55. Ben Moore, "Media Education," 173.

56. Ibid., 181.

3. Ordinary People: Material Culture and the Everyday

1. Raymond Williams, "Culture Is Ordinary" (1985), in Robin Gable, ed., *Resources of Hope: Culture, Democracy, Socialism* (London and New York: Verso, 1989), 5–6.

2. Thomas Popkewitz, *A Political Sociology of Educational Reform: Power/Knowledge in Teaching, Teacher Education, and Research* (New York: Teachers College Press, 1991), 222.

3. As James Clifford has noted, reducing a culture in writing resembles ritual sacrifice, in that it simultaneously creates the culture as a physical text and destroys its oral life. See James Clifford, "On Ethnographic Allegory," in James Clifford and George Marcus, eds., *Writing Culture: The Poetics and Politics of Ethnography* (Berkeley and Los Angeles: University of California Press, 1986), 98–121.

4. Cary Nelson, Paula A. Treichler, and Lawrence Grossberg, "Cultural Studies: An Introduction," in Grossberg, Nelson, and Treichler, eds., *Cultural Studies* (New York: Routledge, 1991), 14.

5. Thomas Crow, "Versions of the Pastoral in Some Recent American Art," in David Ross and Alan Shestack, eds., *American Art in the Late 80s: The Bi-national* (Boston: Institute for Contemporary Art, 1988), 25–26.

6. Judith Williamson, "Woman Is an Island: Femininity and Colonization," in Tania Modleski, ed., *Studies in Entertainment: Critical Approaches to Mass Culture* (Bloomington and Indianapolis: Indiana University Press, 1986), 99–118.

7. Stuart Hall, "Ethnicity: Identity and Difference," *Radical America* 23, no. 4 (June 1991): 16.

8. Roland Barthes, *Mythologies*, trans. Annette Lavers (New York: Hill and Wang, 1972), 62.

9. John Clarke, Stuart Hall, Tony Jefferson, and Brian Roberts, "Sub Cultures, Cultures, and Class" (1976), in Stuart Hall and Tony Jefferson, eds., *Resistance through Rituals: Youth Sub Cultures in Post-war Britain* (London: Unwin Hyman, 1976), 56–57

10. Dick Hebdige, *Subculture: The Meaning of Style* (New York: Methuen, 1979).

11. Pierre Bourdieu, *Outline of a Theory of Practice* (1972), trans. Richard Nice (Cambridge: Cambridge University Press, 1977), 3

12. Susan Strasser, *Satisfaction Guaranteed: The Making of the American Mass Market* (New York: Pantheon, 1989), 3–28. See also Arjun Appadurai, ed., *The Social Life of Things: Commodities in Cultural Perspective* (London and New York: Cambridge University Press, 1986).

13. Susan Willis, *A Primer for Daily Life* (New York and London: Routledge, 1991).

14. Georg Wilhelm Friedrich Hegel, *Phenomenology of the Spirit*, trans. A. V. Miller (Oxford: Clarendon Press, 1977).

15. Karl Marx, *Grundisse: Foundations of the Critique of Political Economy*, trans. Martin Nicolaus

(Harmondsworth: Penguin, 1973); Karl Marx, *Capital* 3 vols., ed. Friedrich Engels, trans. Samuel Moore and Edward Aveling (London: Lawrence and Wishart, 1974).

16. Jürgen Habermas, *Knowledge and Human Interests*, trans. Jeremy J. Shapiro (London: Heinemann, 1972).

17. Anthony Giddens, *Profiles and Critiques in Social Theory* (Berkeley: University of California Press, 1982), 86.

18. Writing in the 1970s, Pierre Bourdieu prescribed a "third mode" of anthropological analysis that could accommodate both phenomenological (Lévi-Strauss) and objectivist (Durkheim) traditions. He explained this as the integration of the knowledge of those researched with that of the researcher. In other words, ethnographers should reposition themselves as they went about understanding other cultures. One viewpoint was seen as incomplete without the other. This argument acknowledges the applicability of empirical rules and structures in the interpretation of culture, but also stresses the importance of subjective agency in revising conventions, violating rules, misrecognizing cues, or simply choosing "not to act." Like the hermeneutic method, it allows ethnographers to alter their questions to avoid reducing research objects to predetermined stereotypes. See Bourdieu, *Outline of a Theory of Practice*, 3. To Anthony Giddens, such an approach protects the researcher from drifting too far into abstraction, and thus affords the scholarship a social relevance. In his own theory of "structuration" Giddens similarly sought to incorporate the lessons of poststructuralism without relinquishing the accountability of human actors. In this model, structuration links "an adequate account of (meaningful) action with the analysis of its unanticipated conditions and unintended consequences. Neither agent nor society are given primacy." See Giddens, *Profiles*, 18.

19. Mark Poster, "Translator's Introduction," in Jean Baudrillard, *The Mirror of Production* (St. Louis: Telos Press, 1975), 5.

20. Jean Baudrillard, *The Mirror of Production*, 132.

21. See Paulo Freire, *Pedagogy of the Oppressed* (1970), trans. Myra Bergman Ramos (New York: Continuum, 1984), 9–25.

22. Renato Rosaldo, *Culture and Truth: The Remaking of Social Analysis* (Boston: Beacon Press, 1989), 21.

23. Kobena Mercer, "Welcome to the Jungle: Identity and Diversity in Postmodern Politics," in Jonathan Rutherford, ed., *Identity: Community, Culture, Difference* (London: Lawrence and Wishart, 1990), 43–71.

24. Meaghan Morris, "The Banality of Cultural Studies," *Block* (1988): 2–28.

25. Michel de Certeau, *The Practice of Everyday Life* (Berkeley: University of California Press, 1984).

26. John Michael Vlach, "The Need for Plain Talk about Folk Art," in John Michael Vlach and Simon J. Bronner eds., *Folk Art and Art Worlds* (Ann Arbor: University of Michigan Press, 1986).

27. John Frow, "Tourism and the Semiotics of Nostalgia," *October* 57 (Summer 1991): 135.

28. Ibid., 136.

29. Theodor Adorno, *The Jargon of Authenticity*, trans. Knut Tarnowski and Frederic Will (Evanston, Ill.: Northwestern University Press, 1973). See also Susan Hiller, ed., *The Myth of Primitivism: Perspectives on Art* (New York: Routledge, 1991).

30. Basil Bernstein, *The Structure of Pedagogic Discourse* (London and New York: Routledge, 1990), 20. Originally published as "Codes, Modalities and the Process of Cultural Reproduction: A Model," *Language and Society* 10 (1981): 327–63.

31. Ibid., 44.

32. Eugene W. Metcalf, "The Politics of the Past in Folk Art History," in John Michael Vlach and Simon J. Bronner, eds., *Folk Art*, 47.

33. John Frow, "Tourism and the Semiotics of Nostalgia," 141–42.

34. Pierre Bourdieu, *Distinction: A Social Critique of the Judgement of Taste*, trans. Richard Nice (Cambridge, Mass.: Harvard University Press, 1984).

35. Quoted in Eugene W. Metcalf, "The Politics of the Past," 30.

36. A recent and extremely lavish example of this phenomenon was the *Parallel Visions* exhibition and catalogue by the Los Angeles County Museum of Art. See Maurice Tuchman, ed., *Parallel Visions: Modern Artists and Outsider Art* (Princeton, N.J.: Princeton University Press, 1992).

37. Ormond Loomis, "Folk Artisans under Glass: Practical and Ethical Considerations for the Museum," in Simon J. Bronner, ed., *American Material Culture and Folklife: A Prologue and Dialogue* (Ann Arbor: University of Michigan Press, 1985), 193–95.

38. Paul Goldberger, "25 Years of Unabashed Elitism," *New York Times,* February 6, 1992, H34.

39. Ibid.

40. Pierre Bourdieu, *Distinction.*

41. Georg Simmel, *The Philosophy of Money,* trans. Tom Bottomore, David Frisby, and Kaethe Mengelberg (London and New York: Routledge, 1990). My account of Simmel's theories is indebted to that of Daniel Miller, *Material Culture and Mass Consumption* (London: Basil Blackwell, 1987). Miller's book also provides an overview of major theories of material culture, and constitutes the most thorough volume on the subject written to date.

42. Renato Rosaldo, *Culture and Truth,* 46–67.

43. See Paul Willis, *Common Culture: Symbolic Work at Play in the Everyday Cultures of the Young* (Boulder and San Francisco: Westview Press, 1990).

44. Quoted in Thalia Gouma-Peterson and Patricia Mathews, "The Feminist Critique of Art History," *Art Bulletin* (September 1987): 333.

45. See Kathryn McGinty, *Miriam Shapiro and the Language of Quilts* (Ann Arbor: University of Michigan Press, 1991).

46. Erica Wilson, *Quilts of America* (Birmingham: Oxmoor House, 1979), 2.

47. Patricia Mainardi, "Quilts: The Great American Art," in Norma Broude and Mary Garrard, eds., *Feminism and Art History* (New York: Harper and Row, 1982), 331–46.

48. Patricia Mainardi, quoted in Kathryn McGinty, *Miriam Shapiro and the Language of Quilts,* 32.

49. Miriam Shapiro and Faith Wilding, "Cunts/Quilts/Consciousness," *Heresies* 6, no. 4 (1989): 13.

50. Thalia Gouma-Peterson, "Faith Ringgold's Narrative Quilts," *Arts* 61 (January 1987): 64–69.

51. Ibid., 65.

52. Ibid., 69

53. Moira Roth, "Suzanne Lacy: Social Reformer and Witch," in Arlene Raven, ed., *Art in the Public Interest* (Ann Arbor: University of Michigan Press, 1989), 161.

54. Douglas Sadownick, "AIDS Quilt Begins National Tour," *High Performance* 11, no. 2 (Spring/Summer 1988): 21.

55. Marita Sturken, "Conversations with the Dead: Bearing Witness in the AIDS Memorial Quilt," *Socialist Review* 92/2 (April-June 1992): 65–97.

56. Quoted in Marita Sturken, "The Wall, the Screen, and the Image: The Vietnam Veterans Memorial," *Representations* 35 (Summer 1991): 123.

57. Ibid., 126.

58. Marianne Sawicki, "Feminist Pedagogy: A Report on Ed 32, Spring Semester 1990," unpublished manuscript.

4. A Change of Address: Homelessness and the Politics of Voice

1. bell hooks, *Sisters of the Yam: Black Women and Self-Recovery* (Boston: South End Press, 1993), 29.

2. Plan International foster parents program, advertisement, *Mother Jones* (April/May 1990).

3. California Aid to Families with Dependent Children (AFDC) tables for 1989.

4. Michael Katz, *The Undeserving Poor: From the War on Poverty to the War on Welfare* (New York: Pantheon, 1989), 130.

5. Philip Farnsworth and Vernon Baker, *Under the Bridge* (New York: Farnsworth and Baker, 1988); Howard Schatz, *Homeless: Portraits of Americans in Hard Times* (San Francisco: Chron-

icle Books, 1993); *Homeless in America*, Families for the Homeless and the National Mental Health Association (Washington, D.C.: Acropolis Books, 1989); *Shooting Back: Photography by and about the Homeless*, Washington Project for the Arts, September 14–November 3, 1990.

6. David Snow and Leon Anderson, *Down on Their Luck: A Study of Homeless Street People* (Berkeley and Los Angeles: University of California Press, 1993), 6.

7. Fred Block, Richard A. Cloward, Barbara Ehrenreich, and Francis Fox Piven, *The Mean Season: The Attack on the Welfare State* (New York: Pantheon, 1987), 72.

8. Elizabeth Swados, "The Story of a Street Person: Remembering My Brother," *New York Times Magazine*, August 18, 1991, 16.

9. Ibid., 41.

10. Michael Harrington, *The Other America* (New York: Macmillan, 1962).

11. For a detailed analysis of this phenomenon, see William Ryan, "The Art of Savage Discovery," in Ira Colby, ed., *Social Welfare Policy* (Chicago: Dorsey Press, 1989), 16–33.

12. Edward Banfield, *The Unheavenly City* (Boston: Little Brown, 1970).

13. George Gilder, *Wealth and Poverty* (New York: Basic Books, 1981).

14. Lawrence Mead, *Beyond Entitlement: The Social Obligations of Citizenship* (New York: Free Press, 1986).

15. Michael Katz, *The Undeserving Poor*, 189.

16. As Sally Stein has pointed out, the significance afforded earlier photographers such as Jacob Riis was largely the retroactive enterprise of an emerging academic field in search of a legitimizing history. See Sally Stein, "Making Connections with the Camera: Photography and Social Mobility in the Career of Jacob Riis," *Afterimage* 10, no. 10 (May 1983): 9–15.

17. Paul Boyer, "Building Character among the Urban Poor," in Ira Colby, ed., *Social Welfare Policy*, 113–34.

18. Herbert Spencer, *The Principles of Ethics*, vol. 1 (New York: Appleton, 1904), 93.

19. Erskine Caldwell and Margaret Bourke-White, *You Have Seen Their Faces* (New York: Viking Press, 1937), 75.

20. Frank Washington, "A Night of Hell at Ground Zero," *Newsweek*, May 11, 1992, 35.

21. Lance Morrow, "Video Warriors in Los Angeles," *Time*, May 11, 1992, 68.

22. Tom Mathews, "The Siege of L.A.," *Newsweek*, May 11, 1992, 30.

23. Quoted in Martha Rosler, "in, around, and afterthoughts (on documentary photography)," *Martha Rosler: 3 Works* (Halifax: Nova Scotia College of Art and Design, 1981), 78. This essay by Rosler remains one of the most thoroughgoing critiques of documentary photographic practice written to date.

24. George Russell, "The American Underclass," *Time*, August 29, 1977, 14–16.

25. Ibid., 14–16.

26. For an extended discussion of the relationship of cultural politics and urban housing, see Rosalyn Deutsche, "Alternative Space," in Brian Wallis, ed., *If You Lived Here: The City in Art, Theory, and Social Activism* (Seattle: Bay Press, 1991), 45–46.

27. Plan International foster parents program advertisement, *Mother Jones* (October 1989).

28. Jim Hubbard, *American Refugees* (Minneapolis: University of Minnesota Press, 1991).

29. Jonathan Kozol, foreword in ibid., xi .

30. Jim Hubbard, preface, *American Refugees*, xiv.

31. Ibid., 109

32. Martha Rosler, "in, around, and afterthoughts," 73.

33. Stephen Shames, *Outside the Dream: Child Poverty in America* (New York: Aperture and the Children's Defense Fund, 1991).

34. Marian Wright Edelman, afterword in Stephen Shames, *Outside the Dream: Child Poverty in America,* 85.

35. Jonathan Kozol, *Death at an Early Age: The Destruction of the Hearts and Minds of Negro Children in the Boston Public Schools* (Boston: Houghton Mifflin, 1967).

36. Jonathan Kozol, *Savage Inequalities: Children in America's Schools* (New York: Crown, 1991).

37. Gordon W. E. Nore, "The Progressive Interview: Jonathan Kozol," *Progressive*, December 1991, 36.

38. See Thomas S. Popkewitz, *A Political Sociology of Educational Reform: Power/Knowledge in Teaching, Teacher Education, and Research* (New York: Teachers College Press, 1991), 217–44.

39. Antonio Gramsci, *Selections from the Prison Notebooks*, ed. and trans. Quintin Hoare and Geoffrey Nowell Smith (New York: International Publishers, 1972).

40. These issues are taken up in depth in Patti Lather, "Postmodernism and the Discourses of Emancipation: Precedents, Parallels and Interruptions," in Patti Lather, *Getting Smart: Feminist Research and Pedagogy with/in the Postmodern* (New York and London: Routledge, 1991), 19–50.

41. Renato Rosaldo, "Subjectivity in Social Analysis," in *Culture and Truth: The Remaking of Social Analysis* (Boston: Beacon Press, 1989), 168–95.

42. The concept of participant observation was developed by Bronislaw Malinowski in *Argonauts of the Western Pacific* (New York: Dutton, 1961).

43. Renato Rosaldo, "Subjectivity," 181.

44. Ibid., 183.

45. See Alexander Kluge, "The Public Sphere," in Brian Wallis, *If You Lived Here*, 67–70.

46. Wall label for *Out of the Studio: Art with Community*, P.S. I, Institute for Art and Urban Resources, Long Island City, N.Y., January 25-March 22, 1987.

47. *Shooting Back: Photography by and about the Homeless*, Washington Project for the Arts, September 14-November 3, 1990. Along with work by professional photographers, the exhibition included over a hundred photographs taken by participants in workshops conducted by the Shooting Back Education and Media Center, founded by Hubbard in 1988. See *Afterimage* (November 1990): 19.

48. Michelle Fine, "Silencing in Public Schools," *Language Arts* 64, no. 2 (February 1987): 157–73. These issues are also taken up at length in Christine Sleeter, ed., *Empowerment through Multicultural Education* (Albany: SUNY Press, 1991).

49. bell hooks, *Yearning: Race, Gender, and Cultural Politics* (Boston: South End Press, 1990), 28.

50. Chandra Talpade Mohanty, "On Race and Voice: Challenges for Liberal Education in the 1990s," *Cultural Critique* (Winter 1989–90): 179–209.

51. Ibid., 184.

52. bell hooks, *Yearning*, 29

53. Micheal A. Susko, ed., *Cry of the Invisible: Writings from the Homeless and Survivors of Psychiatric Hospitals* (Boston and Montreal: Conservatory Press, 1991).

54. Ibid., xiii.

55. Bruce Whitcomb, "Bruce Whitcomb's Story," in ibid., 37.

56. Detailed analyses of Lonidier's works are found in Allan Sekula, "Dismantling Modernism, Reinventing Documentary (Notes on the Politics of Representation)," in Allan Sekula, *Photography against the Grain: Essays and Photo Works, 1973–1983* (Halifax: Nova Scotia College of Art and Design, 1984), 53–75; and Grant H. Kester, "Toward a New Social Documentary," *Afterimage* (March 1987): 9–12.

57. Fred Lonidier, "Working with Unions," in Douglas Kahn and Diane Neumaier, eds., *Cultures in Contention* (Seattle: Real Comet Press, 1985), 102–15.

58. Yvonne Rainer, "Preface: The Work of Art in the (Imagined) Age of the Unalienated Exhibition," in Brian Wallis, ed., *If You Lived Here*, 12.

59. Artists' Television Access, press release for the "Ungentrification Project" (of which *Who's the Landlord?* was one part), September 1989.

60. Spain Rodriguez, "The Crack House Is the White House/Public Housing: Who's in Control?" Special supplement to *North Mission News*, August 1, 1990.

1. June Jordan, quoted in Pratiba Parmar, "Black Feminism: The Politics of Articulation," in Jonathan Rutherford, ed., *Identity, Community, Culture, Difference* (London: Lawrence and Wishart, 1990), 110.
2. John Callahan, *Digesting the Child Within, and Other Cartoons to Live By* (New York: William Morrow, 1991), 9.
3. Ibid., 17.
4. Ibid., 47.
5. Micki McGee, "The Overextended Family," in Connie Butler and Micki McGee, eds., *Reframing the Family* (New York: Artists' Space, 1991), 21.
6. Andrew Ross, *Strange Weather: Culture, Science, and Technology in the Age of Limits* (New York: Routledge, 1991), 15–74.
7. James Davison Hunter, *Culture Wars: The Struggle to Define America* (New York: Basic Books, 1991), 176–96. Within his larger discussion of the "war of positions" in U.S. culture, this chapter of Hunter's book specifically outlines the evolution of current controversies surrounding the family.
8. Lawrence Grossberg, *We Gotta Get Outta This Place: Politics and Popular Culture in Contemporary America* (New York: Routledge, 1992).
9. As reproduced in Marcy Darnovsky, "The New Traditionalism: Repackaging Ms. Consumer," *Social Text* no. 29 (1991): 72–91. Although somewhat determinist in its view of ideological transmission, Darnovsky's article provides an informative reading of the New Traditionalist promotional campaign.
10. Mary Ellen Mark, *Streetwise* (Philadelphia: University of Pennsylvania Press, 1988); Mary Ellen Mark, *Faukland Road* (New York: Knopf, 1981); Mary Ellen Mark, *Ward 81* (New York: Simon and Schuster, 1979).
11. Marcy Darnovsky, "The New Traditionalism," 76.
12. Julia Hirsch, *Family Photographs: Content, Meaning, and Effect* (New York and Oxford: Oxford University Press, 1981).
13. Andrew Parker, Mary Russo, Doris Sommer, and Patricia Yeager, introduction to Andrew Parker et al., eds., *Nationalisms and Sexualities* (New York and London: Routledge, 1992), 6.
14. Nancy Gibbs, "The War against Feminism," *Time*, March 9, 1992, 50.
15. Susan Faludi, *Backlash: The Undeclared War against American Women* (New York: Crown, 1991).
16. Nancy Gibbs, "The War against Feminism," 51.
17. One of the most influential (and outrageous) commentators on the family is former Reagan administration policy adviser George Gilder, to whom the family represents the bedrock of both moral value and economic motivation. Gilder asserted in his well-known 1981 essay "The Nature of Poverty" that the true cause of economic misfortune is unbridled male (hetero)sexuality, not racism or discrimination. See George Gilder, "The Nature of Poverty," in Ira Colby, ed., *Social Welfare Policy: Perspectives, Patterns, Insights* (Chicago: Dorsey Press, 1989), 47–58. According to Gilder, critiques of racism are "at once false and invidious. Not only does it slander white Americans, it deceives and demoralizes blacks" (49). Instead the problem stems from a lack of discipline resulting from an inability to defer sexual pleasure. This results in laziness and irresponsibility. Marriage harnesses men to economic responsibility, contains their sexual drives, and forces them to consider the interests of their offspring. Citing Edwin Banfield's widely read analysis of urban poverty, *The Unheavenly City*, Gilder concludes that "man disciplines his sexuality and extends it into the future through the womb of a woman" (53).
18. Lawrence M. Mead, *The New Politics of Poverty: The Nonworking Poor in America* (New York: Basic Books, 1992).
19. See "Spheres of Influence," a special issue of *Afterimage* (Summer 1988) devoted to the family, with essays by Cynthia Chris, Coco Fusco, Laura Hoptman, Lorraine Kenny, Joanne Lukitsh, Laura Marks, Nadine McGann, Patricia Zimmerman, and Fenton Johnson, among others.

20. Jonathan Green, introduction to Jonathan Green, ed., *The Snapshot* (New York: Aperture, 1974), 3.

21. Robert Young, *White Mythologies: Writing History and the West* (London and New York: Routledge, 1990), 15.

22. "The Pleasures and Terrors of Domestic Comfort," Museum of Modern Art, New York, September 26-December 31, 1991.

23. Peter Galassi, introduction to Peter Galassi, ed., *Pleasures and Terrors of Domestic Comfort* (New York: Museum of Modern Art and Harry N. Abrams, 1991), 6–24.

24. Ibid., 15.

25. The sixty-three photographers exhibited in *Pleasures and Terrors* included Tina Barry, Ellen Brooks, James Casebere, William Eggleston, Larry Fink, Mary Frey, Lee Friedlander, Nan Goldin, Frank Majore, Sally Mann, Nic Nicosia, Nicholas Nixon, Lorie Novak, Cindy Sherman, Laurie Simmons, Sage Sohier, Joel Sternfeld, Larry Sultan, JoAnn Verberg, Carrie Mae Weems, and Neil Winokur.

26. Peter Galassi, *Pleasures and Terrors*, 12.

27. Ibid.

28. David Cohen, ed., *The Circle of Life: Rituals from the Human Family* (New York: HarperCollins, 1991). The traveling exhibition version of the project was first shown November 1-30, 1991, at the California Academy of Arts and Sciences, San Francisco.

29. Ibid., 12. *The Family of Man* was an exhibition organized by Edward Steichen at New York's Museum of Modern Art in 1955. Comprising photographs of people from around the world, the exhibit was initially praised and later criticized for its highly dramatized message of shared human values.

30. *Circle of Life* participants included Sam Abell, Shelby Lee Adams, Carol Beckwith, Douglas Kirkland, Peter Korniss, Mary Ellen Mark, Rudi Meisel, Susan Meiselas, Claus Meyer, and Stephen Trimble.

31. Roland Barthes, *Mythologies*, trans. Annette Lavers (New York: Hill and Wang, 1972), 101.

32. David Cohen, *Circle of Life*, 6.

33. See Allan Sekula, "The Traffic in Photographs," in Allan Sekula, *Photography against the Grain: Essays and Photo Works, 1973–1983* (Halifax: Nova Scotia College of Art and Design, 1984), 77–101. Sekula's essay remains the most thorough critique of "The Family of Man" written to date. See also Christopher Phillips, "The Judgement Seat of Photography," *October* 22 (1982): 27–63.

34. Michel Foucault, *The History of Sexuality, Vol. I: An Introduction*, trans. Robert Hurley (New York: Vintage Books, 1980), 123.

35. The implications of Foucault's theories regarding women and children are elaborated on at length in "The Violence of Rhetoric: Considerations on Representation and Gender," in Teresa de Lauretis, *Technologies of Gender: Essays on Theory, Film and Fiction* (Bloomington and Indianapolis: Indiana University Press, 1987), 31–51.

36. Michel de Certeau, *The Practice of Everyday Life* (Berkeley: University of California Press, 1984).

37. Nancy Fraser has noted that the very concept of separate "private" and "public" spheres naturalizes and depoliticizes certain kinds of gendered work within the domestic realm. See Nancy Fraser, *Unruly Practices: Power, Discourse, and Gender in Contemporary Social Theory* (Minneapolis: University of Minnesota Press, 1989).

38. Patricia Holland, "Introduction: History, Memory, and the Family Album," in Jo Spence and Patricia Holland, eds., *Family Snaps: The Meanings of Domestic Photography* (London: Virago, 1991), 1.

39. Julia Hirsch, *Family Photographs*, 44.

40. Don Slater, in *Family Snaps*, 50.

41. Simon Watney, in *Family Snaps*, 28

42. Jo Spence, in *Family Snaps*, 203.

43. Sigmund Freud, "The Sexual Life of Human Beings," in *Introductory Lectures on Psychoanalysis* (Harmondsworth: Penguin, 1972), 353.

44. Simon Watney, "School's Out," in Diana Fuss, ed., *Inside/Outside: Lesbian Theories, Gay Theories* (New York and London: Routledge, 1991), 387–404.

45. This would include the ways students actively produce knowledge from what is offered to them in school.

46. See Christine Sleeter, ed., *Empowerment through Multicultural Education* (Albany: SUNY Press, 1991).

47. A detailed account and analysis of these circumstances appears in Brian Goldfarb, "Video Activism and Critical Pedagogy: Sexuality at the End of the Rainbow Curriculum," *Afterimage* 20, no. 10 (May 1993): 4–8.

48. Mariamne H. Whatley, "Raging Hormones and Powerful Cars: The Construction of Men's Sexuality in School Sex Education and Popular Adolescent Films," *Journal of Education* 170, no. 3 (1988): 100–121. See also J. Sears, ed., *Sexuality and Curriculum* (New York: Teachers College Press, 1992).

49. Michael W. Apple, *Teachers and Texts: A Political Economy of Class and Gender Relations in Education* (New York: Routledge, 1989), 92.

50. Ibid., 95.

51. Ibid., 98

52. The most famous discussion of this phenomenon is found in Judith Williamson, "How Does Girl Number 20 Understand Ideology?" *Screen Education* 40 (Autumn-Winter 1981–82), reprinted in *exposure* 28, nos. 1/2 (1991): 51–56. A slightly more optimistic outlook is found in the more recent work by Lois Weis, who asserts that the increased presence of women in the workforce has changed students' attitudes toward marriage and child rearing. See Lois Weis, *Working Class without Work: High School Students in a De-industrialized Economy* (New York and London: Routledge, 1990).

53. Lois Weis, "Disempowering White Working Class Females," in Christine Sleeter, ed., *Empowerment*, 95–124.

54. The Group Material *Democracy* project originated at the DIA Art Foundation in New York City. Its three components "Democracy: Education," "Democracy and Electoral Politics," and "Democracy: AIDS," each entailed a central installation composed of works by dozens of artists and community groups, as well as town meetings. The Kiss and Tell Collective from Vancouver, British Columbia, organized the traveling exhibition, *Drawing the Line*, which presented a sequence of images of lesbian lovemaking arranged in increasing increments of intensity and detail. Women viewers were encouraged to "draw the line" by indicating in pencil on the wall where they thought the sequence should end—and by adding whatever commentary they thought appropriate. Santa Barbara, California, artist Richard Bolton's traveling installation, *The Emperor's New Clothes*, presented erotic imagery from artworks, advertising, and the pornography industry, along with commentary written by prominent participants in the censorship debate. On comment sheets on the walls and in public forums, Bolton asked viewers to add their own viewpoints to the discussion. These projects are discussed at length in David Trend, *Cultural Pedagogy: Art/Education/Politics* (New York: Bergin and Garvey, 1992).

55. "Family Stories," Snug Harbor Cultural Center, Staten Island, N.Y., April 28-September 2, 1990. See Eleanor Heartney, *Afterimage* 18, no. 4 (October 1990): 1–20.

56. Celia Alvarez Muñoz, "Stories your mother never told you," in Olivia Georgia, ed., *Family Stories* (Staten Island: Snug Harbor Cultural Center, 1990), 24.

57. Clarissa Sligh, *Reading Dick and Jane with Me* (Rochester, N.Y.: Visual Studies Workshop Press, 1989). In this work Sligh inserts African-American children into the familiar story of two white children. See Laura U. Marks, "Reinscribing the Self: An Interview with Clarissa Sligh," *Afterimage* 17, no. 5 (December 1989): 6–9. The *Birth of a Candy Bar* tapes were produced in 1989–1990 by students working in an after-school pregnancy prevention program with video artist Branda Miller. See David Trend, "To Tell the Truth: Strategies for Media Literacy," *Afterimage* 18, no. 8 (March 1991): 12–14.

58. See Henry A. Giroux, *Schooling and the Struggle for Public Life* (Minneapolis: University of Minnesota Press, 1989).

59. Constance Clayton, "We Can Educate All Our Children," *Nation*, July 24–31, 1989, 132.

60. Paula A. Treichler, "Teaching Feminist Theory," in Cary Nelson, ed., *Theory in the Classroom* (Urbana and Chicago: Illinois University Press, 1986), 57–128.

6. READ MY LIPS: BUREAUCRATIC RHETORIC AND TEXTUAL AUTHORITY

1. Victor Burgin, *The End of Art Theory: Criticism and Postmodernity* (Atlantic Highlands, N.J.: Humanities Press, 1986), 190.

2. For an excellent summary of these issues, see Brian Wallis, "Democracy and Cultural Activism," in Brian Wallis, ed., *Democracy: A Project by Group Material* (New York: Dia Art Foundation, 1990), 5–12.

3. Ibid., 5.

4. See Cleo H. Cherryholmes, *Power and Criticism: Poststructural Investigations in Education* (New York: Teachers College Press, 1988).

5. Max Weber, "The Leveling of Social Differences," in H. Gerth and C. Wright Mills, eds., *Max Weber: Essays in Sociology* (New York: Oxford University Press, 1981), 224.

6. Ibid., 235.

7. David Tyack, "'Restructuring' in Historical Perspective: Tinkering Toward Utopia," *Teachers College Record* 92, no. 2 (Winter 1990): 174.

8. See Robert Young, *White Mythologies: Writing History and the West* (London and New York: Routledge, 1990), 126.

9. For an extensive elaboration of these issues, see Nancy Fraser, "Struggle over Needs: Outline of a Socialist-Feminist Critical Theory of Late Capitalist Political Culture," in Nancy Fraser, *Unruly Practices: Power, Discourse and Gender in Contemporary Social Theory* (Minneapolis: University of Minnesota Press, 1989), 161–87.

10. This process is discussed at length in Hubert L. Dreyfus and Paul Rabinow, *Michel Foucault: Beyond Structuralism and Hermeneutics* (Chicago: University of Chicago Press, 1982), 196.

11. National Commission for Excellence in Education, *A Nation at Risk: The Imperative for Educational Reform* (Washington, D.C.: U.S. Publications Office, 1983).

12. See Michael Apple, *Teachers and Texts: A Political Economy of Class and Gender Relations in Education* (New York: Routledge, 1988), 139.

13. Philip Corrigan, *Social Forms and Human Capacities: Essays in Authority and Difference* (London and New York: Routledge, 1989), 201.

14. See Dennis K. Mumby, *Communication and Power in Organizations: Discourse, Ideology, and Domination* (New York: Ablex, 1988).

15. Nancy Fraser, *Unruly Practices*, 154.

16. U.S. Department of Education, *America 2000: An Education Strategy* (Washington, D.C.: U.S. Government Printing Office, 1991); The Independent Commission on the National Endowment for the Arts, "Report to Congress on the National Endowment for the Arts," *Journal of Arts Management and Law* 20, no. 3 (Fall 1990): 7–70.

17. National Commission for Excellence in Education, *A Nation at Risk*, 5.

18. George Bush, "Remarks by the President at the Presentation of the National Education Strategy," in *America 2000*, 4.

19. See Wayne J. Urban, "Is There a New Teacher Unionism?" *Educational Theory* 41, no. 3 (Summer 1991): 331–38.

20. Dennis K. Mumby, *Communication and Power*, 17.

21. These campaigns are described at length in Richard Bolton, "The Cultural Contradictions of Conservativism," *New Art Examiner* 17, no. 10 (June 1990): 24–29. In the article Bolton details some AFA activities: "Wildmon's first success came in 1981, when he convinced Proctor and

Gamble, the largest advertiser on television, to withdraw advertising support for 50 shows. He went on to convince the FCC to regulate Dial-A-Porn, and he organized a boycott of Holiday Inns because the motels provided televised pornography. Over the decade, he has campaigned against a score of television programs, including *The Thorn Birds* (in which a Catholic Priest breaks a vow of chastity), *Saturday Night Live* (for too many uses of the word 'penis')....Recent headlines in his newsletter point to new targets: 'Kellogg, Sara Lee Promote Christian Buffoons on ABC,' 'GM, Revlon Help ABC with Child Sex Theme' (referring to an episode of *The Wonder Years*), and 'Pro-homosexual Show Sponsored by Chrysler on NBC's *L.A. Law*'" (25).

22. These issues are taken up at length in Kenneth M. Zeichner, 'Contradictions and Tensions in the Professionalization of Teaching and the Democratization of Schools," *Teachers College Record* 92, no. 3 (Spring 1991): 363–79.
23. *America 2000*, 2.
24. The Independent Commission on the National Endowment for the Arts, "A Report to Congress on the National Endowment for the Arts," 7–70.
25. Michel Foucault, *Discipline and Punish* (New York: Penguin, 1979), 179.
26. See Anthony Wilden, ed., *The Rules Are No Game* (London: Routledge and Kegan Paul, 1987).
27. Milbrey W. McLaughlin, "Where's the Community in America 2000?" in *Voices from the Field: 30 Expert Opinions on America 2000, the Bush Administration Strategy to "Reinvent" America's Schools* (Washington, D.C.: William T. Grant Foundation, 1991), 42.
28. See Stephen J. Ball, *Foucault and Education: Disciplines and Knowledge* (New York: Routledge, 1990), 158.
29. *America 2000*, 2.
30. Ibid., 10.
31. Ibid., 59
32. Ibid., 4
33. Franklin Parrasch, "NEA Independent Commission Report," *New Art Examiner* 18, no. 3 (November 1990): 13.
34. "Report to Congress," 55.
35. Stephen J. Ball, *Foucault*, 157.
36. Max Weber, "Leveling of Social Differences," 235.
37. "Report to Congress," 49.
38. Ibid., 40.
39. *America 2000*, 1.
40. "Report to Congress," 22.
41. Ibid., 49.
42. Ibid., 51.
43. Ibid., 49.
44. Robert H. Knight, "The National Endowment for the Arts: Misusing Taxpayers' Money," *Heritage Foundation Backgrounder* 803 (1991): 2.

7. **THE COLOR OF MONEY: CULTURAL POLICY AND THE PUBLIC INTEREST**

1. Carole S. Vance, "The War on Culture," *Art in America* (September 1989). Reprinted in Richard Bolton, ed., *Culture Wars: Documents from the Recent Controversies in the Arts* (New York: New Press, 1992), 112.
2. See Richard Bolton, ed., *Culture Wars: Documents*; James Davison Hunter, *Culture Wars: The Struggle to Define America* (New York: Basic Books, 1992); Ira Schor, *Culture Wars: School and Society in the Conservative Restoration, 1969–1985* (London and New York: Routledge, 1986); William J. Bennett, *The De-Valuing of America: The Fight for Our Culture and Our Children* (New York: Summit Books, 1992); Richard Wightman Fox and J. T. Jackson Lewis, *The Power of Culture: Critical Essays in American History* (Chicago: University of Chicago Press, 1993);

Bruce Robbins, ed., *The Phantom Public Sphere* (Minneapolis: University of Minnesota Press, 1993).

3. Raymond Williams, *Keywords* (London: Fontana, 1976), 80. This distinction is taken up in relation to public policy in Tony Bennett, "Putting Policy into Cultural Studies," in Lawrence Grossberg, Cary Nelson, and Paula Treichler, eds., *Cultural Studies* (New York and London: Routledge, 1992), 23–33.

4. Terry Eagleton, *The Ideology of the Aesthetic* (New York and London: Basil Blackwell, 1990), 3.

5. Ibid., 13.

6. Steven C. Dubin, *Bureaucratizing the Muse: Public Funding and the Cultural Worker* (Chicago and London: University of Chicago Press, 1987), 175. See also W. McNeil Lowery, introduction to W. McNeil Lowery, ed., *The Arts and Public Policy in the United States* (Englewood Cliffs, N.J.: Prentice Hall, 1984), 6.

7. Ralph Waldo Emerson, "The American Scholar" (1837), in R. E. Spiller, ed., *Selected Essays, Lectures and Poems of Ralph Waldo Emerson* (New York: Simon and Schuster, 1965), 63.

8. Pierre Bourdieu, *Distinction: A Social Critique of the Judgement of Taste*, trans. Richard Nice (Cambridge, Mass.: Harvard University Press, 1986).

9. Quoted in Edward Arian, *The Unfulfilled Promise: Public Subsidy of the Arts in America* (Philadelphia: Temple University Press, 1989), 23.

10. Timothy W. Luke, *Shows of Power: Power, Politics, and Ideology in Art Exhibitions* (Durham, N.C.: Duke University Press, 1992), 1.

11. Herbert Marcuse, *An Essay on Liberation* (Boston: Beacon Press, 1969), 21.

12. bell hooks, "Talking Back," in Russell Ferguson, Martha Gever, Trinh T. Minh-ha, and Cornel West, eds., *Out There: Marginalization in Contemporary Cultures* (Cambridge, Mass.: MIT Press, 1990), 341.

13. See Paulo Freire, *Literacy: Learning to Read the World* (South Hadley, Mass.: Bergin and Garvey, 1987); Paulo Freire, *Pedagogy of the Oppressed*, trans. Myra Bergman Ramos (New York: Continuum, 1970); Paulo Freire, *Politics of Education: Culture, Power, and Liberation* (South Hadley, Mass.: Bergin and Garvey, 1985); Peter McLaren and Peter Leonard, eds., *Paulo Freire: A Critical Encounter* (New York and London: Routledge, 1993).

14. Edward Banfield, *The Democratic Muse: Visual Arts and the Public Interest* (New York: Basic Books, 1984), 8.

15. Ibid., 7.

16. Ibid., 6.

17. Ibid., 6–7.

18. Samuel Lipman, "Cultural Policy: Wither America, Wither Government?" *New Criterion* 3, no. 3 (November 1984): 11.

19. The role of indirect subsidies is taken up at length in Alan L. Feld, Michael O'Hare, and J. Mark Davidson Schuster, *Patrons Despite Themselves: Taxpayers and Arts Policy* (New York and London: New York University Press, 1983).

20. Frank Hodsoll, "Chairman's Statement," *National Endowment for the Arts 1986 Annual Report* (Washington, D.C.: NEA, 1987), 1.

21. Dick Netzer, *The Subsidized Muse: Public Support for the Arts in the United States* (London and New York: Cambridge University Press, 1978).

22. Justin Lewis, *Art, Culture, and Enterprise: The Politics of Art and the Cultural Industries* (London and New York: Routledge, 1990).

23. Ibid., 26. These issues are contextualized in Janet Wolff, *The Social Production of Art* (New York: New York University Press, 1981). Wolff's book remains the most comprehensive analysis of the material and social origins of current perceptions of "creativity" and the aesthetic.

24. John P. Robinson, "Assessing the Artist's Condition: Some Quantitative Issues," in C. Richard Swaim, ed., *The Modern Muse: Support and Condition of Artists* (New York: American Council for the Arts, 1989), 33.

25. Michael Straight, *Twigs for an Eagle's Nest: Government and the Arts, 1965–1978* (New York and Berkeley: Devon Press, 1979), 51–68.

26. *NEA Application Guidelines Fiscal Year 1990*, 1.
27. *NEA Application Guidelines Fiscal Year 1988*, 1.
28. Michael Straight, *Twigs for an Eagle's Nest*, 85. This is exactly the principle that has been violated in recent legislation introducing federal oversight of project content on the basis of decency or political intent.
29. Ibid., 76.
30. The program categories at the NEA include Dance, Design Arts, Expansion Arts, Folk Arts, Inter-Arts, Literature, Media Arts:Film/Radio/Television, Museum, Music, Opera-Musical Theater, Theater, and Visual Arts.
31. Hilton Kramer, "Criticism Endowed," *New Criterion* 2, no. 3 (November 1983): 3.
32. Michael Straight, *Twigs for an Eagle's Nest*, 77.
33. Robert Hughes, "Whose Art Is It, Anyway?" *Time*, June 4, 1990, 46.
34. *National Endowment for the Arts Annual Report 1990* (Washington, D.C.: NEA, 1991), 241.
35. Michael S. Joyce, "The National Endowments for the Humanities and the Arts," in Charles L. Heatherly, ed., *Mandate for Leadership* (Washington, D.C.: Heritage Foundation, 1981), 1040–41.
36. Edward Arian, *Unfulfilled Promise*, 42–44.
37. *NEA Annual Report 1988*, 239.
38. National Endowment for the Arts, "Multicultural Impact of Endowment Grant-Making," unpublished report (1992).
39. Ruby Lerner, *Comprehensive Organizational Assistance for Artists' Organizations* (Washington, D.C.: National Association of Artists' Organizations, 1988).
40. Grant Kester, "Rhetorical Questions: The Alternative Arts Sector and the Imaginary Public," *Afterimage* 20, no. 6 (January 1993): 12.
41. Ibid., 11.
42. Samuel Lipman, "Cultural Policy," 14.
43. National Endowment for the Arts, *The National Endowment for the Arts: Five Year Plan, 1986–1990* (Washington, D.C.: NEA, 1986), 33.
44. David B. Pankratz, "Aesthetic Welfare, Government, and Educational Policy," *Design for Arts Education* (July/August 1986): 18.
45. Ibid., 19.
46. See Getty Center for Education in the Arts, *Beyond Creating: The Place for Art in America's Schools* (Los Angeles: Getty Center for Education in the Arts, 1985); Elliot W. Eisner, *The Role of Discipline-Based Art Education in America's Schools* (Los Angeles: Getty Center for Education in the Arts, 1987).
47. Elliot W. Eisner, "Discipline-Based Art Education: Conceptions and Misconceptions," *Educational Theory* 40, no. 4 (Fall 1990): 424.
48. Donald Arnstine, "Art, Aesthetics, and the Pitfalls of Discipline-Based Art Education," *Educational Theory* 40, no. 4 (Fall 1990): 412–22.
49. National Endowment for the Arts, *Toward Civilization: A Report on Arts Education* (Washington, D.C.: NEA, 1988), 44.
50. U.S. Department of Education, *The Nation's Report Card* (Washington, D.C.: U.S. Government Printing Office, 1987), 45.
51. Steven Dubin, *Bureaucratizing the Muse*, 10–19.
52. Ibid., 15.
53. People for the American Way, *The American Public's Perspective on Federal Support for the Arts, and the Controversy over Funding for the National Endowment for the Arts* (Washington, D.C.: People for the American Way, 1990).
54. Quoted in Terri Lynn Cornwell, *Democracy and the Arts: The Role of Participation* (New York: Praeger, 1990), xi.
55. Justin Lewis, *Art, Culture, Enterprise*, 50.
56. W. McNeil Lowery, "How Many Muses? Government Funding for the Multicultural," *Journal of Arts Management and Law* 21, no. 3 (Fall 1991): 264–71.

57. These issues are explored in depth in Doug Blandy and Kristin G. Condon, eds., *Art in a Democracy* (New York: Teachers College Press, 1987). The thirteen essays in this volume explore the varied applications of art as education and democratic practice. See also David Trend, *Cultural Pedagogy: Art/Education/Politics* (New York: Bergin and Garvey, 1992), and Terri Lynn Cornwell, *Democracy and the Arts*.

58. Jeanette Ingberman, Exit Art press release, December 1992.

59. William Honan, "U.S. Arts Panel May Be Revived," *New York Times*, November 20, 1992, A19.

60. Don Adams and Arlene Goldbard, "Learning to Read the World," *exposure* 28, nos. 1/2 (1991): 12–17. See also Don Adams and Arlene Goldbard, *Crossroads: Reflections on the Politics of Culture* (Talmage, Calif.: DNA Press, 1990).

61. Paulo Freire, *Cultural Action for Freedom* (Cambridge, Mass.: Center for the Development for Social Change, 1970), 27.

62. Sara Evans and Harry Boyte, *Free Spaces: The Sources of Democratic Change in America* (New York: Harper and Row, 1986).

8. Rethinking Media Activism: Why the Left Is Losing the Culture War

1. Edward Said, *Culture and Imperialism* (New York: Knopf, 1993), 323.

2. Patrick Buchanan, "In the War for America's Culture, Is the 'Right' Side Losing?" *Richmond News Leader*, June 24, 1989. Republished in Richard Bolton, *Culture Wars: Documents from the Recent Controversies in the Arts* (New York: New Press, 1992), 31–33.

3. See Richard Bolton, *Culture Wars: Documents*; James Davison Hunter, *Culture Wars: The Struggle to Define America* (New York: Basic Books, 1992); Ira Schor, *Culture Wars: School and Society in the Conservative Restoration, 1969–1985* (London and New York: Routledge, 1986); William J. Bennett, *The De-Valuing of America: The Fight for Our Culture and Our Children* (New York: Summit Books, 1992); Margaret Heins, *Sex, Sin, and Blasphemy* (New York: New Press, 1993).

4. Quoted in Richard Bolton, *Culture Wars: Documents*, 32.

5. In a recent development that has mortified free speech advocates, in March 1993 the Clinton administration appealed the federal court decision that struck down the National Endowment for the Arts's "decency clause." Like George Bush, Clinton is arguing that content restrictions of federally funded art are legal. It is worth noting that during his election campaign, Clinton staunchly insisted that he would lift all such restrictions. See C. Carr, "Artful Dodging: The NEA Funds the Defended Four," *Village Voice*, June 15, 1993, 30–31.

6. As one commentator responded to Bill Clinton's nomination of Sheldon Hackney to head the National Endowment for the Humanities, "Once you have convinced people, as the right wing has, that multiculturalism and deconstruction are barbaric forms of nihilism, how can you expect an NEH nominee to speak favorably of them in public?" See Stephen Burd, "Hackney Attacked and Praised for Criticizing Literary Theory," *Chronicle of Higher Education*, July 14, 1993, A21.

7. David Rieff, "Multiculturalism's Silent Partner," *Harper's*, August 1993, 64.

8. Quoted in ibid., 65.

9. Ben J. Bagdikian, *The Media Monopoly*, 3rd ed. (Boston: Beacon Press, 1990). Important materialist analysis of media also appears in Herbert I. Schiller, *Mass Communications and American Empire* (Boston: Beacon Press, 1969); John Tomlinson, *Cultural Imperialism: A Critical Introduction* (Baltimore: Johns Hopkins University Press, 1991); and Sut Jhally, *The Codes of Advertising: Fetishism and the Political Economy of Meaning in Consumer Society* (London and New York: Routledge, 1990).

10. Elayne Rapping, "Who Needs the Hollywood Left?" *Progressive*, September 1993, 34.

11. Admittedly, during the initial decades following the patenting of the daguerreotype in 1839 photographic equipment was expensive , the chemical processes were complex, and its practi-

tioners tended to be wealthy. But by the turn of the century photography had become a commonly available technology, which George Eastman quickly adapted to mass production and amateur use.

12. In fact, the perceived boom in cultural studies is an illusion. Although a handful of cultural studies practitioners have attracted some publicity, cultural studies (and media studies) has failed to gain a substantial foothold in the academy as a whole. Although cultural studies courses are taught in some schools, less than half a dozen universities have elevated the endeavor to the status of a department. A recent discussion of this situation appears in Liz McMillen, "New York U. Becomes a Magnet for Scholars in Cultural Studies," *Chronicle of Higher Education*, July 28, 1993, A10.

13. See Teresa Ebert, "Ludic Feminism, the Body, Performance, and Labor: Bringing Materialism Back into Feminist Cultural Studies," *Cultural Critique* 23 (Winter 1992–93): 17. In this remarkably reductive essay, Ebert collapses the work of such diverse thinkers as Judith Butler, Nancy Fraser, Donna Haraway, Kobena Mercer, Ernesto Laclau, Diana Fuss, Andrew Ross, and Fredric Jameson into a category she identifies as "ludic" postmodernism.

14. In the early writing of Jean Baudrillard the dual logics of materialist and textualist positions fuse in the figure of the "commodity sign." Like Marx, Baudrillard blames the representation of commodities for generating an "abstract" exchange value from a "concrete" use value. In this manner Baudrillard identifies signification as the central logic of late capitalism. As seen in much of consumer society, the rendering of the commodity as text becomes the driving force of objectification, surplus valuation, and, ultimately, alienation. See Mark Poster, "Translator's Introduction," in Jean Baudrillard, *The Mirror of Production* (St Louis: Telos Press, 1975), 5.

15. Selected examples of the culture-as-substitute argument resurface in Teresa Ebert, "Ludic Feminism"; Margaret Heins, *Sex, Sin, and Blasphemy*; Barbara Epstein, "Political Correctness and Collective Powerlessness," *Socialist Review* 21, nos. 3/4 (July-December 1991): 13–37; and Thomas Crow, "I'll Take the High Road, You Take the Low Road," *Artforum* 19 (January 1991): 104–7.

16. Mable Haddock and Chiquita Mullins, "Whose Multiculturalism? PBS, the Public, and Privilege," *Afterimage* 21, no. 1 (Summer 1993): 14–19.

17. Michael Berubé, "Exegencies of Value," *Minnesota Review* 36 (Fall/Winter 1992/93): 63–87.

18. This has been made apparent in Hillary Rodham Clinton's concern, following that of *Tikkun* editor Michael Lerner, over what has been termed the "politics of meaning."

19. Quoted in Richard Bolton, *Culture Wars: Documents*, 33.

20. Quoted in Richard Bolton, "The Cultural Contradictions of Conservatism," *New Art Examiner* 17, no. 10 (June 1990): 26.

21. Ruby Lerner, *Comprehensive Organizational Assistance for Artists' Organizations* (Washington, D.C.: National Association of Artists' Organizations, 1988).

22. Robert Samuelson, "Highbrow Pork Barrel, Washington Post, August 16, 1989," in Richard Bolton, ed., *Culture Wars: Documents*, 95.

23. Michael Denning, "The Academic Left and the Rise of Cultural Studies," *Radical History Review* 54 (1992): 21–47.

24. Quoted in Eric Barnou, *Documentary: A History of the Non-Fiction Film* (New York: Oxford University Press, 1983), 5.

25. Herbert Marcuse, *An Essay on Liberation* (Boston: Beacon Press, 1969), 21.

26. Grant Kester, "Rhetorical Questions: The Alternative Arts Sector and the Imaginary Public," *Afterimage* 20, no. 6 (January 1993): 11.

27. Martha Rosler, "in, around, and afterthoughts (on documentary photography)," *Martha Rosler: 3 Works* (Halifax: Nova Scotia College of Art and Design, 1981).

28. Among these programs were the Resettlement Administration and the Farm Security Administration, both of which commissioned numerous documentaries.

29. See John Hess, "Notes on U.S. Radical Film, 1967–80," in Peter Steven, ed., *Jumpcut: Hollywood, Politics, CounterCinema* (New York: Praeger, 1985), 134–51.

30. Quoted in Michael Renov, "Early Newsreel: The Construction of a Political Imaginary for the New Left," *Afterimage* 14, no. 7 (February 1987): 12–15.

31. Andrew Kopkind, "The Rising of the Wretched," *Nation*, May 6, 1991, 588.

32. Pat Aufderheide, "Charting Cultural Change: The Role of the Critic," in Mark O'Brien and Craig Little, eds., *Reimaging America: The Arts of Social Change* (Santa Cruz, Calif.: New Society, 1990), 359.

33. Specifically, reader response theorists would include such diverse personas as Jonathan Culler, Stanley Fish, Linda Hutcheon, Susan Suleiman, and Wolfgang Iser. The application of this work to media viewing is traced in Anthony Easthope, *Literary into Cultural Studies* (New York and London: Routledge, 1991), and Manuel Alvarado, Edward Buscombe, and Richard Collins, eds., *The Screen Education Reader* (New York: Columbia University Press, 1993). Representative works on critical TV consumption include Robert Allen, ed., *Channels of Discourse: Television and Contemporary Criticism* (Chapel Hill: University of North Carolina Press, 1987), and Henry Jenkins, *Textual Poachers: Television Fans and Participatory Culture* (New York and London: Routledge, 1992). Three valuable books on the pedagogy of media education are Len Masterman, *Teaching the Media* (London: Comedia, 1985); David Lusted, ed., *The Media Studies Book: A Guide for Teachers* (New York and London: Routledge, 1991); and bell hooks, *Talking Back; Thinking Feminist, Thinking Black* (Boston: South End Press, 1989).

34. Antonio Gramsci, *Selections from the Prison Notebooks*, ed. and trans. Quintin Hoare and Jeffrey Nowell Smith (New York: International Publishers, 1972).

35. David Armstrong, *A Trumpet to Arms: Alternative Media in America* (Boston: South End Press, 1981), 71.

36. See Michael Shamberg and the Raindance Corporation, *Guerrilla Television* (New York: Holt, Rinehart, and Winston, 1971).

37. Martha Gever, "Video Politics: Early Feminist Projects," in Diane Neumaier and Douglas Kahn, eds., *Cultures in Contention* (Seattle: Real Comet Press, 1985), 92–101. The overwhelming dominance of white men in the New Left is taken up in Alice Echols, "We Gotta Get Out of This Place: Notes toward Remapping the Sixties," *Socialist Review* 22, no. 2 (April-June 1992): 9–33.

38. Dorothy Todd Hénaut, "Asking the Right Questions: Video in the Hands of Citizens," unpublished manuscript, National Film Board of Canada (1975).

39. bell hooks, *Talking Back*.

40. Quoted in Deedee Halleck, "Paper Tiger Television," in Diane Neumaier and Douglas Kahn, eds., *Cultures in Contention*, 35.

41. Paper Tiger organizer Jesse Drew, telephone interview with author (July 27, 1993).

42. Lawrence Daressa, "The Politics of Distribution," *Afterimage* 15, no. 2 (September 1987): 8–9.

43. Michele Shapiro, "ITVS Trial by Fire," *Independent* 16, no. 2 (March 1993): 10–12.

44. Jeffrey Chester and Kathryn Montgomery, "Technology in Transition: From Video Dialtone to DBS—Where Do Independents Fit In?" *Independent* 16, no. 3 (April 1993): 29.

45. A thorough discussion of the need for activists in different spheres to consider new sites for their political work appears in Henry A. Giroux, *Border Crossings: Cultural Workers and the Politics of Education* (New York: Routledge, 1992). Specific discussions of these concerns as they relate to media and arts activism appear in David Trend, *Cultural Pedagogy: Art/Education/Politics* (New York: Bergin and Garvey, 1992). The important issue of dialogue was prominently introduced to the Left community in Paulo Freire, *Pedagogy of the Oppressed*, trans. Myra Bergman Ramos (New York: Continuum, 1970). These ideas have recently been examined at length in Peter McLaren and Peter Leonard, eds., *Paulo Freire: A Critical Encounter* (New York: Routledge, 1993).

9. Pedagogy and Ethics: Notes for a Radical Democracy

1. Chantal Mouffe, "Radical Democracy: Modern or Postmodern," in Andrew Ross, ed., *Universal Abandon* (Minneapolis: University of Minnesota Press, 1988), 42.

2. Ernesto Laclau and Chantal Mouffe, *Hegemony and Socialist Strategy: Towards a Radical Democratic Politics*, trans. Winston Moore and Paul Cammack (London: Verso, 1985), 189.

3. See Jürgen Habermas, *The Theory of Communicative Action*, trans. Thomas McCarthy (Boston: Beacon Press, 1984).

4. See John Dewey, *Democracy and Education* (New York: Macmillan, 1910), 321–60.

5. See Philip R. D. Corrigan, "Towards a Celebration of Difference(s): Notes for a Sociology of a Possible Everyday Future (1981)," in Philip R. D. Corrigan, *Social Forms/Human Capacities* (New York: Routledge, 1990), 130–53. Of course, on another level the Right is very much committed to supporting the differences that install people at varying points in the meritocratic social hierarchy.

6. See David Johnson, "Stormy Days and Sleepless Nights for 'Lightning Rod' at Arts Agency," *New York Times*, May 3, 1991, A14; Brian Wallis, "Slow Burn at the NEA," *Art in America* 79, no. 2 (February 1991): 37; Richard Bolton, "The Cultural Contradictions of Conservativism," *New Art Examiner* 17, no. 10 (Summer 1990): 24–29; Carole S. Vance, "The War on Culture," *Art in America* 77, no. 8 (September 1989): 39–45.

7. Samuel Bowles and Herbert Gintis, *Schooling in Capitalist America: Educational Reform and the Contradictions of Economic Life* (New York: Basic Books, 1976), 20–26.

8. Richard Rorty, *The Consequences of Pragmatism: Essays, 1972–1980* (Minneapolis: University of Minnesota Press, 1982).

9. A critique of Rorty following this argument is found in Nancy Fraser, *Unruly Practices: Power, Discourse, and Gender in Contemporary Social Theory* (Minneapolis: University of Minnesota Press, 1989), 93–112. Fraser develops a considered critique of Rorty, which problematizes his effort to sustain pragmatic and romantic autonomy.

10. This issue is discussed at length in a chapter entitled "Management as Moral Technology: A Luddite Analysis," in Stephen J. Ball, *Foucault and Education: Disciplines and Punish* (New York: Routledge, 1990), 153–66.

11. John Rawls, *A Theory of Justice* (Cambridge, Mass.: Harvard University Press, 1971). An important series of reconsiderations of Rawls appears in Milton Fisk, ed., *Justice* (Atlantic Highlands, N.J.: Humanities Press, 1993).

12. Emmanuel Levinas, *Totality and Infinity: An Essay on Exteriority*, trans. Alphonso Lingis (Pittsburgh: Duquesne University Press, 1969), 21.

13. Robert Young, *White Mythologies: Writing History and the West* (London and New York: Routledge, 1990), 16.

14. Quoted in ibid.

15. Stuart Hall and David Held, "Citizens and Citizenship," in Stuart Hall and Martin Jacques, eds., *New Times: The Changing Face of Politics in the 1990s* (London: Verso, 1990), 173–74.

16. Quoted in ibid., 173.

17. Cornel West, "The New Cultural Politics of Difference," in Martha Gever, Russell Ferguson, Trinh T. Minh-ha, and Cornel West, eds., *Out There: Marginalization and Contemporary Culture* (Cambridge, Mass.: MIT Press, 1990), 35. See also David Purpel, *The Moral and Spiritual Crisis in Education* (New York: Bergin and Garvey, 1989).

18. Robert Young, *White Mythologies*, 1–20.

19. Kobena Mercer, "Welcome to the Jungle: Identity and Diversity in Postmodern Politics," in Jonathan Rutherford, ed., *Identity: Community, Culture, Difference* (London: Lawrence and Wishart, 1990), 43–71.

20. Paulo Freire, *Pedagogy of the Oppressed*, trans. Myra Bergman (New York: Continuum, 1970).

21. Homi Bhabha, "The Third Space," in Jonathan Rutherford, ed., *Identity*, 207–39.

22. Edward Said, in Phil Mariani and Jonathan Cracy, "In the Shadow of the West: An Interview with Edward Said," in Russell Ferguson, William Olander, Marcia Tucker, and Karen Fiss,

eds., *Discourses: Conversations in Postmodern Art and Culture* (Cambridge, Mass.: MIT Press, 1990), 94.

23. Philip R. D. Corrigan, "Celebration of Differences."

24. Benedict Anderson, *Imagined Communities: Reflections on the Origin and Spread of Nationalism* (London: Verso, 1983), 12.

25. Allan Bloom, *The Closing of the American Mind* (New York: Simon and Schuster, 1987); E. D. Hirsch, Jr., *Cultural Literacy: What Every American Needs to Know* (New York: Random House, 1987); and William J. Bennett, *James Madison High School: A Curriculum for American Students* (Washington, D.C.: U.S. Department of Education, 1988).

26. Samuel Lipman, "Redefining Culture and Democracy," *New Criterion* 8, no. 4 (December 1989), 16.

27. This is not, of course, to suggest that individual practitioners in these traditions (John Dewey, for example) have not tried to modify their ethical strategies to make them more responsive to changing circumstances. What I want to stress is the foundationalist character of most ethical argument and the inherent politics that such foundationalism typically carries.

28. Cornel West, *The Ethical Dimensions of Marxist Thought* (New York: Monthly Review Press, 1991), 1.

29. See Chantal Mouffe, "Radical Democracy," 31–45. What is interesting here is the way Mouffe follows Habermas in seeking to salvage the Enlightenment hope for progress, while discarding its rationalist baggage. See also Chantal Mouffe, "The Civics Lesson," *New Statesman & Society* (October 7, 1988): 28–31; and Chantal Mouffe, "Towards a Radical Democratic Citizenship," *Democratic Left* 17, no. 2 (March/April, 1989): 6–7.

30. An example of the rigidly foundationalist ethics I am arguing against is found in John Wilson, *A New Introduction to Moral Education* (London: Cassell Education, 1990). In this work Wilson argues for a form of ethical reasoning free of the subjective influence of culture and politics. In assuming that such a position is possible, this kind of ethics replicates the age-old tradition of authority to deny its enabling structures, and thereby to mystify its workings.

31. Chelda Sandoval, "U.S. Third World Feminism: The Theory and Method of Oppositional Consciousness in the Postmodern World," *Genders* 10 (Spring 1991): 1–24.

32. Nancy Fraser's remarks about activist vanguardism are useful in this context: "Think of intellectuals first and foremost as members of social groups and as participants in social movements. Think of them, in other words, as occupying specifiable locations in social space rather than free-floating individuals who are beyond ideology.... Think of them as potentially capable of utilizing these skills both in specialized institutions like a university and in various larger cultural and political public spheres. Think of them, thus, as participants on several fronts in struggles for cultural hegemony. Think of them, also, alas, as mightily subject to delusions of grandeur." Nancy Fraser, *Unruly Practices*, 108.

33. Gayatri Chakravorty Spivak, *The Post-Colonial Critic: Interviews, Strategies, Dialogues*, ed. Sarah Harasym (London and New York: Routledge, 1990), 9.

34. Chantal Mouffe, "Democratic Politics Today," in Chantal Mouffe, ed., *Dimensions of Radical Democracy: Pluralism, Citizenship, Community* (London: Verso, 1992), 4.

democracy: cultural aspects, 129, 142; political aspects, 5, 8, 10, 28, 91–92, 129, 147; radical 15, 138, 140–42, 145–48
Democratic Muse (Banfield), 108
Dia Art Foundation, 72–73
dialogue, 13, 121, 141
difference, 5–7, 17, 38, 40, 139
Digesting the Child Within (Callahan), 75
Discipline–Based Art Education (DBAE), 115–16

Eagleton, Terry, 106–7
Ebert, Teresa, 124
education: art, 101, 113–17; definitions of, 1–5; hidden curriculum, 12; history, 12–14; resistance, 12, 17; school policies, 84, 94, 96–104
Eisner, Eliot, 115
Enlightenment, 16, 59, 147
Exit Art, 119–20
expert knowledge, 92, 94

false consciousness, 14, 44
Faludi, Susan, 77
Falwell, Rev. Jerry, 98
family, 75–84
"Family of Man," 80–81
Family Snaps: The Meanings of Domestic Photography (Holland and Spence), 82–84
"Family Stories," 87–89
feminism, 1, 13, 52, 76–78, 140
Ferguson, Russell, 3
Finley, Karen, 25
folk art, 43, 45–51
Foucault, Michel, 4–5, 81, 99
Frankfurt School, 11, 127
Fraser, Nancy, 95–96
Freire, Paulo, 13, 144
Freud, Sigmund, 84
Friedlander, Lee, 79–80, 121
Frow, John, 44

Galassi, Peter, 79
gay men, 1, 11, 70, 76, 85, 107
gay rights, 2, 76
Generation X, 8
Getty Center for Education in the Arts, 115–16
Gintis, Herbert, 12
Giroux, Henry, 13, 14, 149 n. 4
Goldbard, Arlene, 121
Good Housekeeping Magazine, 76, 81
Gore, Jennifer, 16
Gramsci, Antonio, 3–4

Grossberg, Lawrence, 17
Group Material, 73, 87

Habermas, Jürgen, 42–43
Hall, Stuart, 1, 39, 142
Harrington, Michael, 62
Hebdige, Dick, 40
Hegel, Georg Wilhelm Friedrich, 42, 143
Heritage Foundation, 103, 112, 123
Hoggart, Richard, 23
Holland, Patricia, 82
Hollywood: industry, 19, 26, 128; left, 130–31
homelessness, 58, 70, 73, 93
homophobia, 45
hooks, bell, 58, 69
Horkheimer, Max ,11
Hubbard, Jim, 65–66
Huntington, Samuel, 7

identity, 4, 12, 15, 44
If You Lived Here: The City in Art, Theory, and Social Activism (Rosler), 72–74
Independent Television Service (ITVS), 136

Jackson, Jesse, 9
Jameson, Fredric, 12
Jordan, June, 75

Katz, Michael, 64
Kenny, Lorraine, 30
Kester, Grant, 113
Kozol, Jonathan, 65–67
Kramer, Hilton, 111, 125

labor, 70–71
Laclau, Ernesto, 4, 9, 138
Lacy, Suzanne, 54–55
language, 89, 94
"language of possibility," 90
Larkin Street Youth Center, 71–72
Latinos, 76
Lauren, Ralph, 37, 46, 49–50, 54, 77
Learning to Labour (Willis), 13
Leavis, F. R., 23
Lenin, V. I., 127
lesbians, 1, 11, 70, 76, 85, 107, 135
Levinas, Emmanuel, 141–42
Lewis, Justin, 109–10, 118
liberalism: definitions of, 5, 7; critiques of, 69, 96, 106, 138–39, 142
Limbaugh, Rush, 2, 122, 131
Lipman, Samuel, 8, 15, 81, 108, 113, 116, 125
Lippard, Lucy, 51

literary canons, 40, 69
Lonidier, Fred, 70–71

MacBride Report, 22
Mandate for Leadership (Heritage Foundation), 123
Marcuse, Herbert, 12, 107
Mark, Mary Ellen, 76–77, 127
Marx , Karl, 11–12, 14, 42–43, 50, 124
Masterman, Len, 36
McLaren, Peter, 13
McLuhan, Marshall, 29
media: activism, 128–29, 132–37; centers, 135–37; education, 18–20, 28–33; monopoly, 25–26, 133; production, 37
Mercer, Kobena, 143
Metcalf, Eugene, 46
Miller, Branda, 89
modernity, 17
Mohanty, Chandra Talpade, 69
Morris, Meagan, 44–45
Mouffe, Chantal, 9, 138
multiculturalism, 2, 18, 40, 84, 122
Muñoz, Celia, 88
Museum of Modern Art (New York), 47–48, 52, 79, 112

Names Project, 55–56
Nation at Risk, 94, 96, 99
National Endowment for the Arts (NEA): censorship, 8, 10, 77, 108, 126; congressional relations, 96, 98–106, 110–11, 135; education policies, 34–35, 112–17, 119
National Film Board of Canada, 133
National Organization for Women, 6, 52
national identity, 3, 18, 23–28, 45, 51
nationalism, 3, 15
Nava, Mica, 14
Netzer, Dick, 109
New Criterion, 108, 116
New Left, 6, 129, 132
New Museum, 88–89
New Traditionalist Woman, 76–77
New World Order, 28, 46, 81
Newsreel, 129–30

Other America (Harrington), 62
Outside the Dream: Child Poverty in America (Shames), 66

Paper Tiger Television, 134–35
pedagogy: and culture, 5, 14, 33, 51, 89, 121;

critical, 13, 36; of difference, 17; feminist, 51; invisible, 46; and politics, 57, 139
People for the American Way, 118
Perot, Ross, 2
Persian Gulf War, 91, 72, 96, 125
phenomenology, 42
photography: activist, 71–72; documentary, 64–67, 123–24; family, 75–84, 86–87
Plan International, 58–59, 65
Pleasures and Terrors of Domestic Comfort (Galassi), 79–81
political economy, 48
post-Fordism, 1
postmodernism, 13
poststructuralism, 10, 40
power, 3–5, 9, 12
primitivism, 39, 48
Public Broadcasting Service, 126, 135
public sphere, 89

Quayle, Dan, 126, 127
Queer Nation, 15
quilts, 41, 51–57

race: affirmative action, 5; and identity, 17, 39, 45; and representation, 11, 29, 32
Rainbow Coalition, 141, 146
Rapping, Elayne, 122
Rawls, John, 141
Reading Dick and Jane with Me (Sligh), 88
Reagan, Ronald: cultural policies, 94, 107, 111, 114, 116, 120, 123; domestic policies, 61–62; education, 94; and the military, 28–29
Reiff, David, 123
Renov, Michael, 129–30
Report to Congress on the National Endowment for the Arts, 96–97, 99–102
Ringgold, Faith, 53
Rockefeller, David, 7
Rockefeller Foundation, 135
Rorty, Richard, 140–41
Rosaldo, Renato, 44, 67–68
Rosenthal, Mel, 68–69
Rosler, Martha, 72–73, 127
Roth, Moira, 54

Said, Edward, 4, 122
Sandoval, Chelda, 146
Savage Inequalities (Kozol), 67
Sawicki, Marianne, 56
Shames, Steven, 66
Shapiro, Miriam, 52, 54
Simmel, Georg, 50

David Trend is executive director of the Center for Social Research and Education in San Francisco and also executive editor of the *Socialist Review*. He is the author of *Cultural Pedagogy: Art/Education/Politics* (1992) and has written numerous articles on cultural workers, cultural wars, new politics of media literacy, tensions in art funding policies, the function of the media in election campaigns, and education and photography.